KICK-ASS 2. Paperback ISBN: 9781781166123 / Hardback ISBN: 9780857687869. Contains material originally published in magazine form as Kick-Ass 2 #1-7. Published by Titan Books, A division of Titan Publishing Group Ltd., 144 Southwark St., London, SE1 0UP. Copyright © 2010-2012 Millarworld Ltd. and John S. Romita. All Rights Reserved. "KICK-ASS," "KICK-ASS 2," the Kick-Ass logo, and all prominent characters and their likenesses featured herein are trademarks of Millarworld Limited & John S. Romita. "Millarworld" and the Millarworld logo are trademarks of Millarworld Limited. No part of this publication may be reproduced, stored in a retrieval system, or transmitted, in any form or by any means, without the prior written permission of the publisher. Names, characters, places and incidents featured in this publication are either the product of the author's imagination or used fictitiously. Any resemblance to actual persons, living or dead (except for satirical purposes), is entirely coincidental.

A CIP catalogue record for this title is available fr

First edition: April 2013

1 3 5 7 9 10 8 6 4

Printed in Spain.

KICK-ASS 2

Writer & Co-Creator
MARK MILLAR

Penciler & Co-Creator
JOHN ROMITA JR.

Inker & Tones
TOM PALMER

Colourist (Issues #1-5 & #7)
DEAN WHITE
with MICHAEL KELLEHER

Colourist (Issue #6)
DAN BROWN

Letterer
CHRIS ELIOPOULOS
with CLAYTON COWLES

Editor
AUBREY SITTERSON
with JOHN BARBER AND CORY LEVINE

Collection Editor: **AUBREY SITTERSON**
Book Designer: **SPRING HOTELING**
Senior Vice President of Sales: **DAVID GABRIEL**
SVP of Business Affairs & Talent Management: **DAVID BOGART**

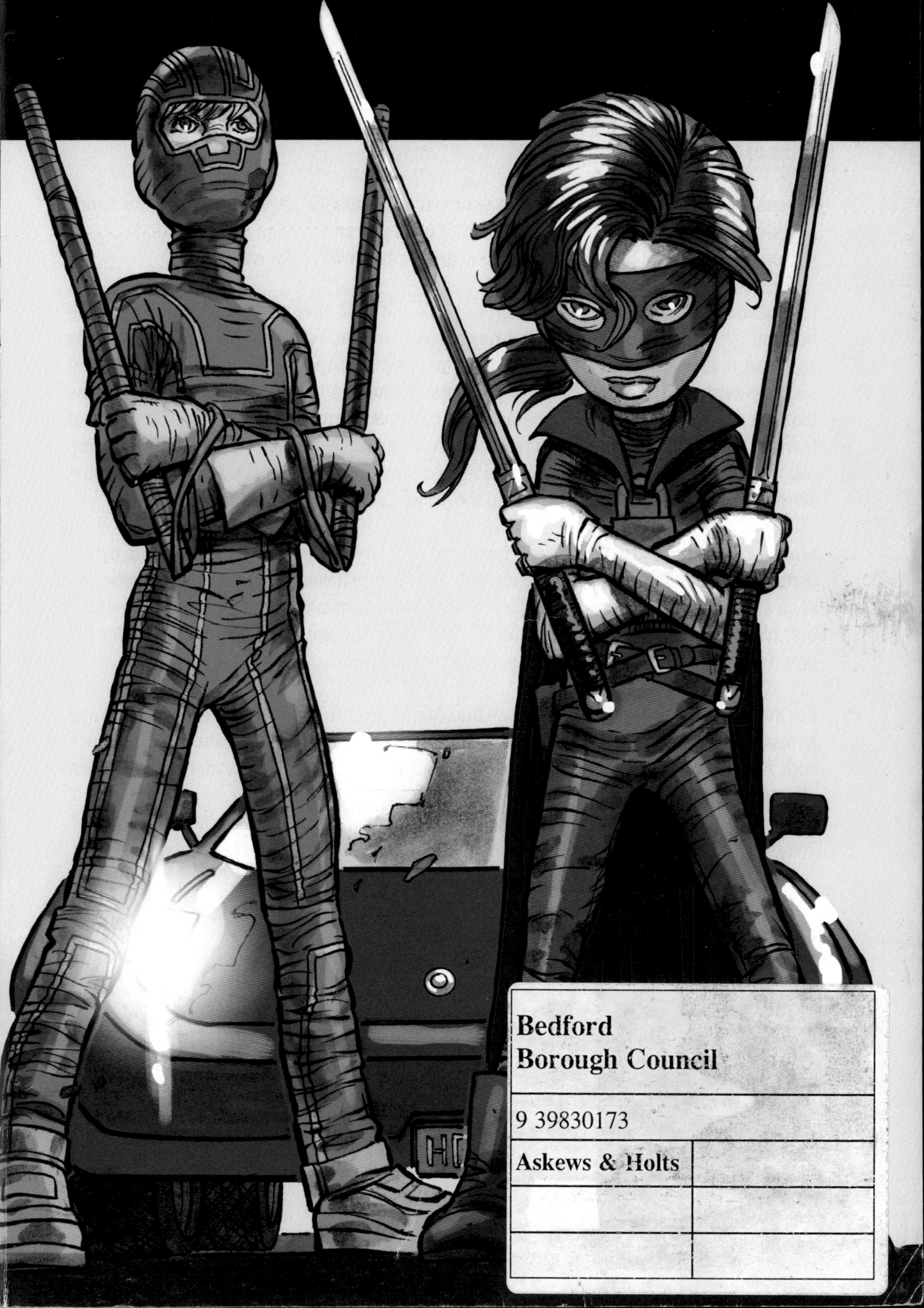

Hey fucker.

Let's face facts, you're one of these fucking fetishistic "fanboy" jerkoffs who secretly wishes that *he* could be Dave Lizewski, beating the shit out of muggers, gangbangers and mob heavies with those akimbo batons as a comely, prepubescent Hit Girl slashes and burns by your side.

It's cool. Me too. I mean good money says most of us already have our dicks in our hands and we're not even out of the intro... but just pace yourself pal and don't pop that nut just yet 'cuz what follows in these pages is one great white *whale* of a wank.

I suppose some basic backstory is in order. Mark and I met where folks not living in an igloo in Bumfuck, Antarctica, tend to meet nowadays... online. Twitter to be precise. Someone reposted (I fucking flat-out refuse to use the word *'Retweet'* for fear that my balls will spontaneously detonate) a Millar passage mentioning his love of *The A-Team* as well as the fact that he had named a character in *Nemesis* "Carnahan" after yours truly. What Mark didn't know, was that I, along with my brother Matt, had been charged with adapting *Nemesis* for Fox but it had all gone sideways under the stewardship of this conniving shithead who singlehandedly torpedoed the project... for the time being.

I reached out to Mark on Twitter and he responded, a fast friendship formed and its cyber-content was reprinted on websites vast and varied where it was poured over and scrutinized at an almost forensic fucking level. The consensus was excitement. It seemed totally natural that two like-minded lads with a mutual taste for shock and awe should team up for the grand guignol-like assault on good taste that is *Nemesis*.

But the bond goes quite a bit deeper than that. Mark and I are of both shared ethnic stock and ancestral discord. We're displaced modern day Celts from a long bloodline chock-a-block with bludgeonings and beheadings. Our forefathers fought Viking invaders on forgotten shores, losing their women, their land and finally, their minds.

They were *The Fraternity Of The Fucked*... and we are their proud descendants.

In keeping that spirit alive and ablaze with wanton bloodlust, my Scottish chum (despite the arrival of another Millar heir and him being dry as a 90-year-old nun's snatch in honor of lent) has nevertheless managed to purge his most putrid cranial pools; the brackish backwaters of the brain where traditional narratives get gang-raped by roid-raging, beer-bellied, gore-soaked gargantuans... to give you sonsabitches yet *another* magnum opus.

In *Kick-Ass 2*, Millar and creative cohort John Romita, Jr. have hotwired the elevator of their frayed mental state to plunge you, fair reader, deeper down into the dripping sub-basement of his perfectly *pitch-black* psychosis. There are no headlamps to light the way down here my lovelies... only the stink of sulfur and suppressed rage. Their off-brand of storytelling is *exactly* the type of perversely, unprintable shit that A.) I love and B.) Affords a battalion's worth of shrinks beachfront homes and Bel Air addresses.

In short, it's a shit-ton of fun.

What you're about to embark on is a true tour de force and the *Kick-Ass* team is in full command of their craft; master illusionists who have perfected the legerdemain of the lewd and vicious, the loathsome and the vile. Blending humor, emotion, sorrow, pain and regret while supercharging the stakes and never forsaking the spirit of what Kick-Ass ultimately is: a kid with a ridiculously outsized dream, who dared to make it a reality... and did.

Gone is the rank teenage ennui of the original and in its place a superheroic dystopia. Dave Lizewski has come to terms with what being a famous public figure is. Larger than life is harder than hell when you're still in high school but growing pains, like a brand new patch of pubes, is par for the course and Dave's willingness to throw himself headlong into shitstorm after shitstorm reconfirms his unbreakable conviction to the ethos of his alter ego, Kick-Ass.

Pushing him ruthlessly along on his journey is the former Red Mist, now rechristened "The Motherfucker." Chris Genovese is no more. The soul-patched nihilist that now inhabits his form thinks nothing of laying waste to an entire suburb for shits and grins or assassinating a sidewalkful of school kids for sport. This "Motherfucker" is the sneering embodiment of society's mindless, amoral masochism.

Rounding out the trifecta is that sweet, chocolate-covered little claymore mine formerly known as "Hit-Girl". Ironically, it's young Mindy Macready that provides the most unlikely moral core for our story. Resigned to a quiet life in relative seclusion with her adopted parents, she reluctantly returns to the mask only when all seems lost, to once again embrace her god-given gifts as a taker of unholy souls, a death machine in overdrive, a living, breathing, paean to pain.

So, with appetites whetted and palms slicked, sit back and have at it kids. What follows is a nightmarish, nuclear meltdown of a mindfuck, lovingly cooked up in the shared mental meth lab of Mark Millar and John Romita, Jr.

Enjoy... *cocksuckers!*

Joe Carnahan
Los Angeles,
March, 2012

ONE

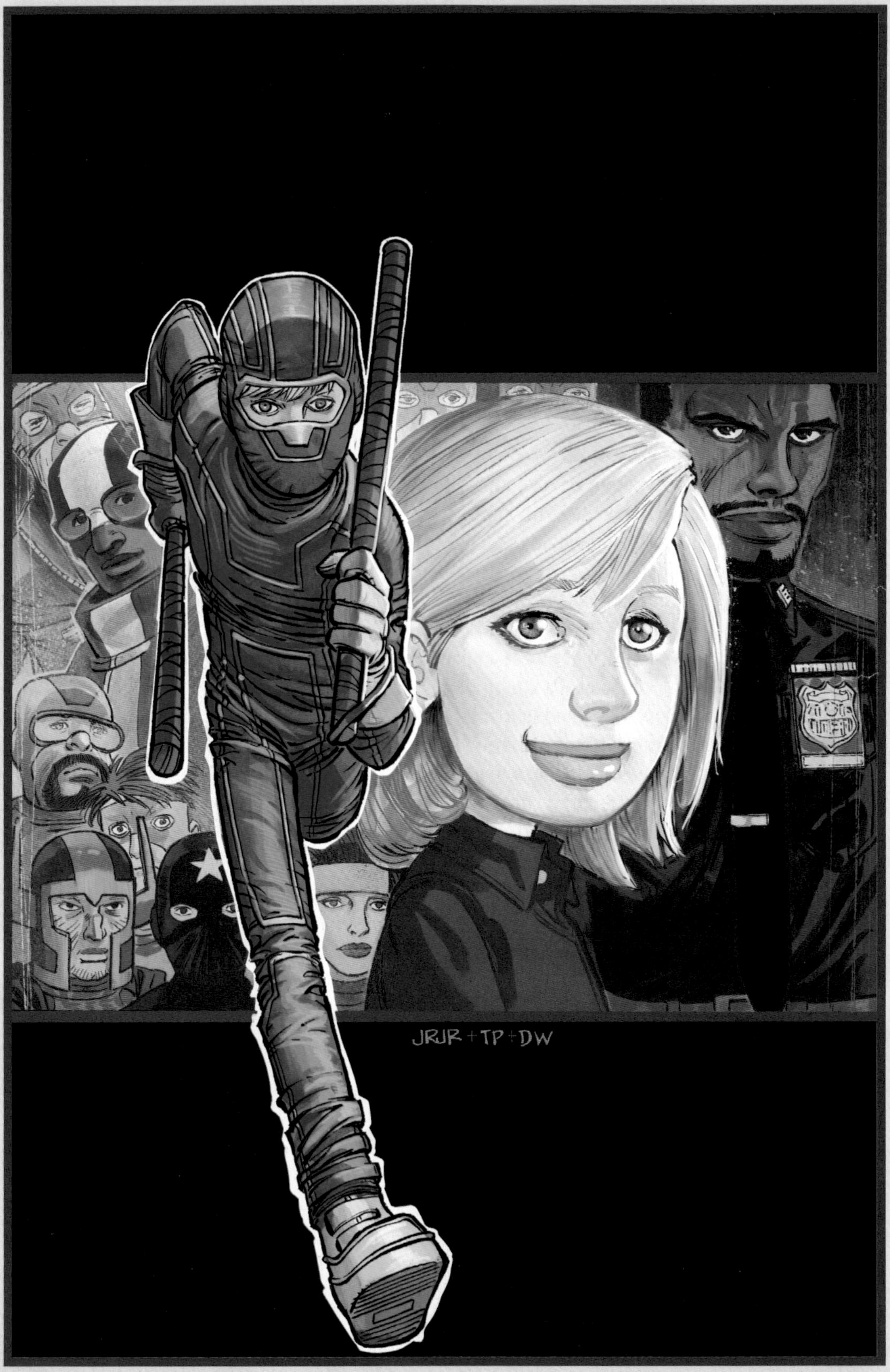
JRJR+TP+DW

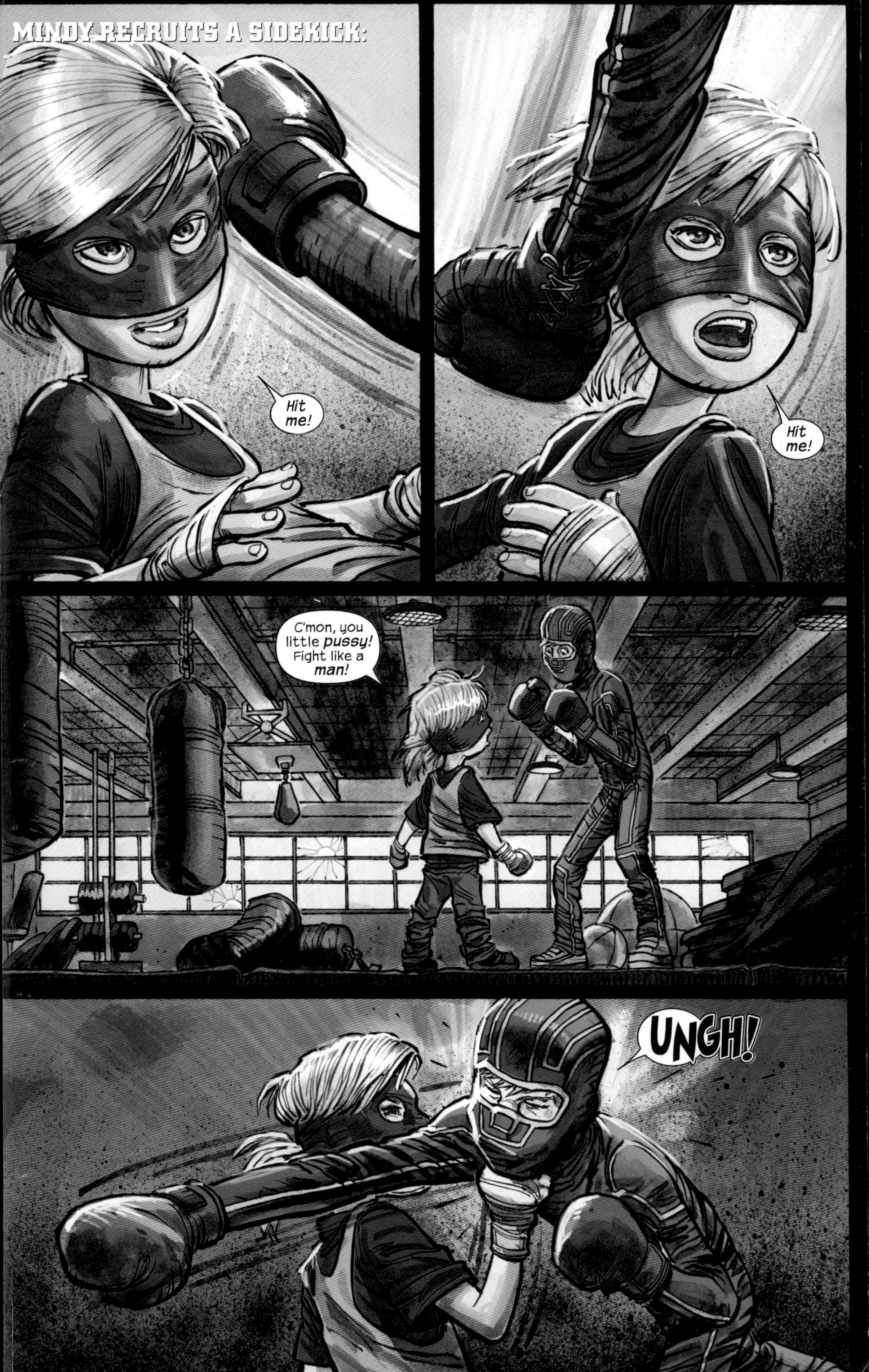
MINDY RECRUITS A SIDEKICK:
Hit me!
Hit me!
C'mon, you little *pussy!* Fight like a *man!*
UNGH!

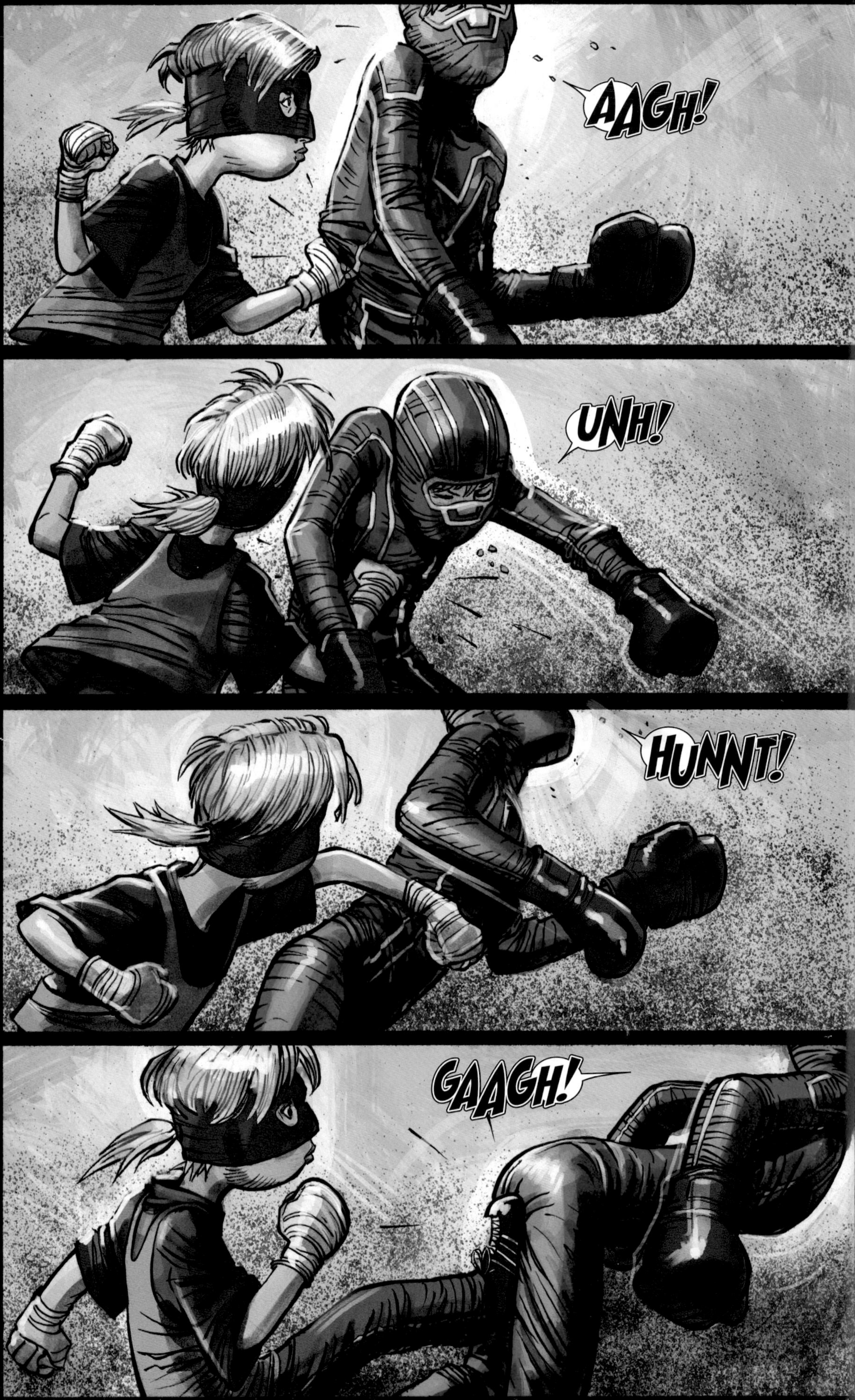
AAGH!
UNH!
HUNNT!
GAAGH!

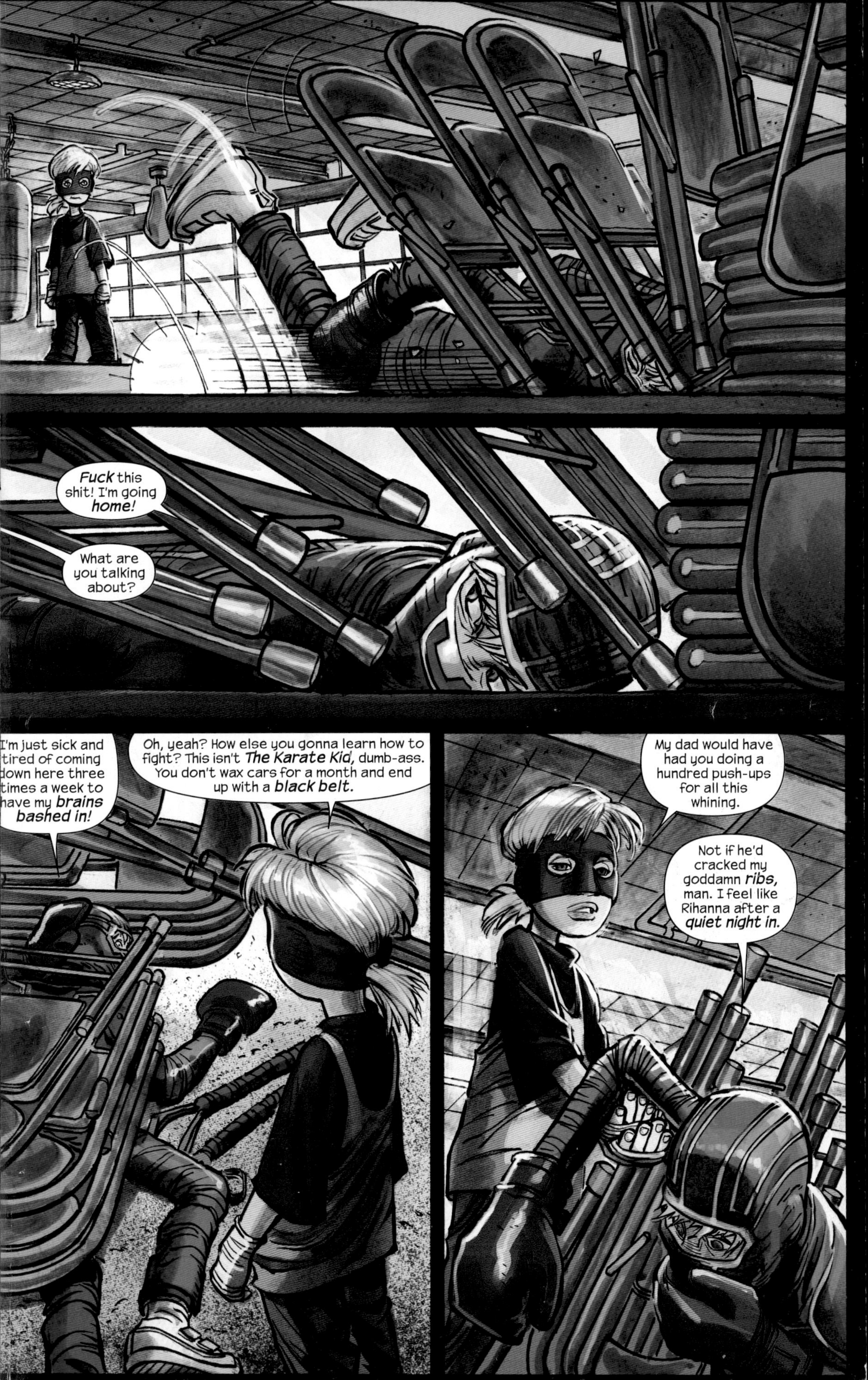

Fuck this shit! I'm going home!
What are you talking about?
I'm just sick and tired of coming down here three times a week to have my brains bashed in!
Oh, yeah? How else you gonna learn how to fight? This isn't The Karate Kid, dumb-ass. You don't wax cars for a month and end up with a black belt.
My dad would have had you doing a hundred push-ups for all this whining.
Not if he'd cracked my goddamn ribs, man. I feel like Rihanna after a quiet night in.

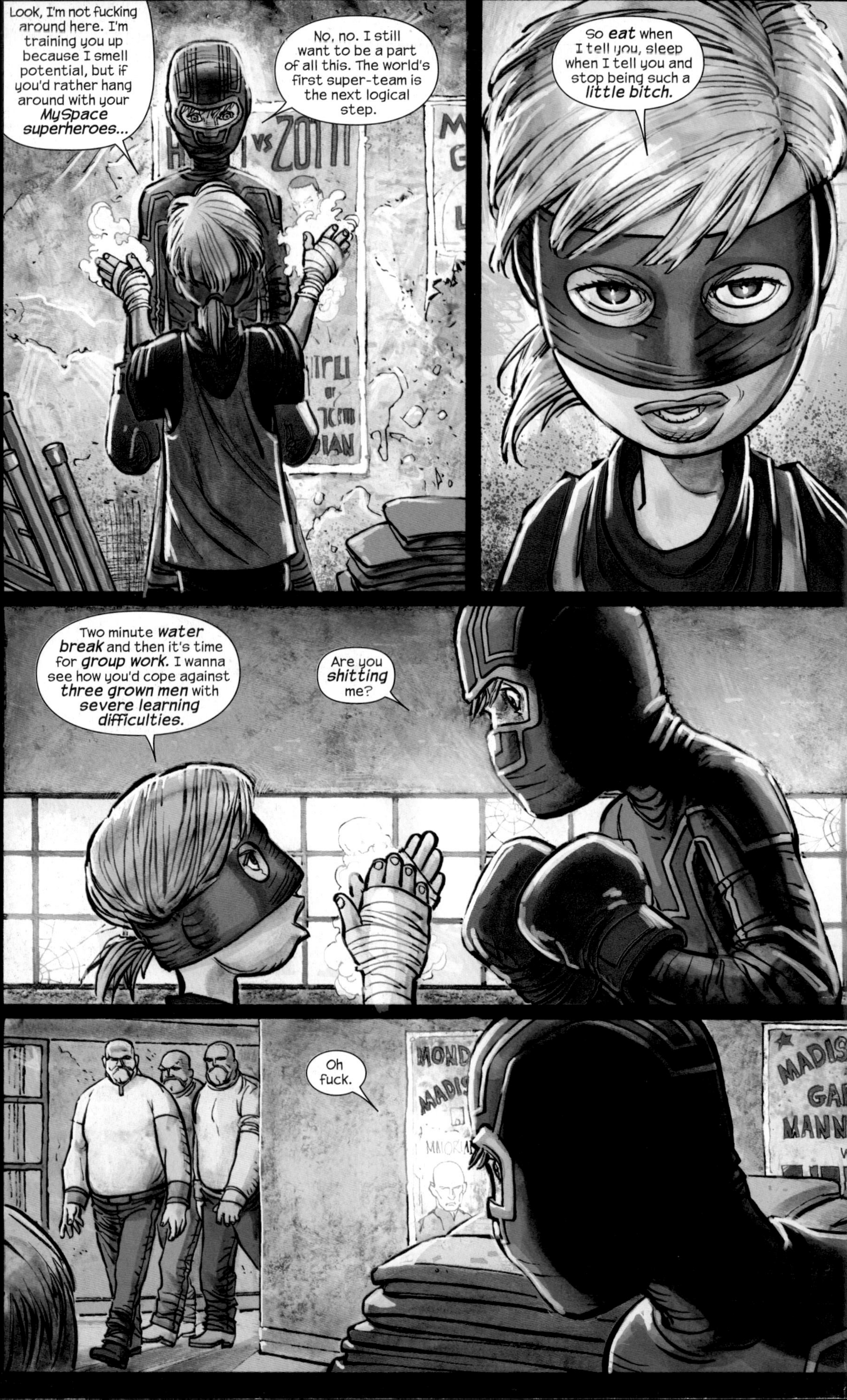
Look, I'm not fucking around here. I'm training you up because I smell potential, but if you'd rather hang around with your MySpace superheroes...
No, no. I still want to be a part of all this. The world's first super-team is the next logical step.
So eat when I tell you, sleep when I tell you and stop being such a little bitch.
Two minute water break and then it's time for group work. I wanna see how you'd cope against three grown men with severe learning difficulties.
Are you shitting me?
Oh fuck.

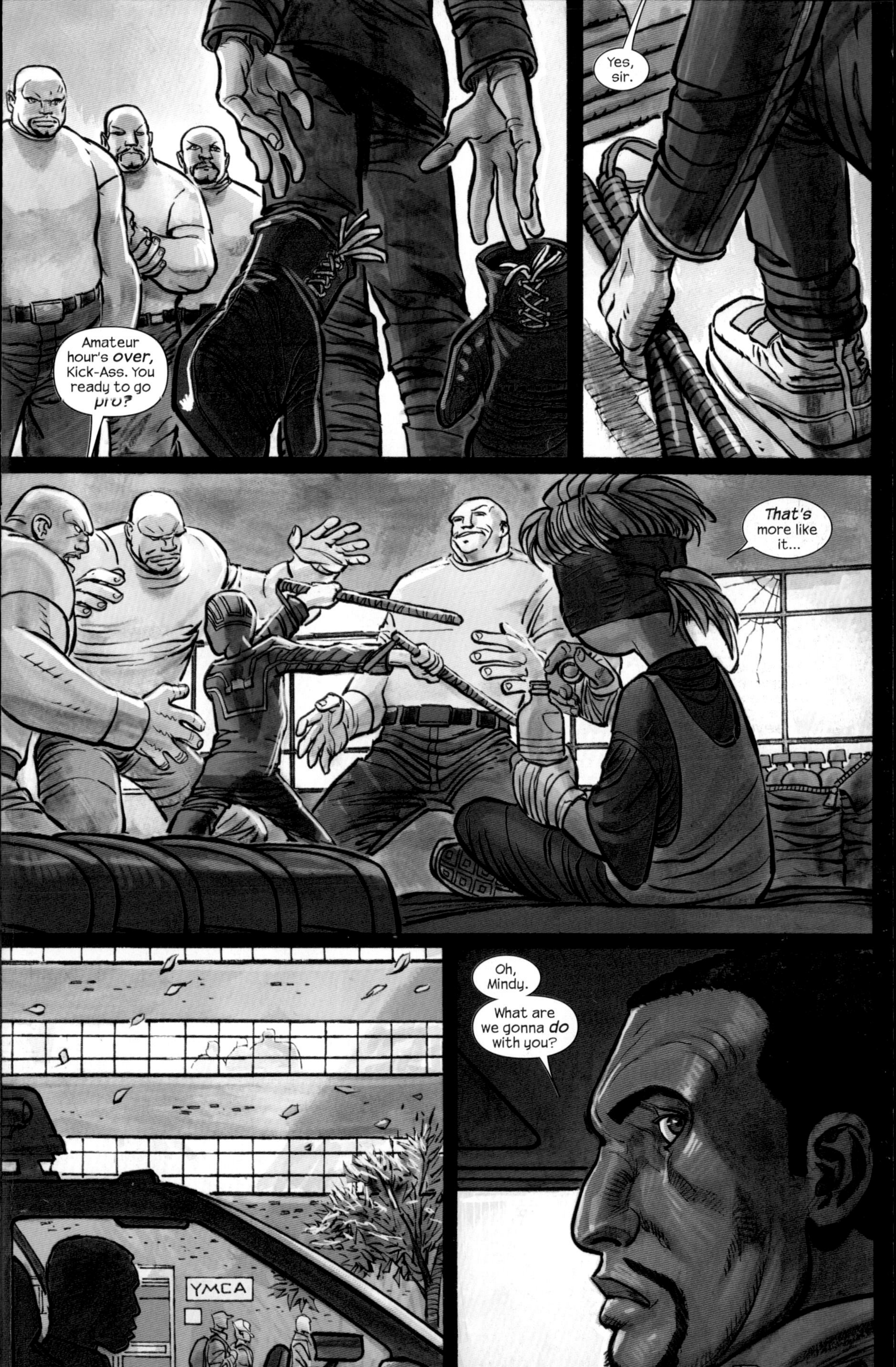
Amateur hour's over, Kick-Ass. You ready to go pro?
Yes, sir.
That's more like it...
Oh, Mindy.
What are we gonna do with you?
YMCA

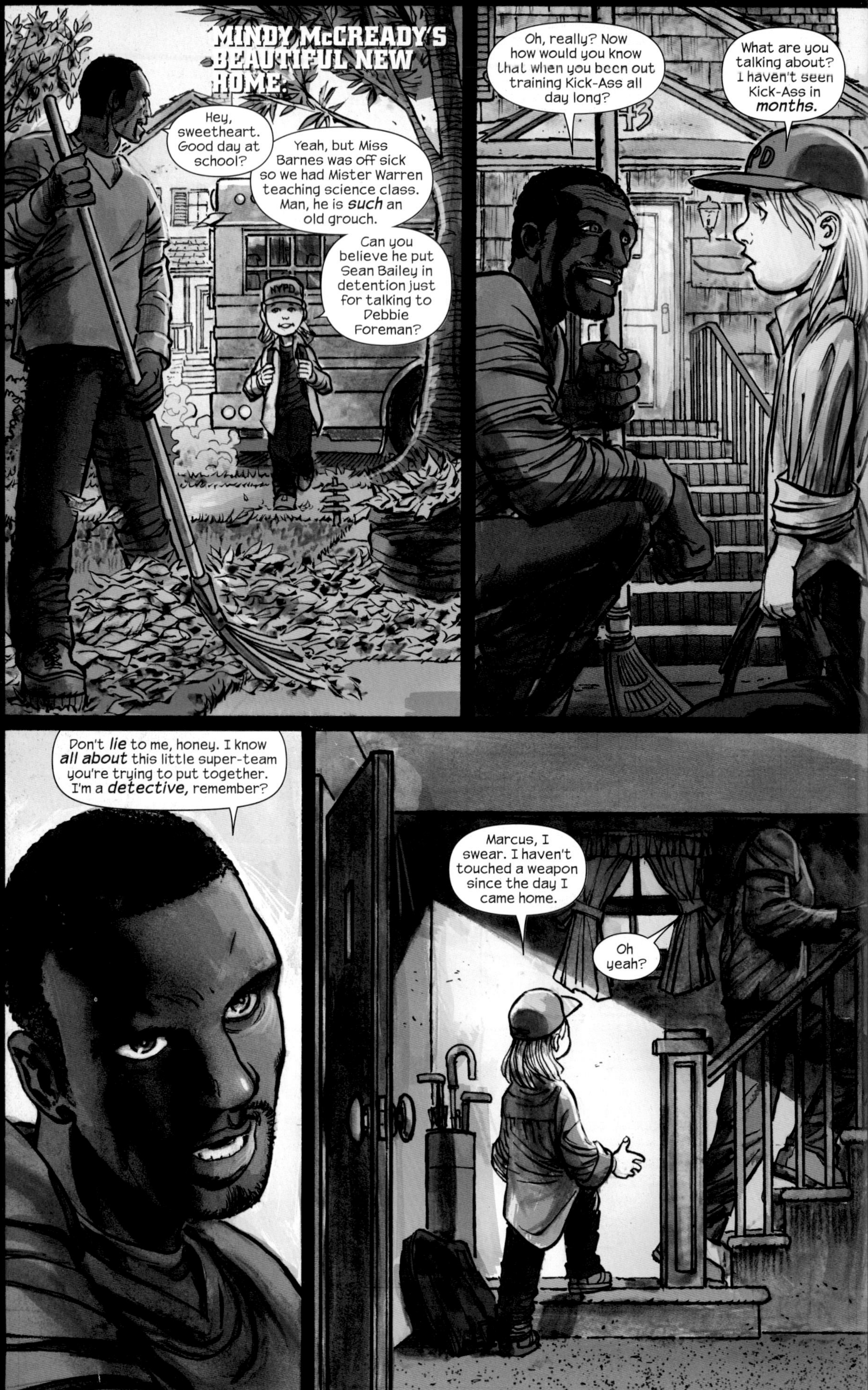

MINDY McCREADY'S BEAUTIFUL NEW HOME:
Hey, sweetheart. Good day at school?
Yeah, but Miss Barnes was off sick so we had Mister Warren teaching science class. Man, he is *such* an old grouch.
Can you believe he put Sean Bailey in detention just for talking to Debbie Foreman?
Oh, really? Now how would you know that when you been out training Kick-Ass all day long?
What are you talking about? I haven't seen Kick-Ass in *months.*
Don't *lie* to me, honey. I know *all about* this little super-team you're trying to put together. I'm a *detective,* remember?
Marcus, I swear. I haven't touched a weapon since the day I came home.
Oh yeah?

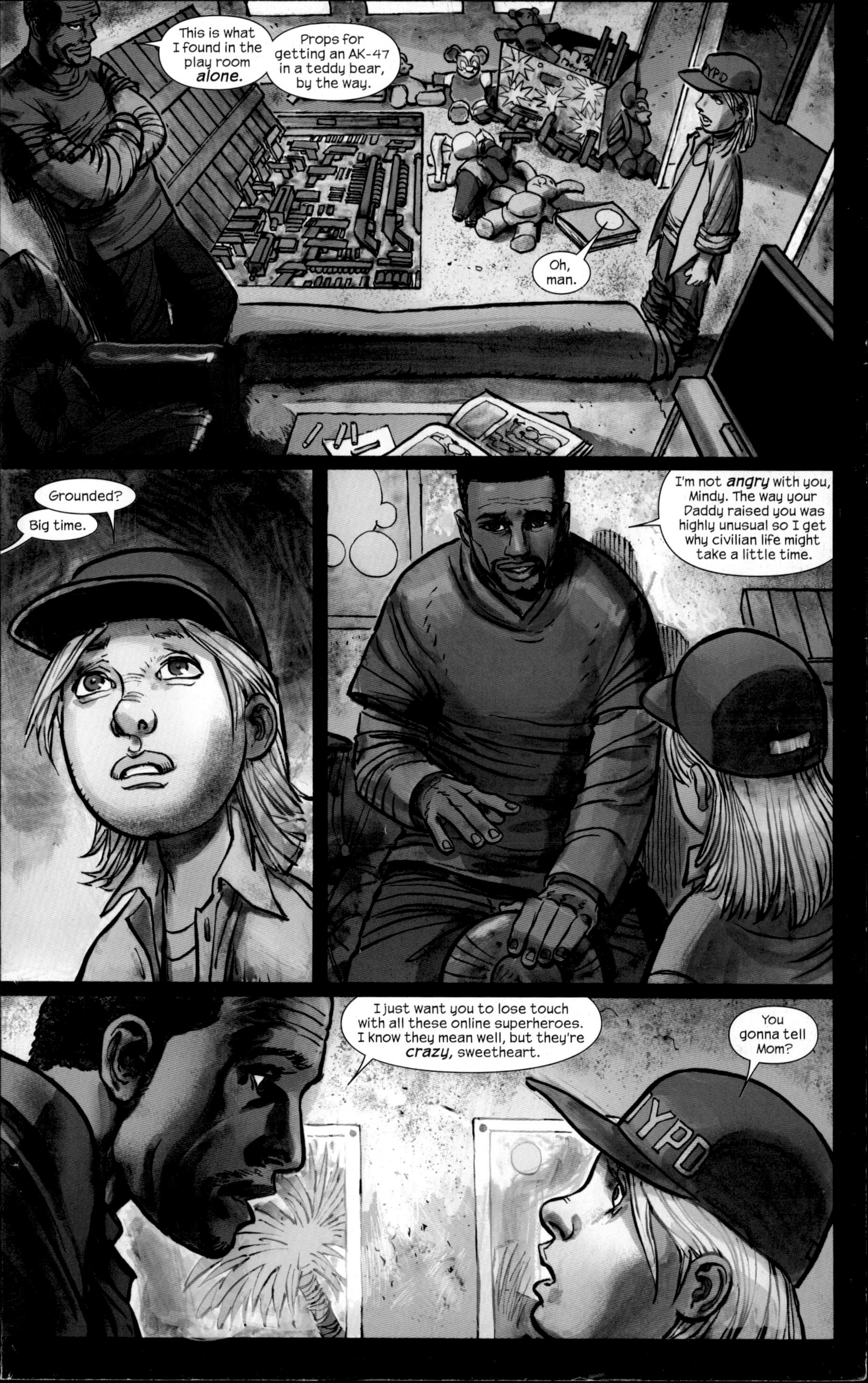
This is what I found in the play room *alone.*
Props for getting an AK-47 in a teddy bear, by the way.
YPD
Oh, man.
Grounded?
Big time.
I'm not *angry* with you, Mindy. The way your Daddy raised you was highly unusual so I get why civilian life might take a little time.
I just want you to lose touch with all these online superheroes. I know they mean well, but they're *crazy,* sweetheart.
You gonna tell Mom?
YPD

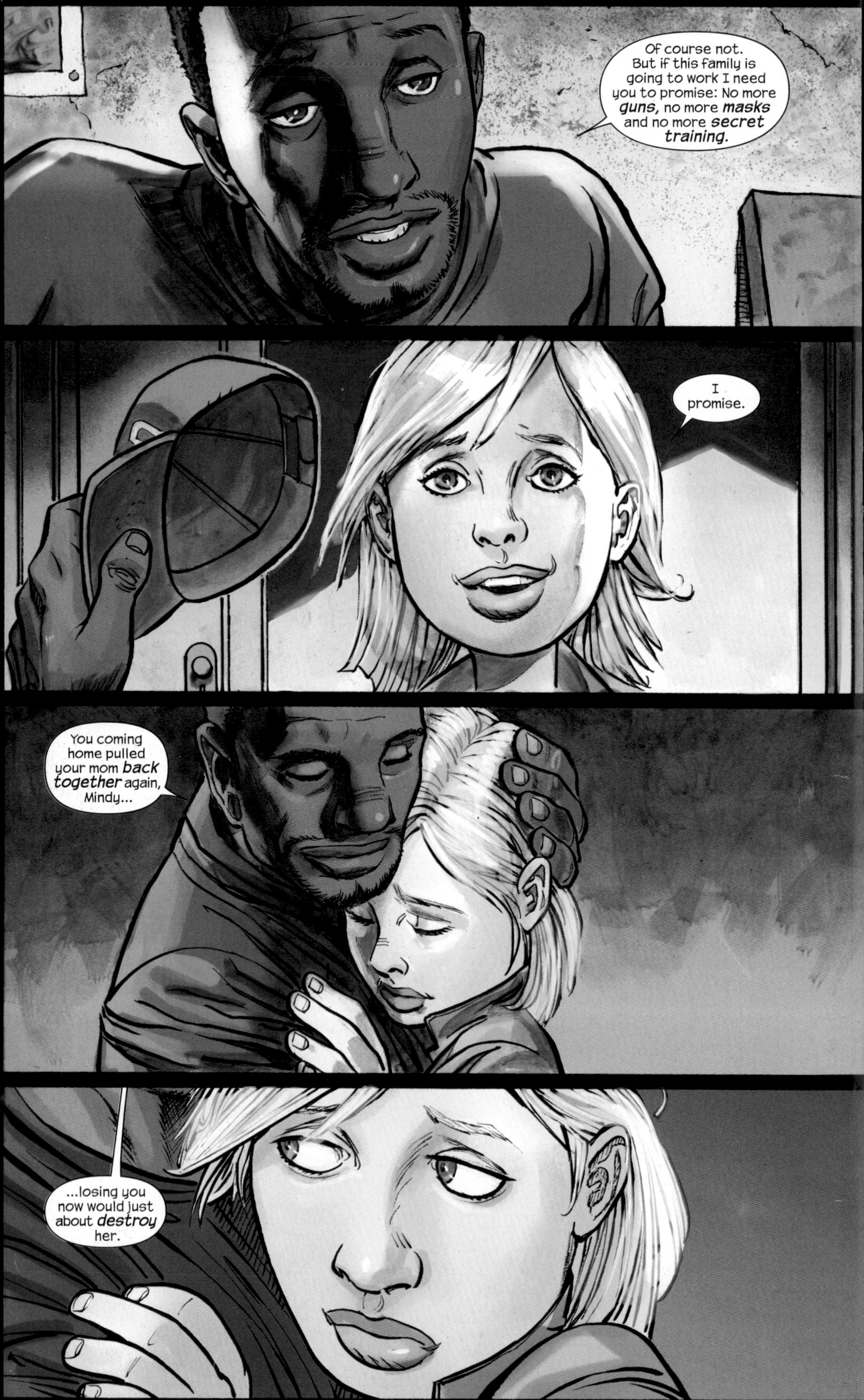
Of course not. But if this family is going to work I need you to promise: No more *guns,* no more *masks* and no more *secret training.*
I promise.
You coming home pulled your mom *back together* again, Mindy...
...losing you now would just about *destroy* her.

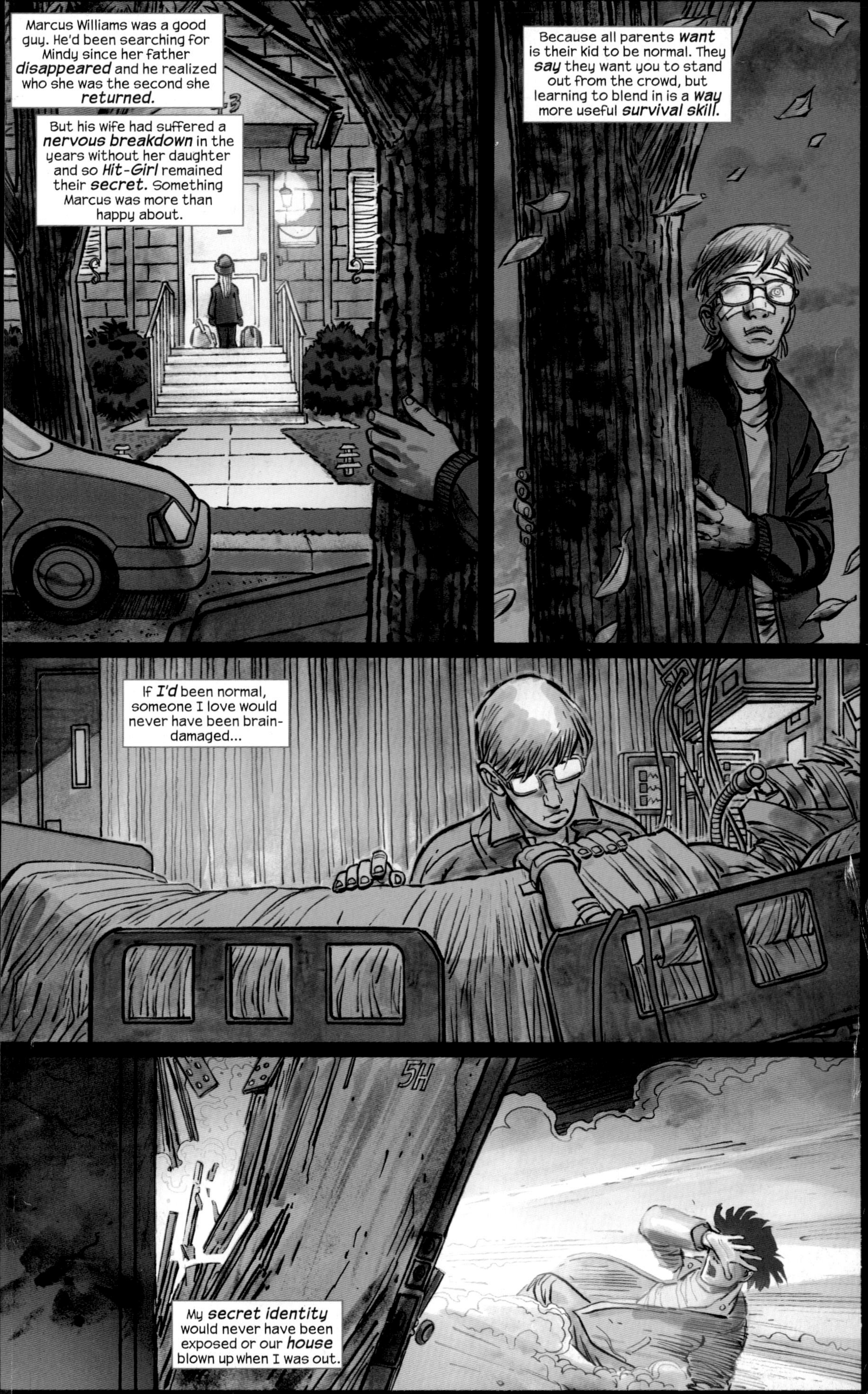
Marcus Williams was a good guy. He'd been searching for Mindy since her father disappeared and he realized who she was the second she returned.
But his wife had suffered a nervous breakdown in the years without her daughter and so Hit-Girl remained their secret. Something Marcus was more than happy about.
Because all parents want is their kid to be normal. They say they want you to stand out from the crowd, but learning to blend in is a way more useful survival skill.
If I'd been normal, someone I love would never have been brain-damaged...
5H
My secret identity would never have been exposed or our house blown up when I was out.

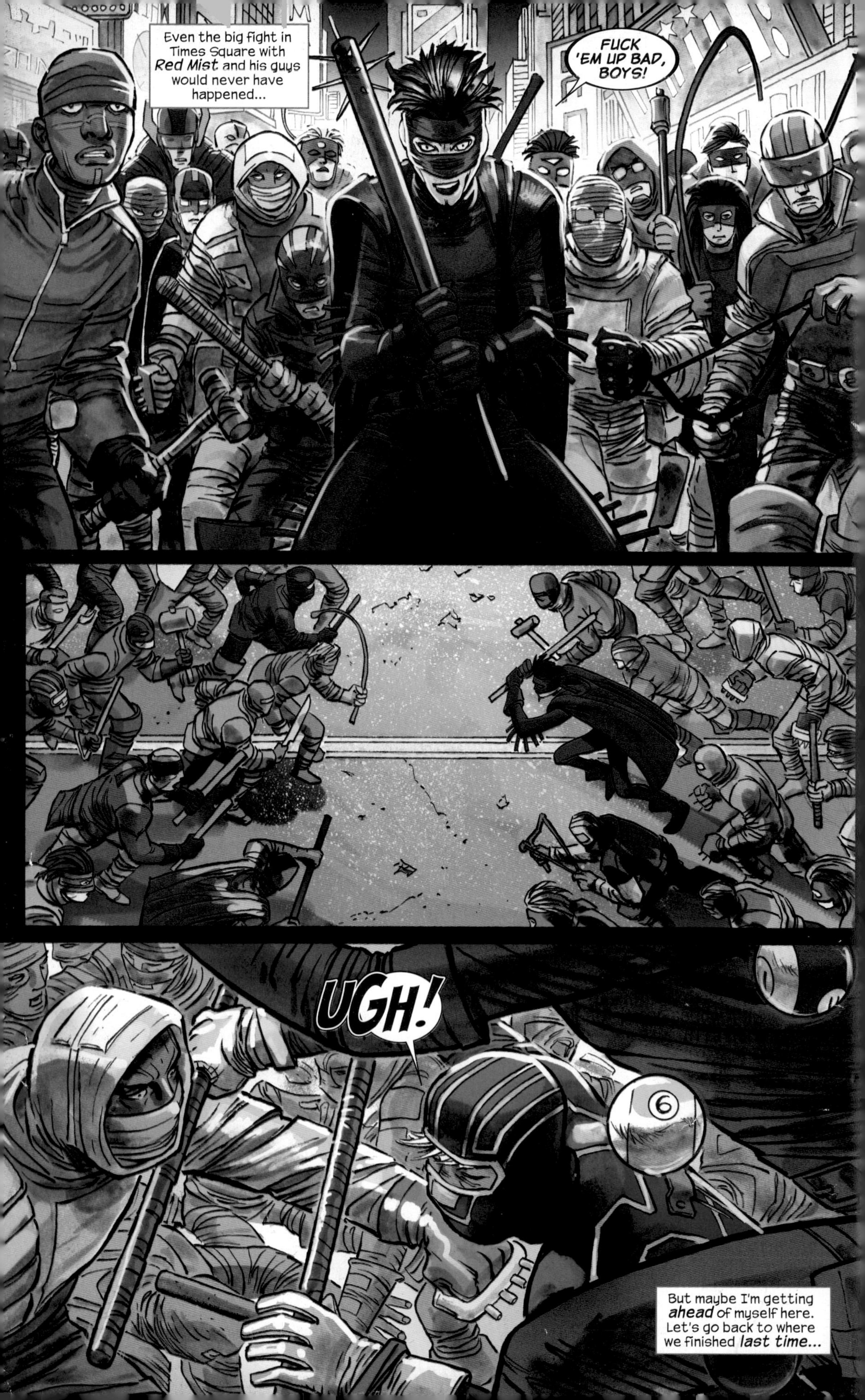
Even the big fight in Times Square with Red Mist and his guys would never have happened...
FUCK 'EM UP BAD, BOYS!
UGH!
But maybe I'm getting ahead of myself here. Let's go back to where we finished last time...

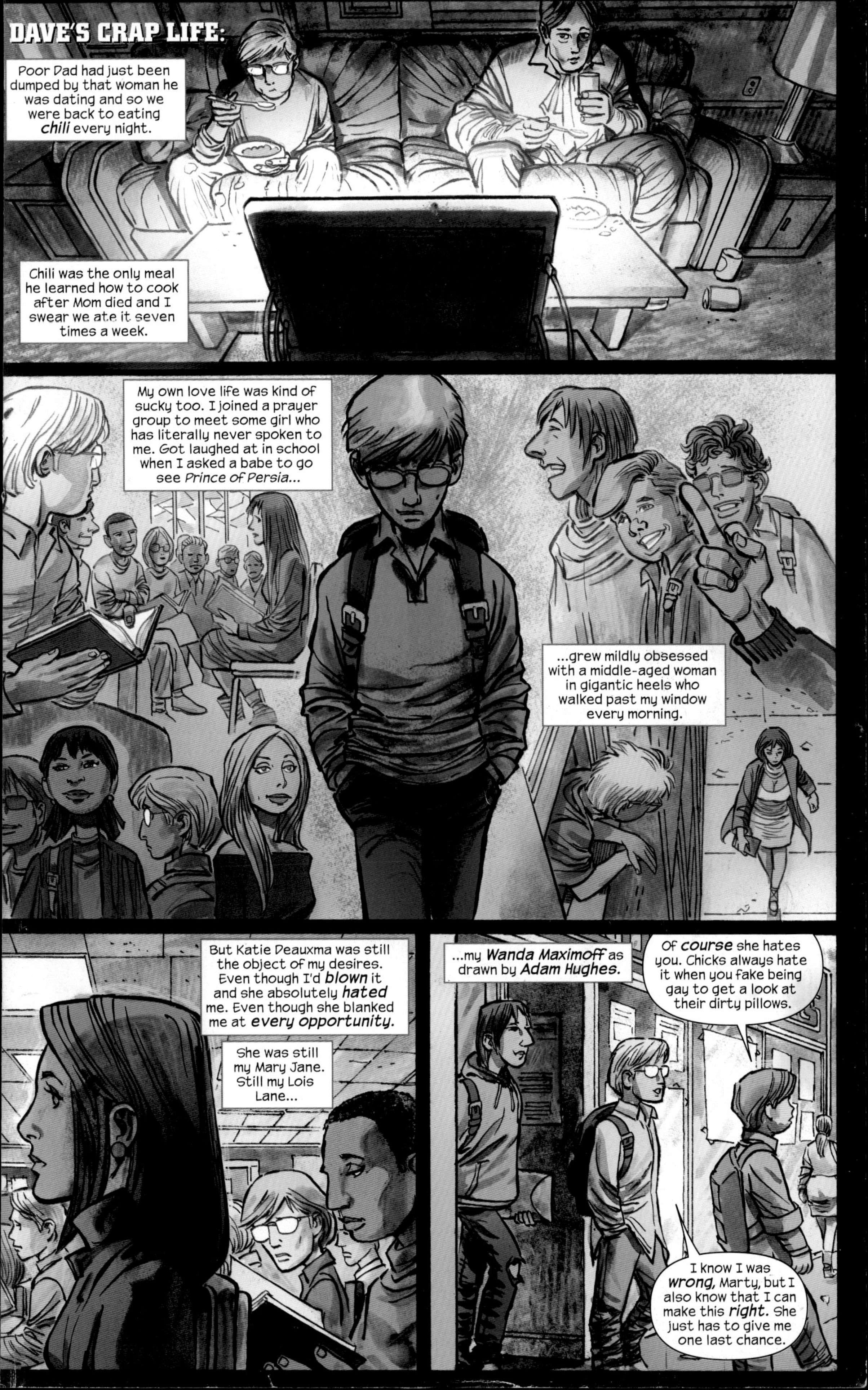

DAVE'S CRAP LIFE:
Poor Dad had just been dumped by that woman he was dating and so we were back to eating chili every night.
Chili was the only meal he learned how to cook after Mom died and I swear we ate it seven times a week.
My own love life was kind of sucky too. I joined a prayer group to meet some girl who has literally never spoken to me. Got laughed at in school when I asked a babe to go see Prince of Persia...
...grew mildly obsessed with a middle-aged woman in gigantic heels who walked past my window every morning.
But Katie Deauxma was still the object of my desires. Even though I'd blown it and she absolutely hated me. Even though she blanked me at every opportunity.
She was still my Mary Jane. Still my Lois Lane...
...my Wanda Maximoff as drawn by Adam Hughes.
Of course she hates you. Chicks always hate it when you fake being gay to get a look at their dirty pillows.
I know I was wrong, Marty, but I also know that I can make this right. She just has to give me one last chance.

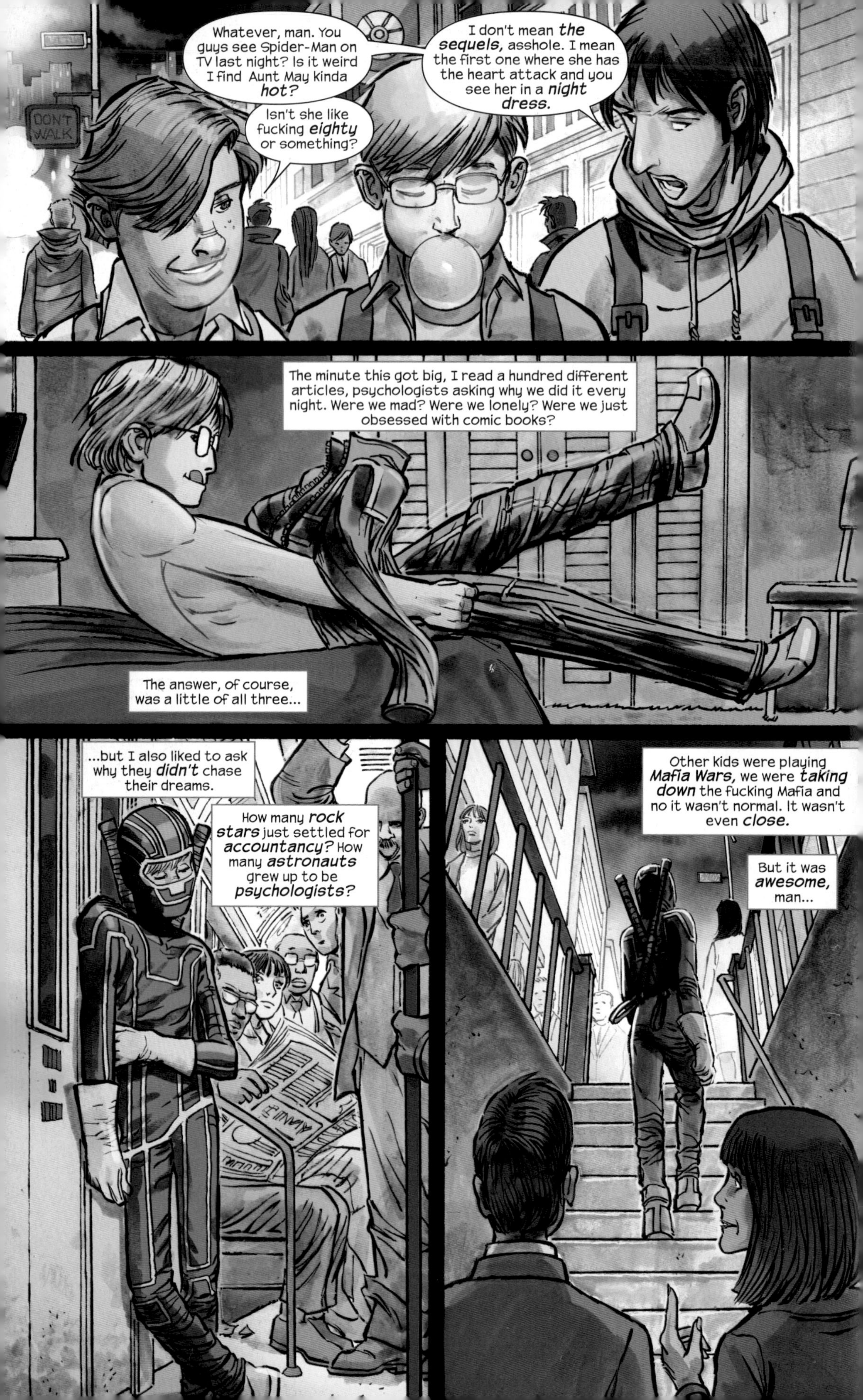

Whatever, man. You guys see Spider-Man on TV last night? Is it weird I find Aunt May kinda hot?
Isn't she like fucking eighty or something?
I don't mean the sequels, asshole. I mean the first one where she has the heart attack and you see her in a night dress.
DON'T WALK
The minute this got big, I read a hundred different articles, psychologists asking why we did it every night. Were we mad? Were we lonely? Were we just obsessed with comic books?
The answer, of course, was a little of all three...
...but I also liked to ask why they didn't chase their dreams.
How many rock stars just settled for accountancy? How many astronauts grew up to be psychologists?
Other kids were playing Mafia Wars, we were taking down the fucking Mafia and no it wasn't normal. It wasn't even close.
But it was awesome, man...

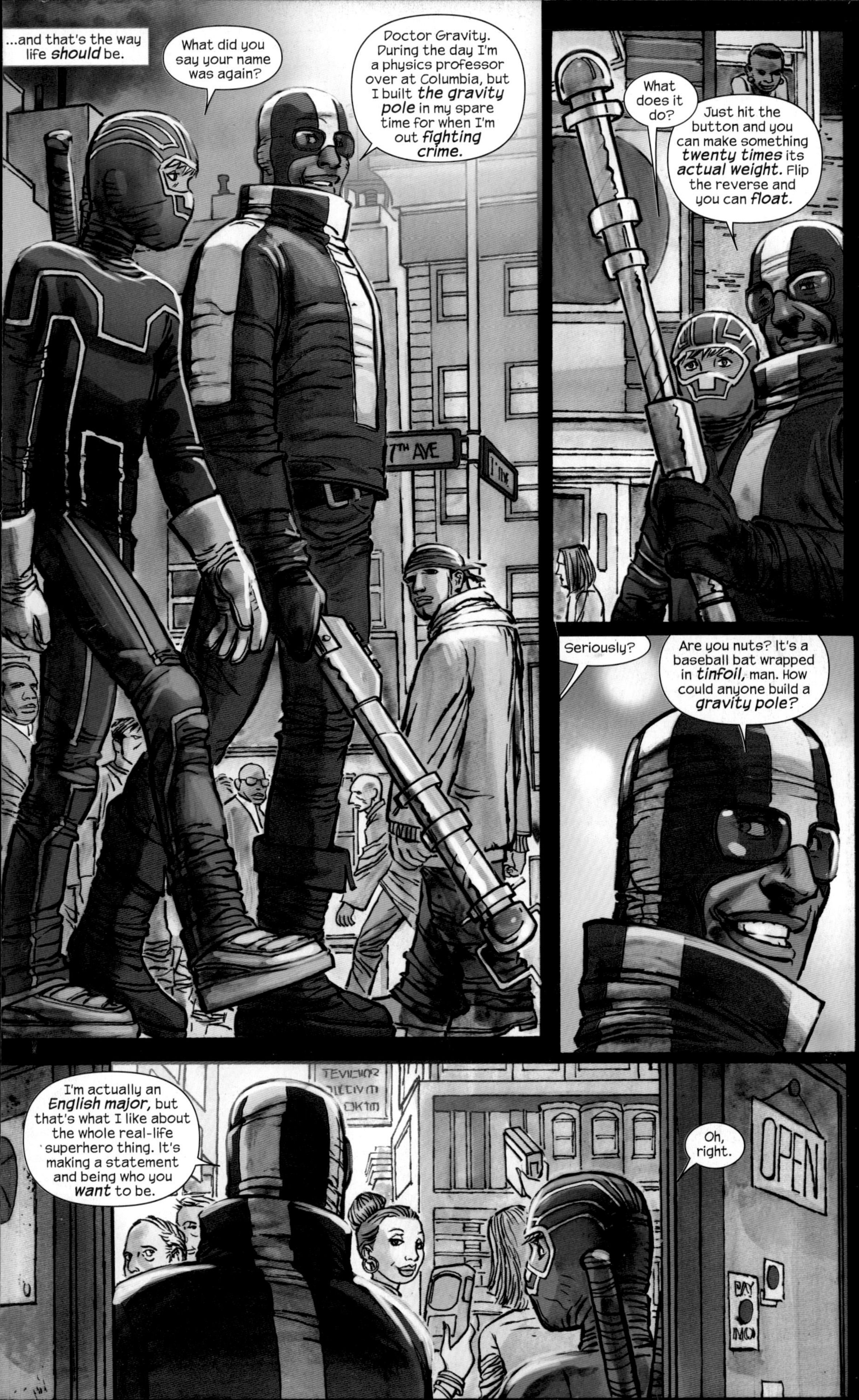

...and that's the way life *should* be.
What did you say your name was again?
Doctor Gravity. During the day I'm a physics professor over at Columbia, but I built *the gravity pole* in my spare time for when I'm out *fighting crime.*
7TH AVE
What does it do?
Just hit the button and you can make something *twenty times* its *actual weight.* Flip the reverse and you can *float.*
Seriously?
Are you nuts? It's a baseball bat wrapped in *tinfoil,* man. How could anyone build a *gravity pole?*
I'm actually an *English major,* but that's what I like about the whole real-life superhero thing. It's making a statement and being who you *want* to be.
Oh, right.
OPEN

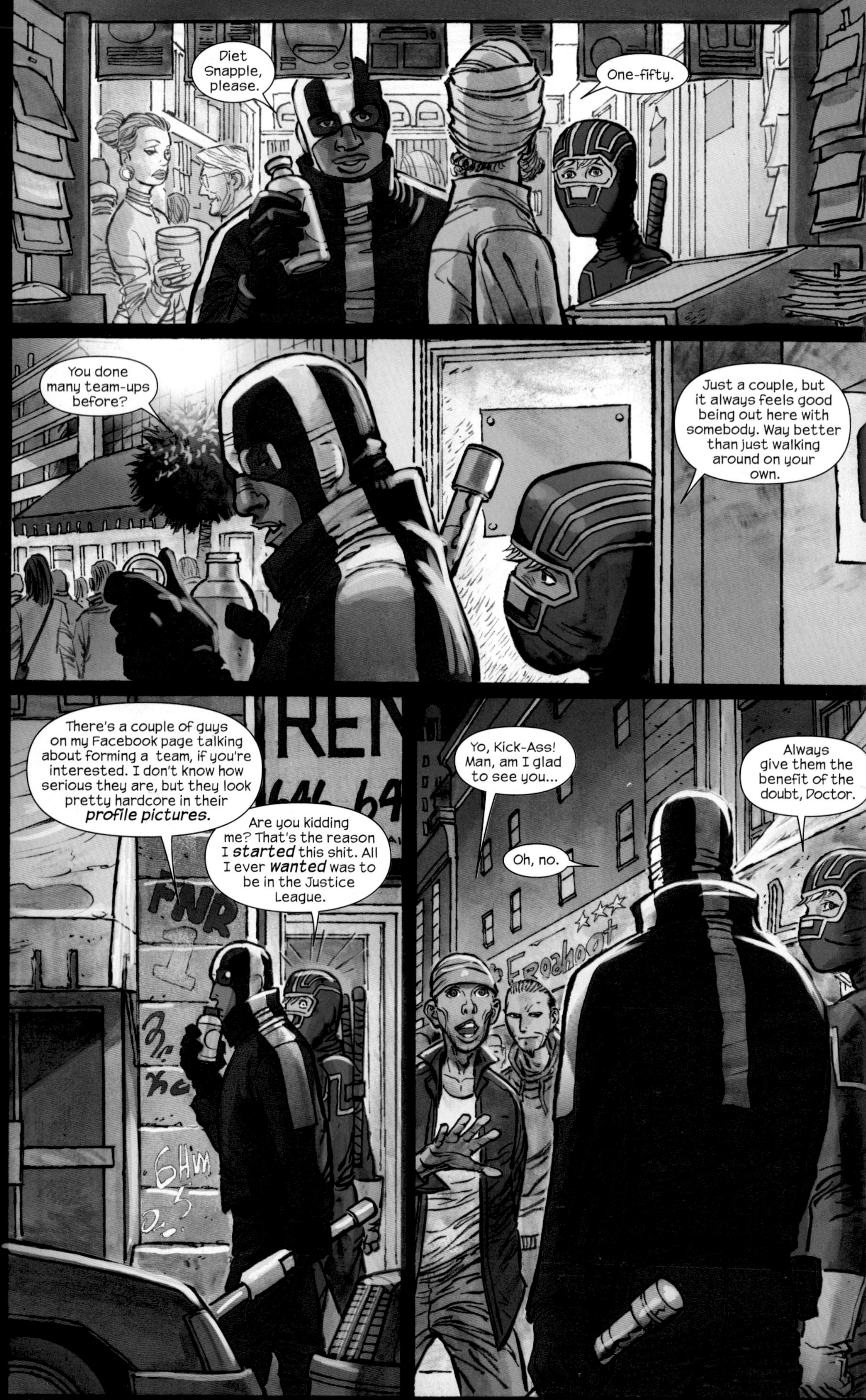

Diet Snapple, please.
One-fifty.
You done many team-ups before?
Just a couple, but it always feels good being out here with somebody. Way better than just walking around on your own.
There's a couple of guys on my Facebook page talking about forming a team, if you're interested. I don't know how serious they are, but they look pretty hardcore in their *profile pictures.*
Are you kidding me? That's the reason I *started* this shit. All I ever *wanted* was to be in the Justice League.
Yo, Kick-Ass! Man, am I glad to see you...
Oh, no.
Always give them the benefit of the doubt, Doctor.

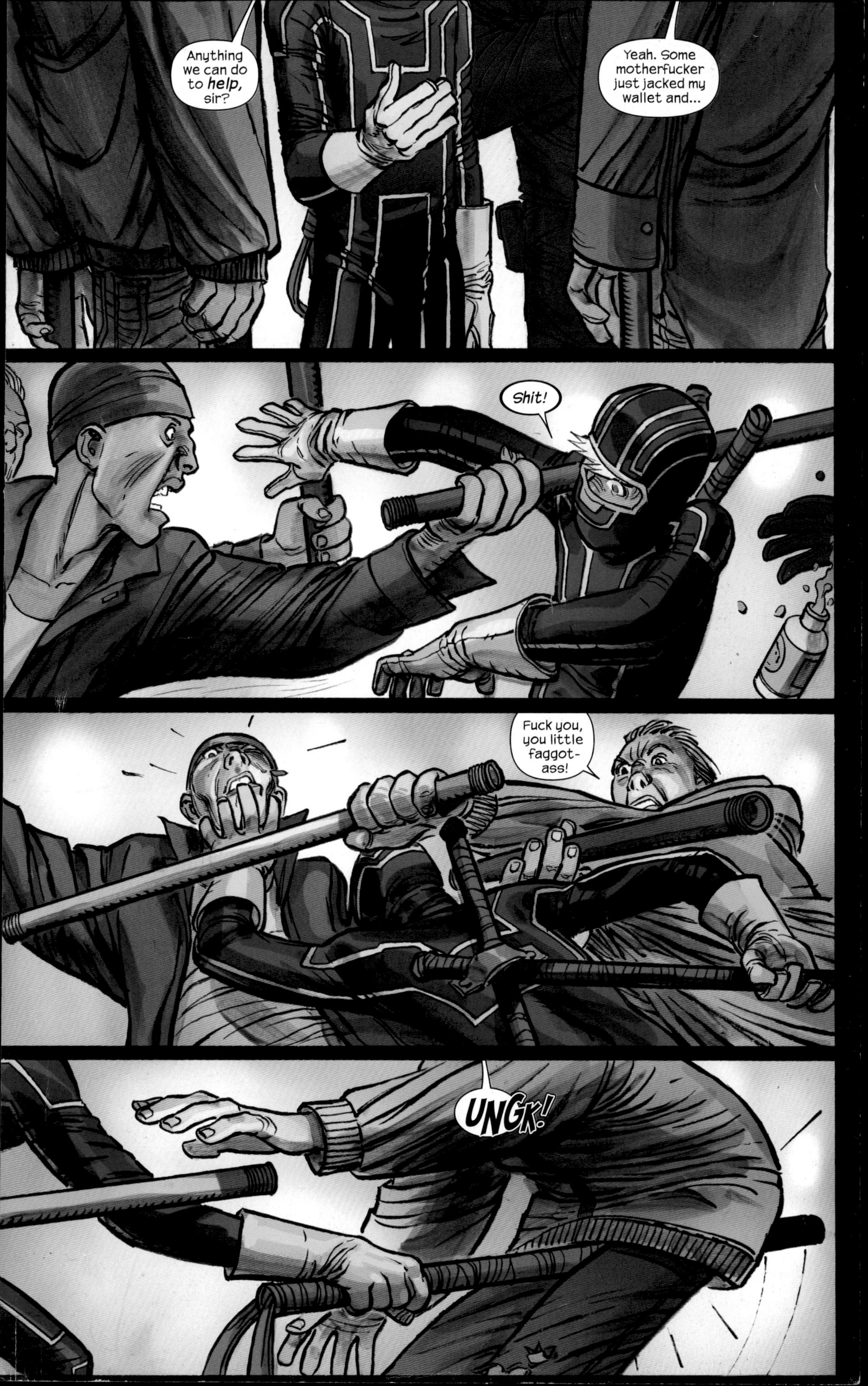
Anything we can do to *help,* sir?
Yeah. Some motherfucker just jacked my wallet and...
Shit!
Fuck you, you little faggot-ass!
UNGK!

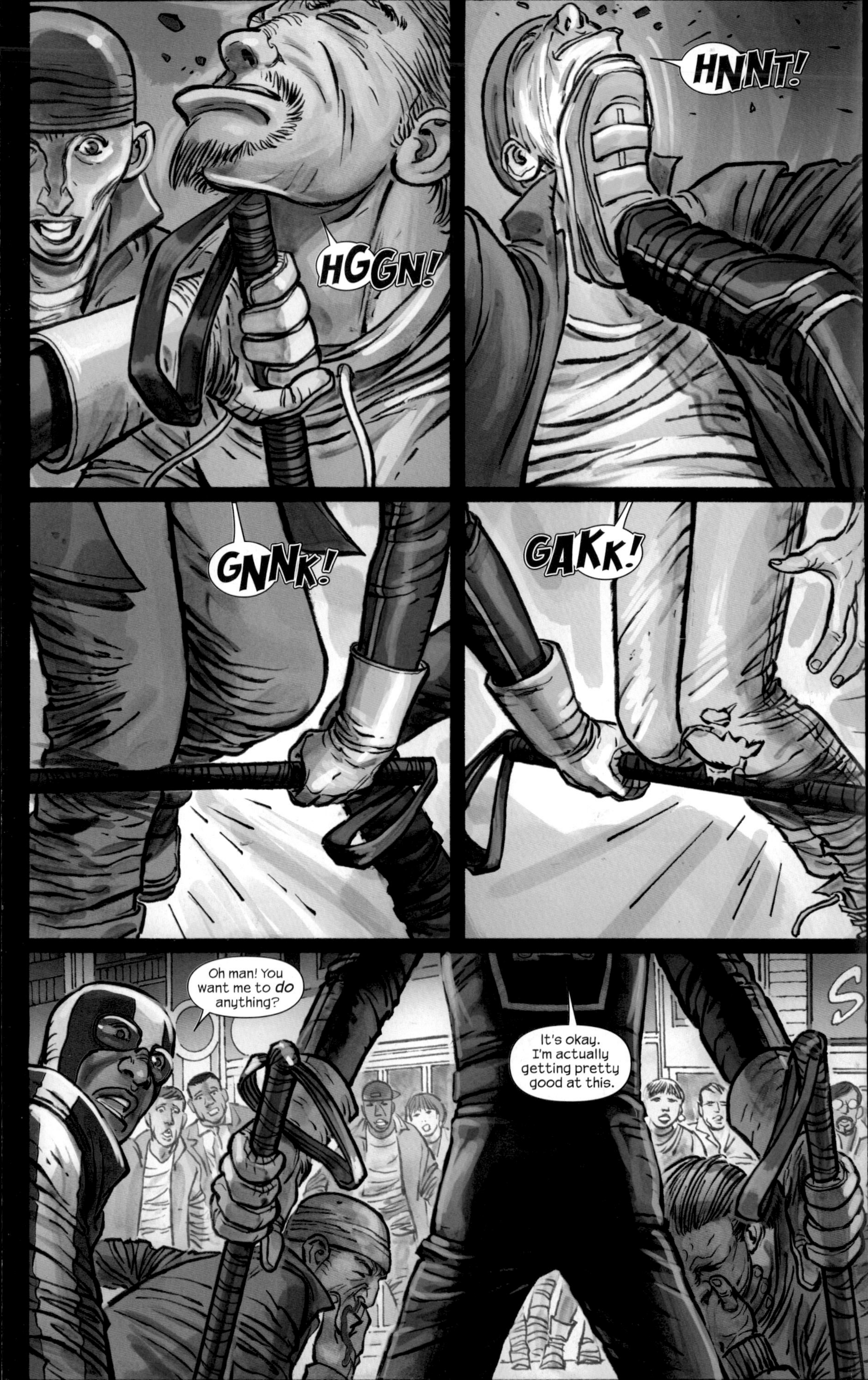
HGGN!
HNNT!
GNNK!
GAKK!
Oh man! You want me to *do* anything?
It's okay. I'm actually getting pretty good at this.

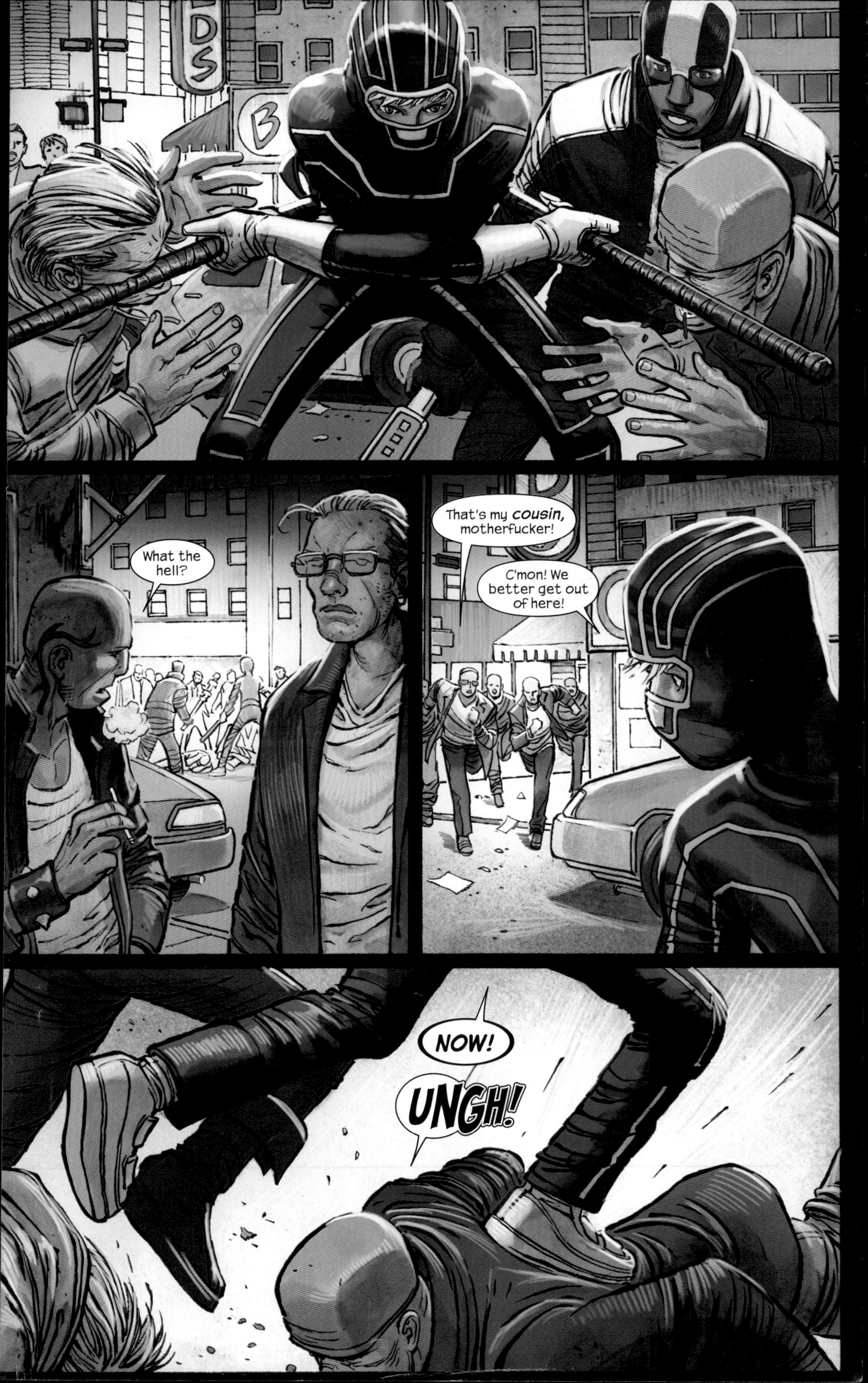
What the hell?
That's my cousin, motherfucker!
C'mon! We better get out of here!
NOW!
UNGH!

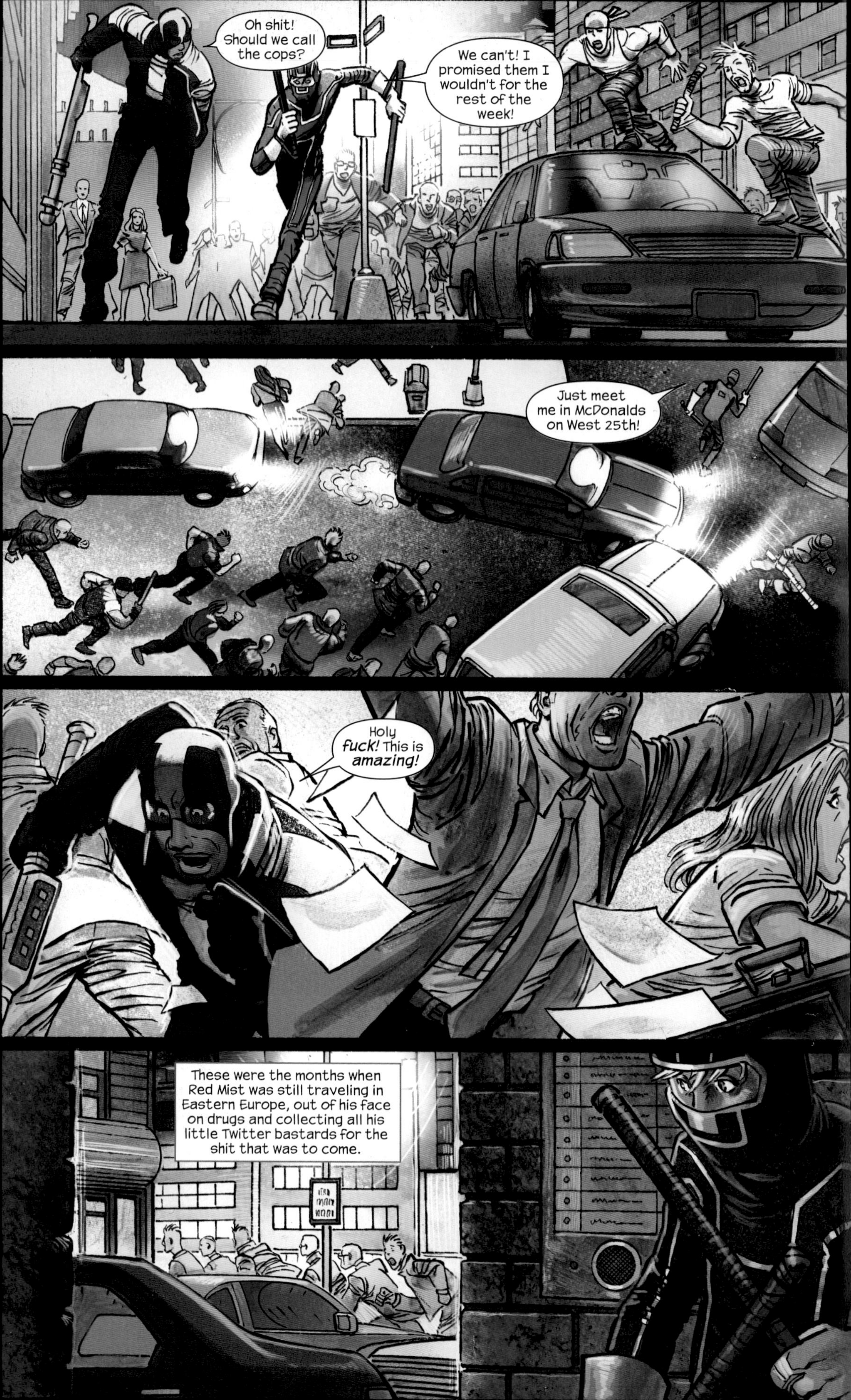
Oh shit! Should we call the cops?
We can't! I promised them I wouldn't for the rest of the week!
Just meet me in McDonalds on West 25th!
Holy *fuck!* This is *amazing!*
These were the months when Red Mist was still traveling in Eastern Europe, out of his face on drugs and collecting all his little Twitter bastards for the shit that was to come.

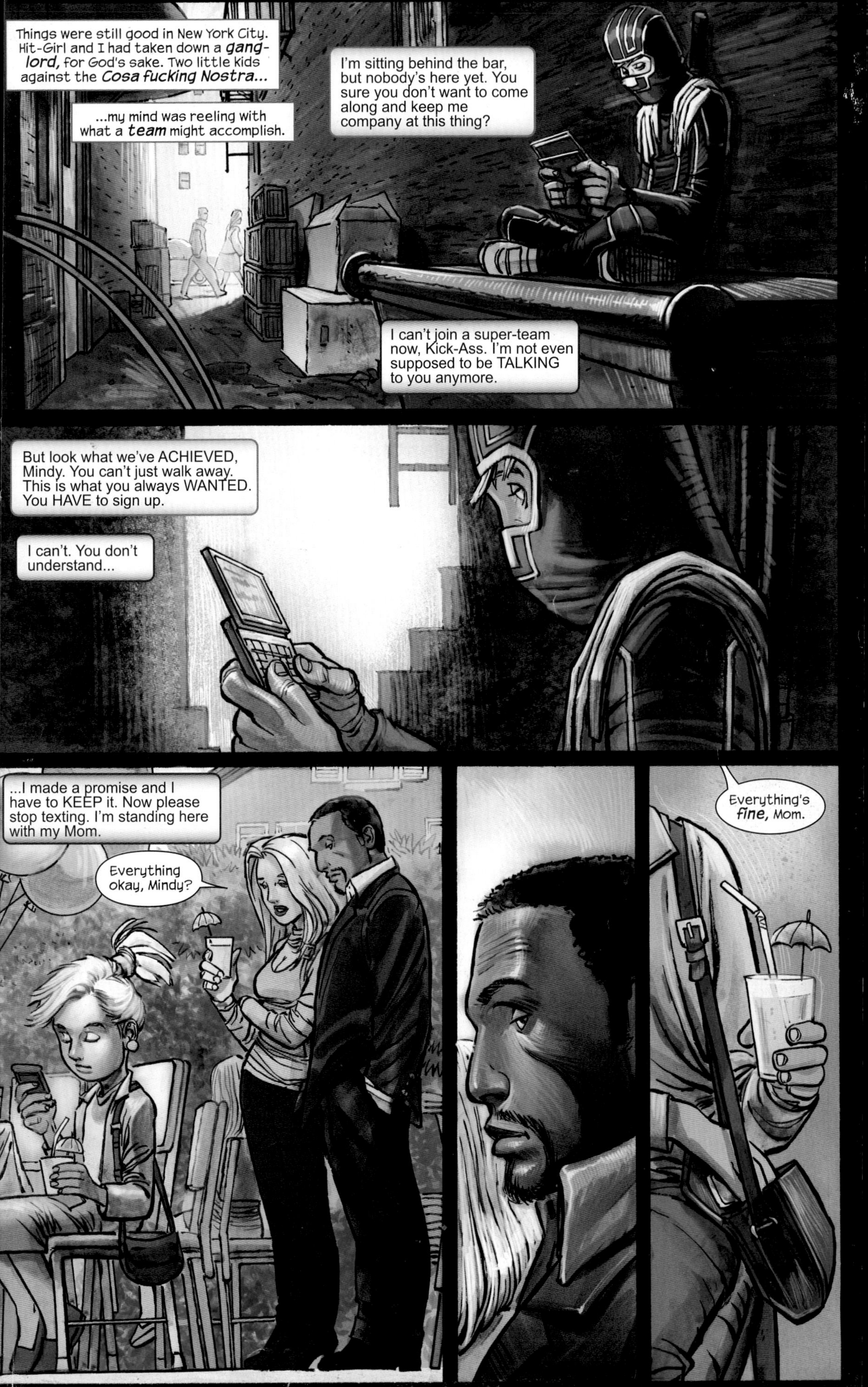
Things were still good in New York City. Hit-Girl and I had taken down a gang-lord, for God's sake. Two little kids against the Cosa fucking Nostra...
...my mind was reeling with what a team might accomplish.
I'm sitting behind the bar, but nobody's here yet. You sure you don't want to come along and keep me company at this thing?
I can't join a super-team now, Kick-Ass. I'm not even supposed to be TALKING to you anymore.
But look what we've ACHIEVED, Mindy. You can't just walk away. This is what you always WANTED. You HAVE to sign up.
I can't. You don't understand...
...I made a promise and I have to KEEP it. Now please stop texting. I'm standing here with my Mom.
Everything okay, Mindy?
Everything's fine, Mom.

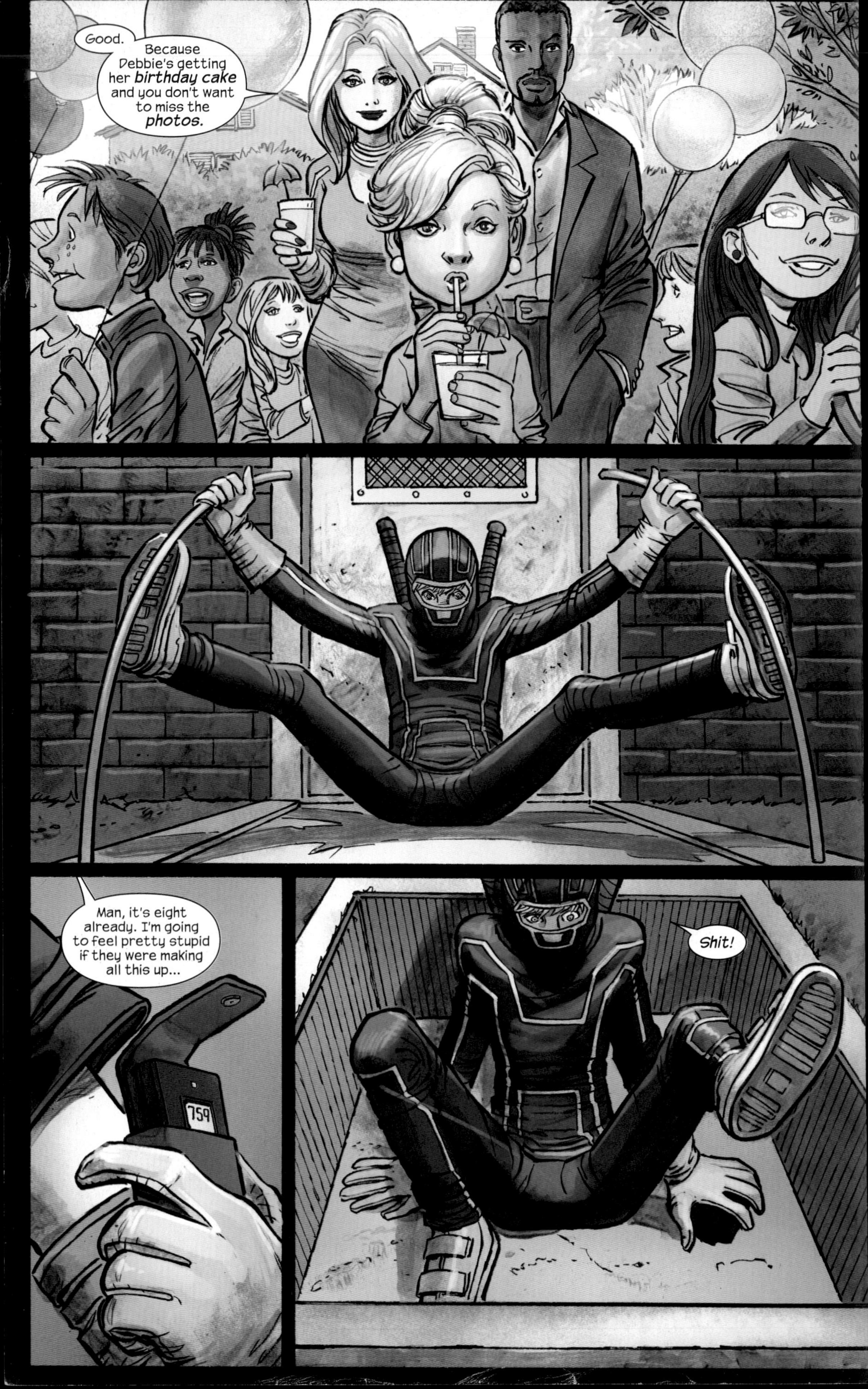
Good.
Because Debbie's getting her birthday cake and you don't want to miss the photos.
Man, it's eight already. I'm going to feel pretty stupid if they were making all this up...
7:59
Shit!

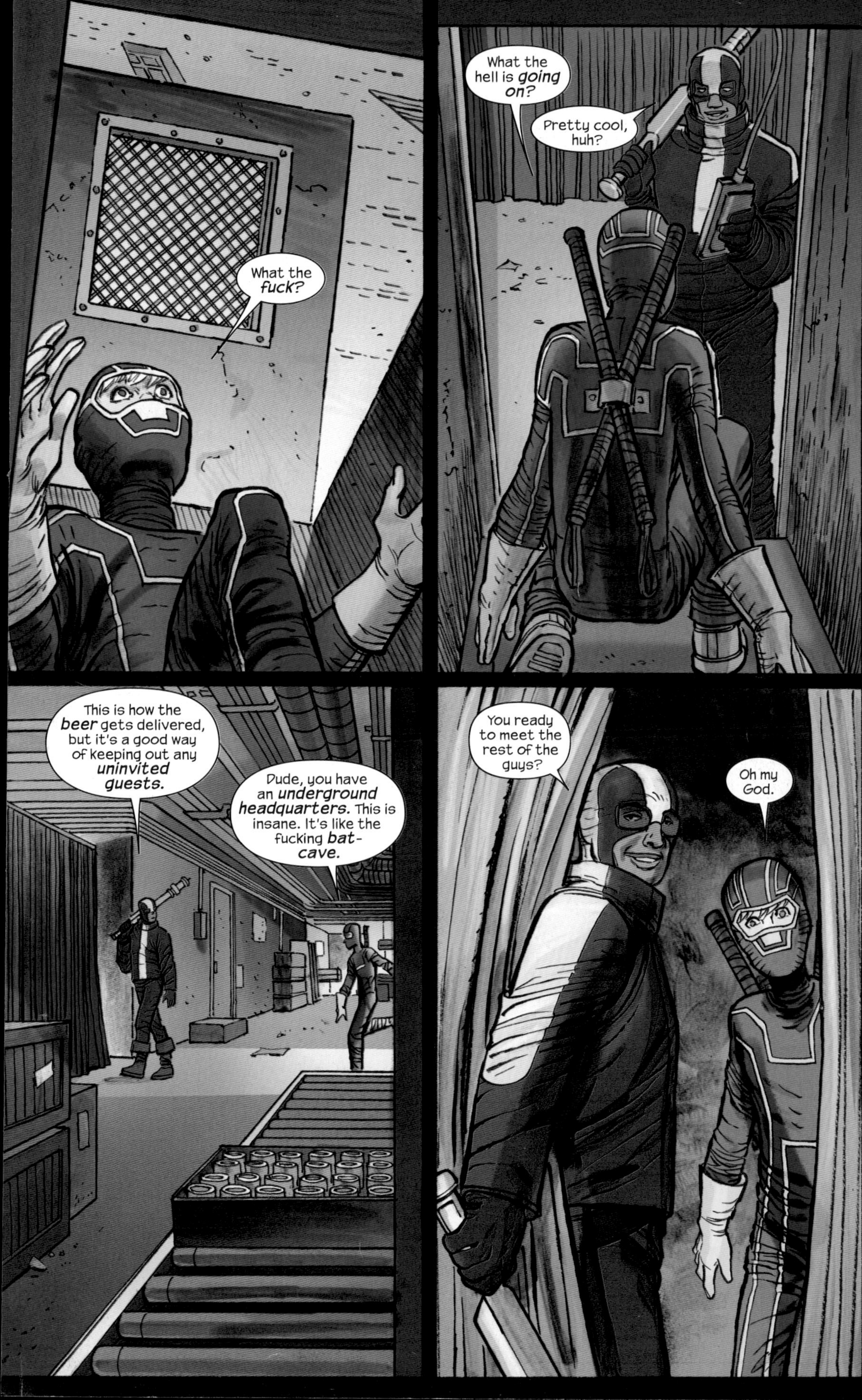

What the *fuck?*
What the hell is *going on?*
Pretty cool, huh?
This is how the *beer* gets delivered, but it's a good way of keeping out any *uninvited guests.*
Dude, you have an *underground headquarters.* This is insane. It's like the fucking *bat-cave.*
You ready to meet the rest of the guys?
Oh my God.

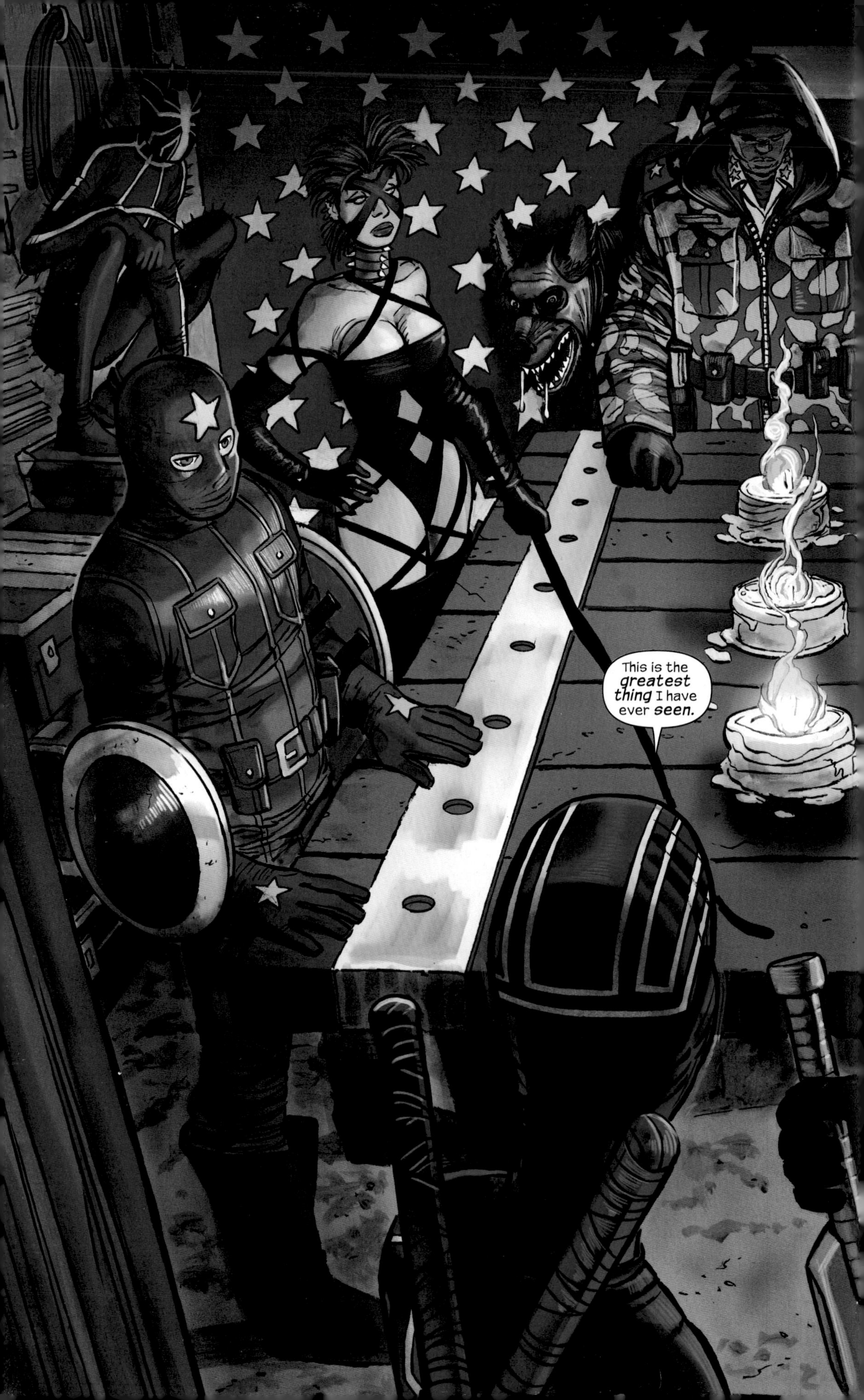
This is the *greatest thing* I have ever *seen.*

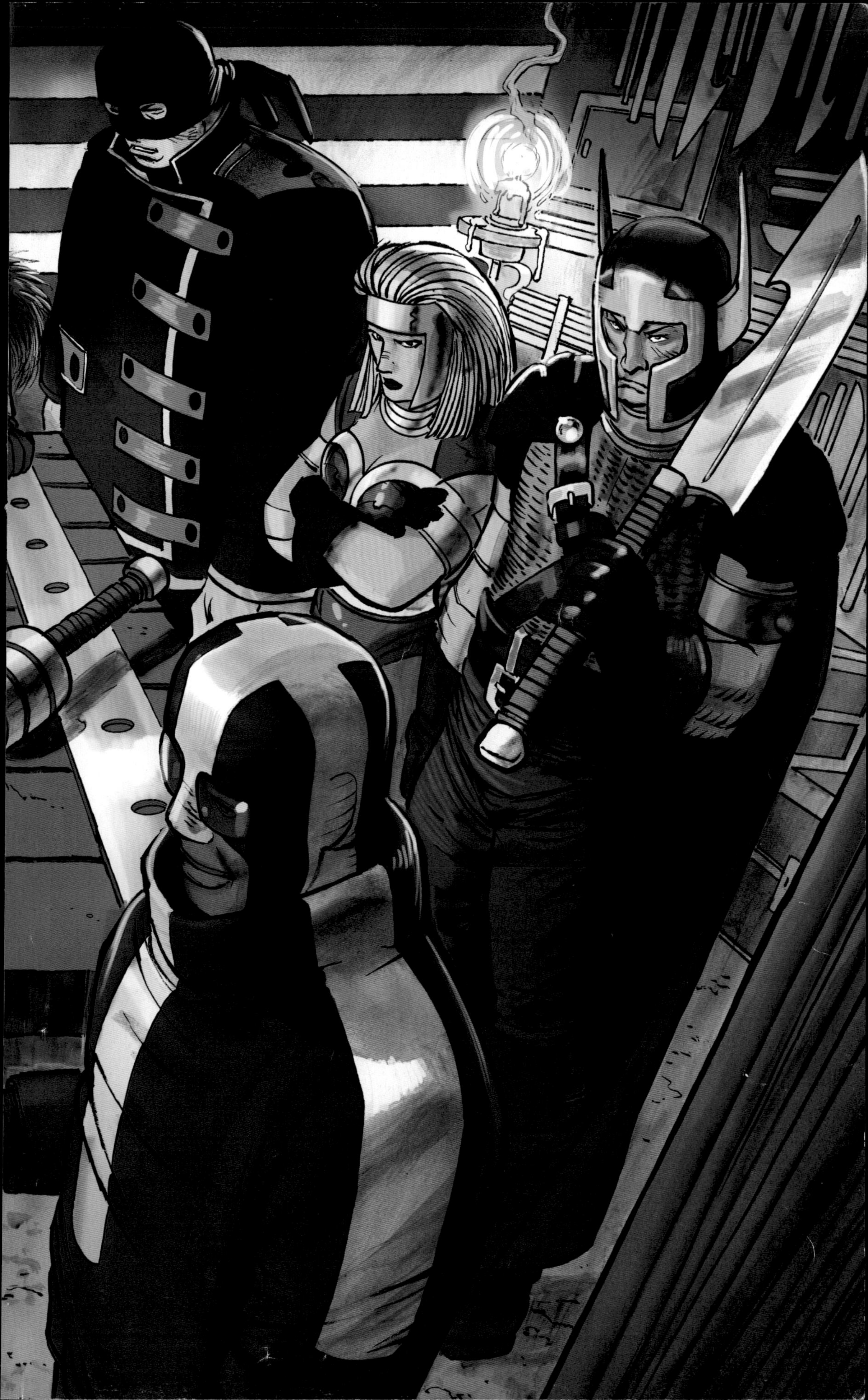

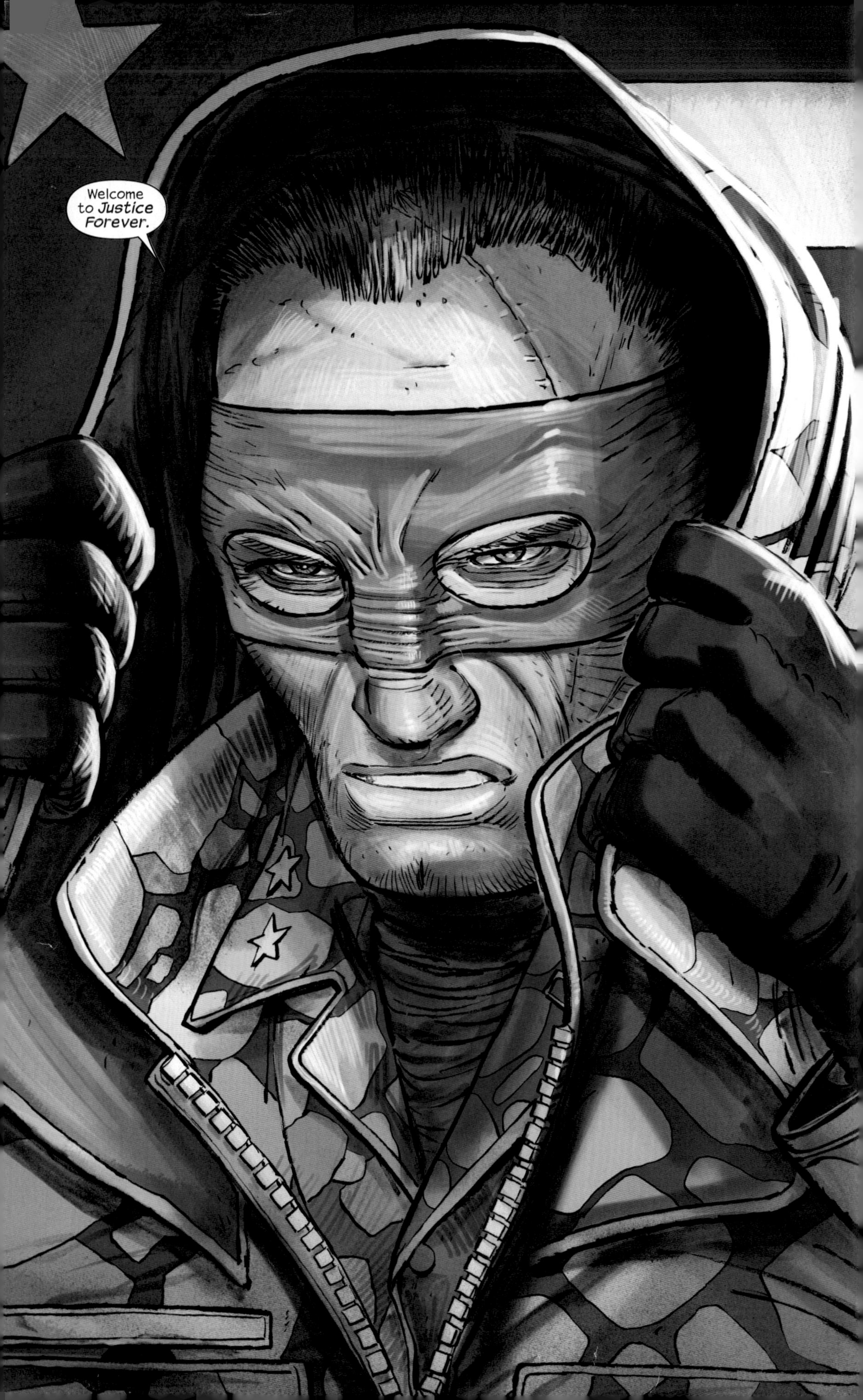
Welcome to *Justice Forever.*

TWO

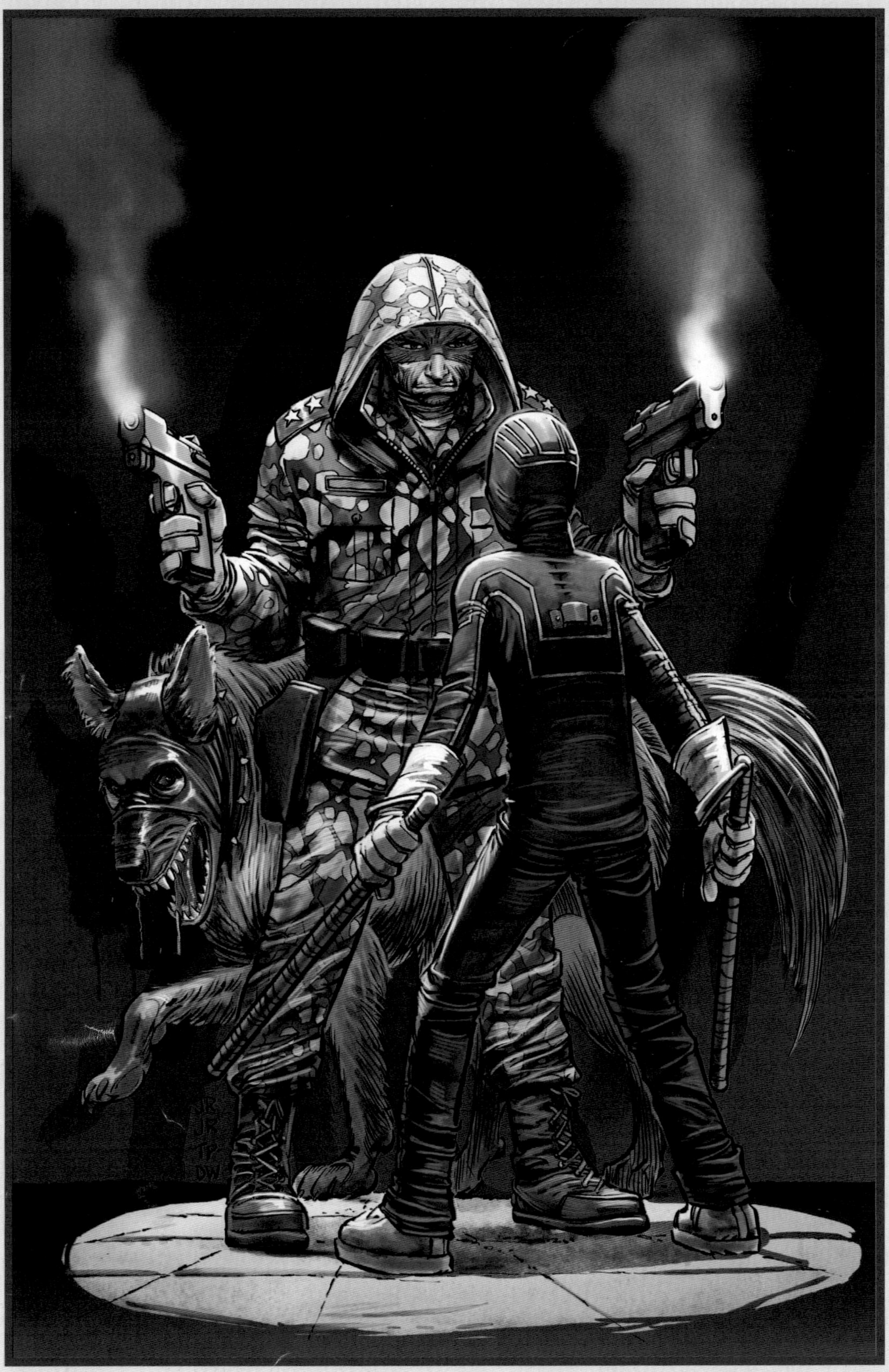

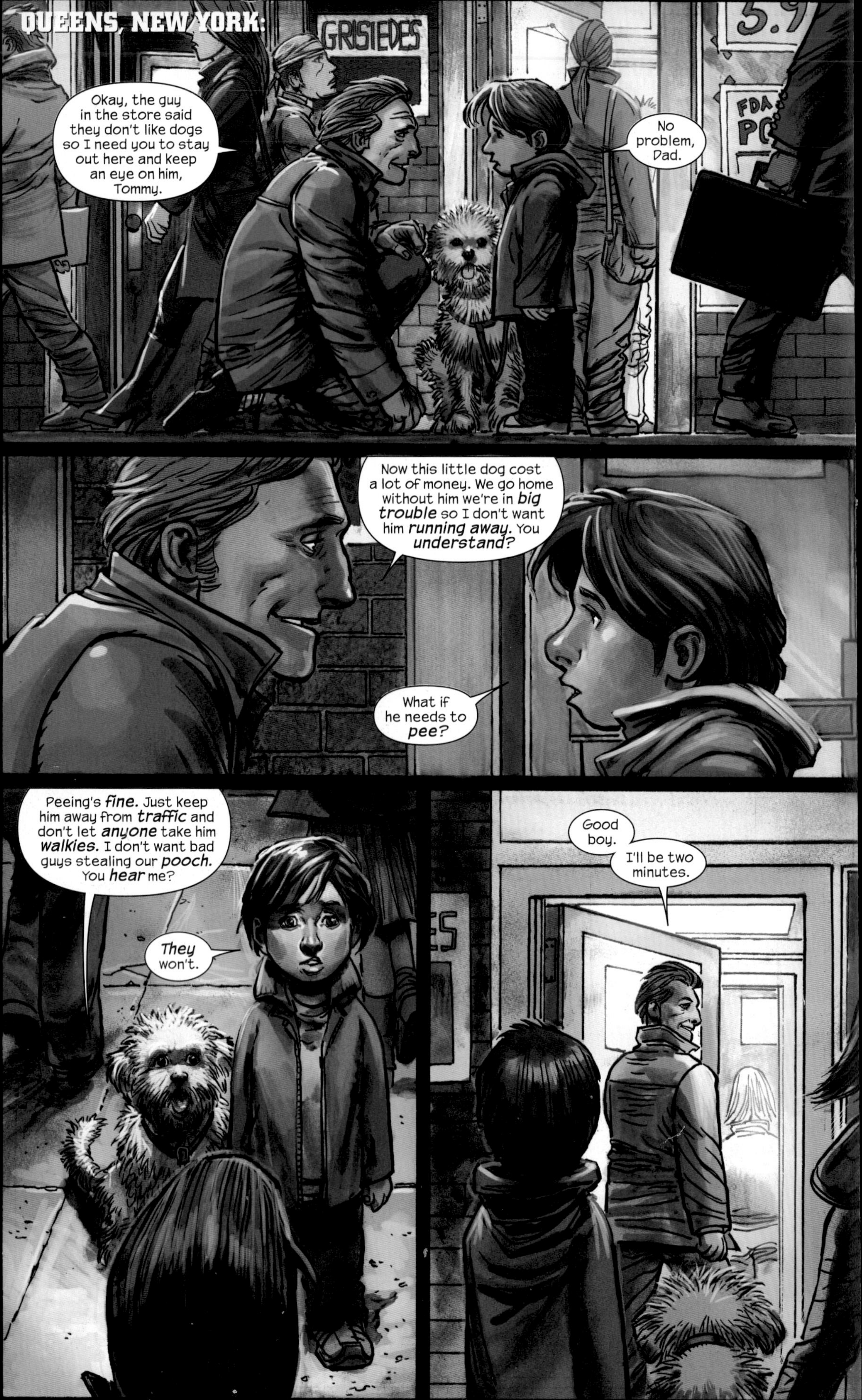
QUEENS, NEW YORK:
GRISTEDES
Okay, the guy in the store said they don't like dogs so I need you to stay out here and keep an eye on him, Tommy.
No problem, Dad.
Now this little dog cost a lot of money. We go home without him we're in *big trouble* so I don't want him *running away.* You *understand?*
What if he needs to *pee?*
Peeing's *fine.* Just keep him away from *traffic* and don't let *anyone* take him *walkies.* I don't want bad guys stealing our *pooch.* You *hear* me?
They won't.
Good boy.
I'll be two minutes.

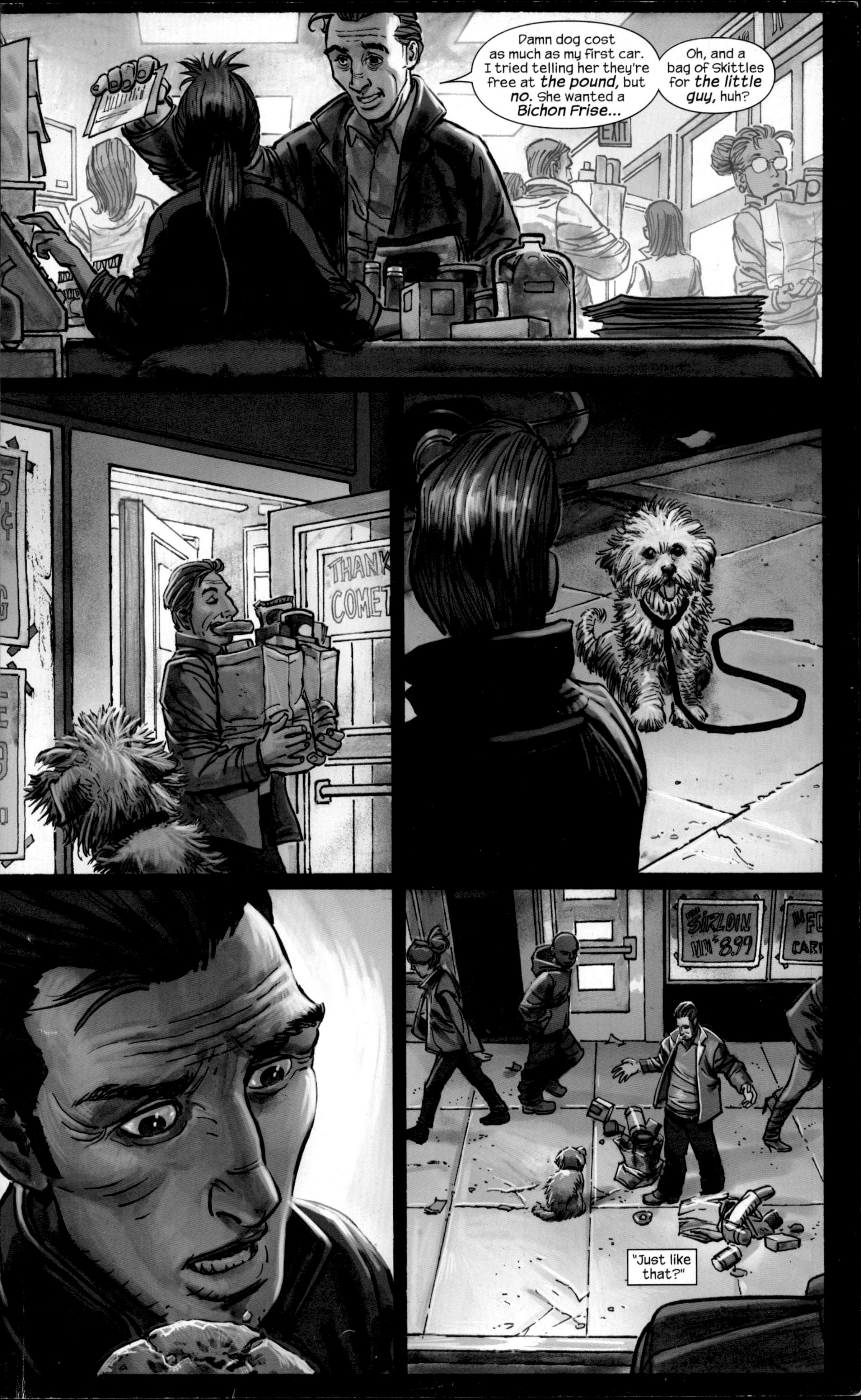
Damn dog cost as much as my first car. I tried telling her they're free at the pound, but no. She wanted a Bichon Frise...
Oh, and a bag of Skittles for the little guy, huh?
EXIT
THANK
COMET
SIRLOIN
$8.99
"Just like that?"

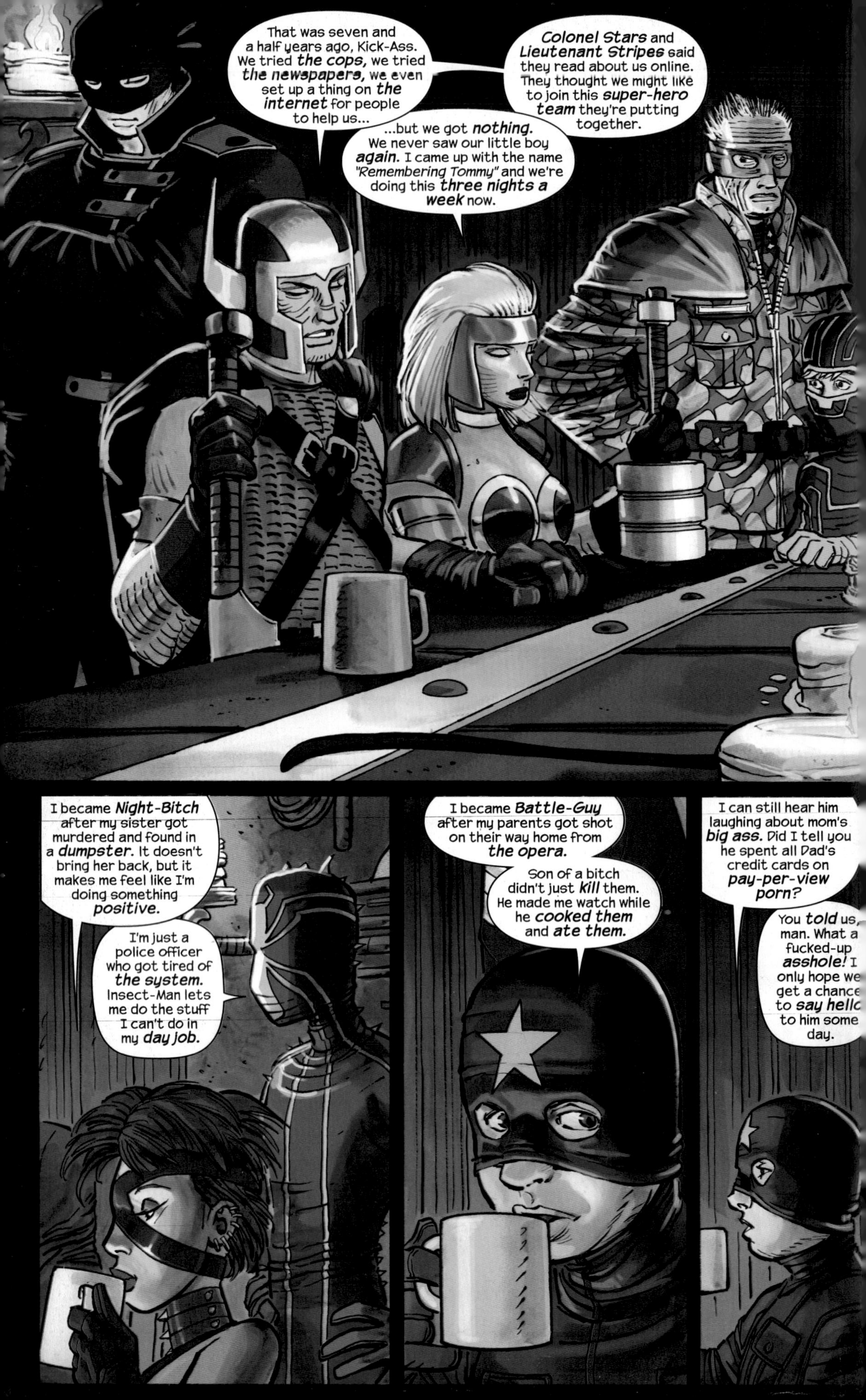

That was seven and a half years ago, Kick-Ass. We tried the cops, we tried the newspapers, we even set up a thing on the internet for people to help us...
...but we got nothing. We never saw our little boy again. I came up with the name "Remembering Tommy" and we're doing this three nights a week now.
Colonel Stars and Lieutenant Stripes said they read about us online. They thought we might like to join this super-hero team they're putting together.
I became Night-Bitch after my sister got murdered and found in a dumpster. It doesn't bring her back, but it makes me feel like I'm doing something positive.
I'm just a police officer who got tired of the system. Insect-Man lets me do the stuff I can't do in my day job.
I became Battle-Guy after my parents got shot on their way home from the opera.
Son of a bitch didn't just kill them. He made me watch while he cooked them and ate them.
I can still hear him laughing about mom's big ass. Did I tell you he spent all Dad's credit cards on pay-per-view porn?
You told us, man. What a fucked-up asshole! I only hope we get a chance to say hello to him some day.

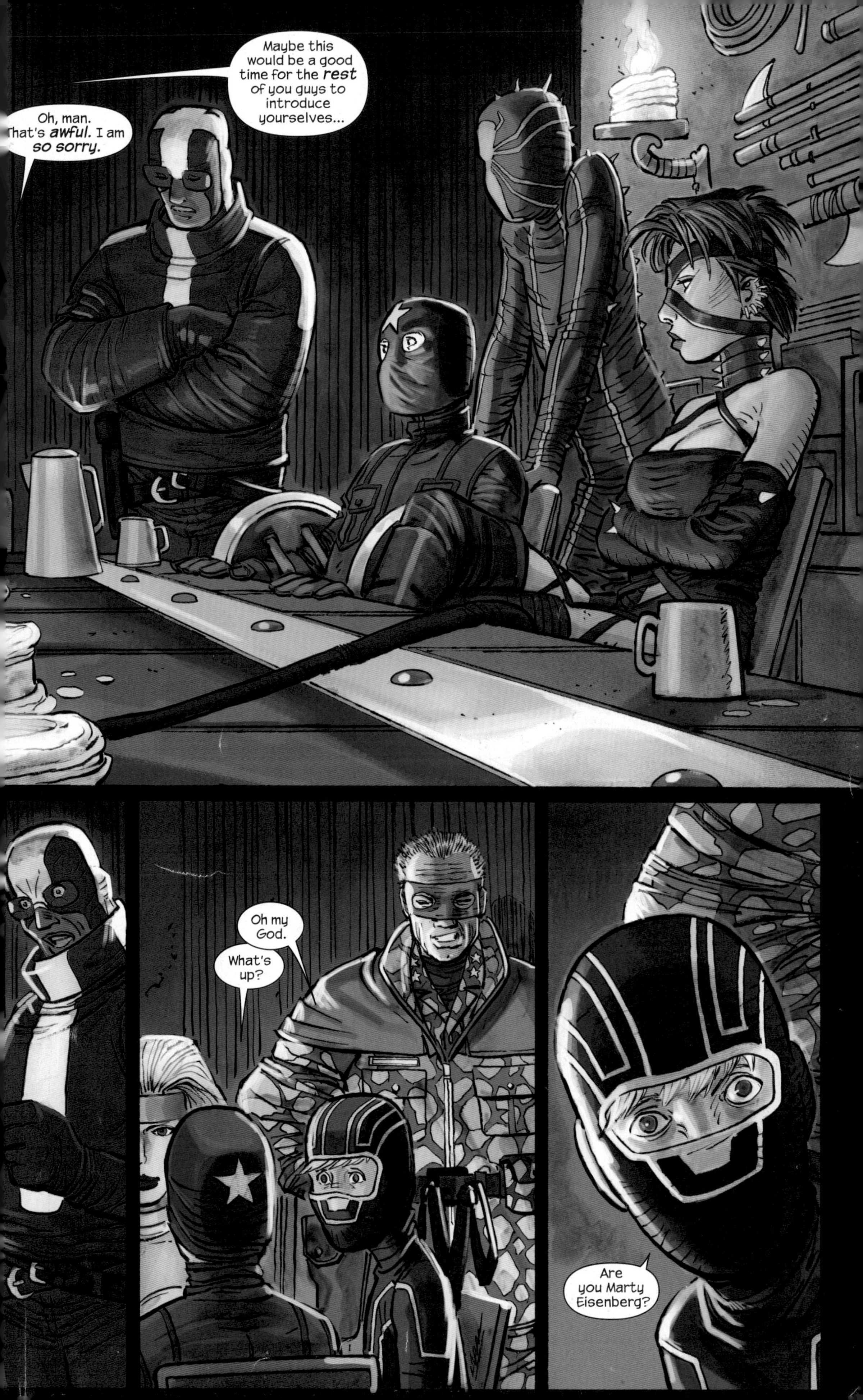
Maybe this would be a good time for the *rest* of you guys to introduce yourselves...
Oh, man. That's ***awful.*** I am ***so sorry.***
Oh my God.
What's up?
Are you Marty Eisenberg?

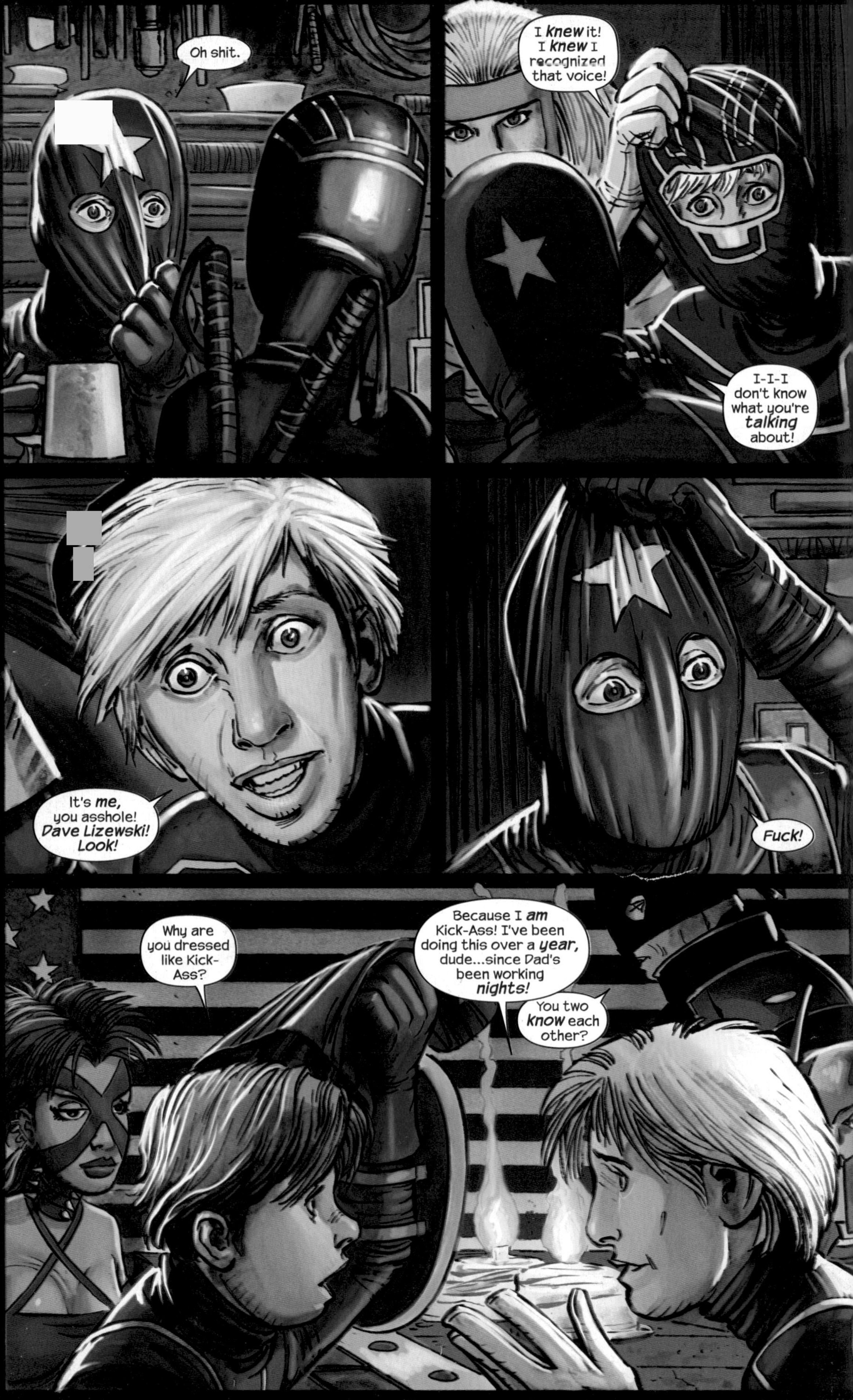
Oh shit.
I *knew* it! I *knew* I recognized that voice!
I-I-I don't know what you're *talking* about!
It's *me,* you asshole! *Dave Lizewski! Look!*
Fuck!
Why are you dressed like Kick-Ass?
Because I *am* Kick-Ass! I've been doing this over a *year,* dude...since Dad's been working *nights!*
You two *know* each other?

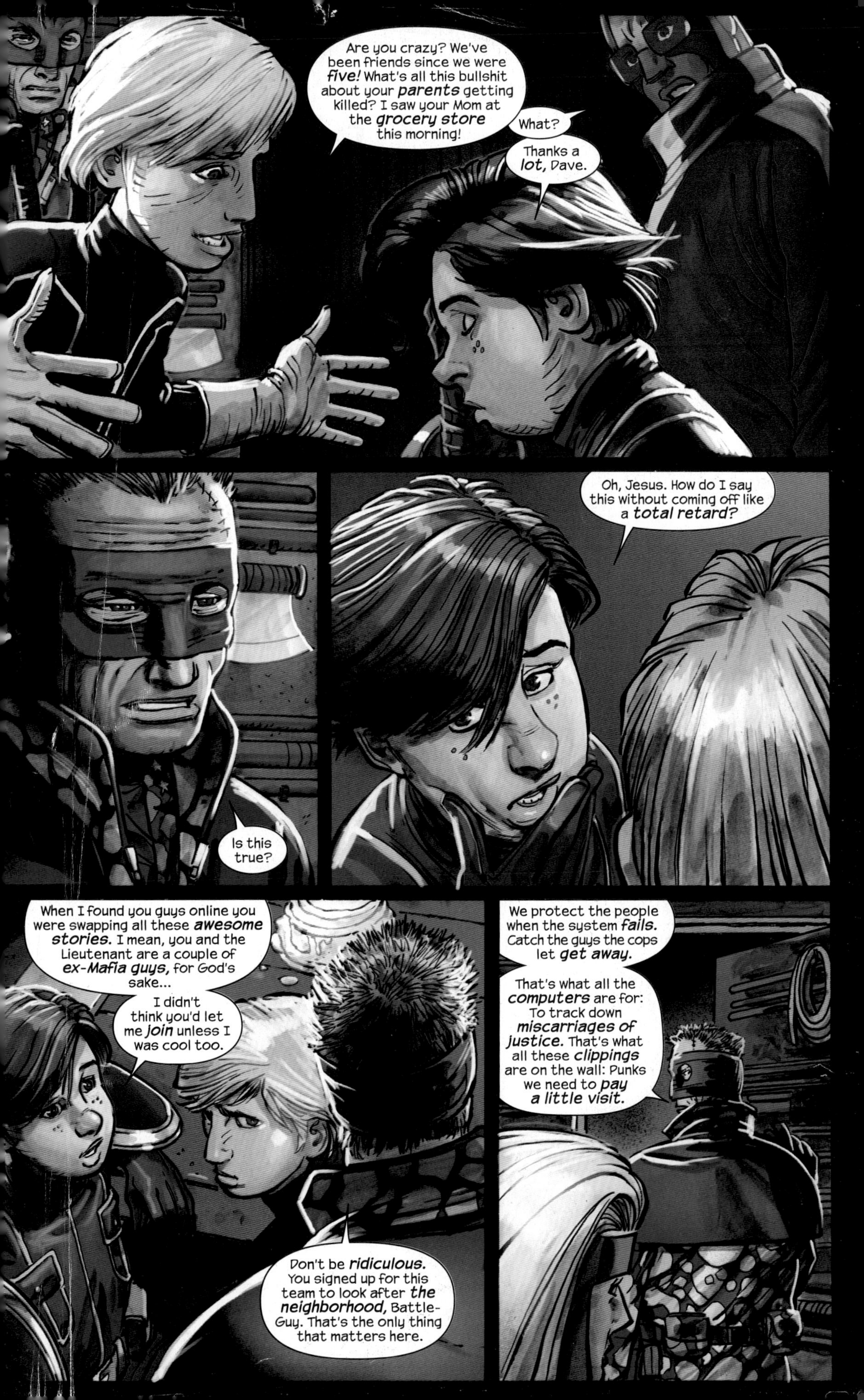
Are you crazy? We've been friends since we were five! What's all this bullshit about your parents getting killed? I saw your Mom at the grocery store this morning!
What?
Thanks a lot, Dave.
Is this true?
Oh, Jesus. How do I say this without coming off like a total retard?
When I found you guys online you were swapping all these awesome stories. I mean, you and the Lieutenant are a couple of ex-Mafia guys, for God's sake...
I didn't think you'd let me join unless I was cool too.
Don't be ridiculous. You signed up for this team to look after the neighborhood, Battle-Guy. That's the only thing that matters here.
We protect the people when the system fails. Catch the guys the cops let get away.
That's what all the computers are for: To track down miscarriages of justice. That's what all these clippings are on the wall: Punks we need to pay a little visit.

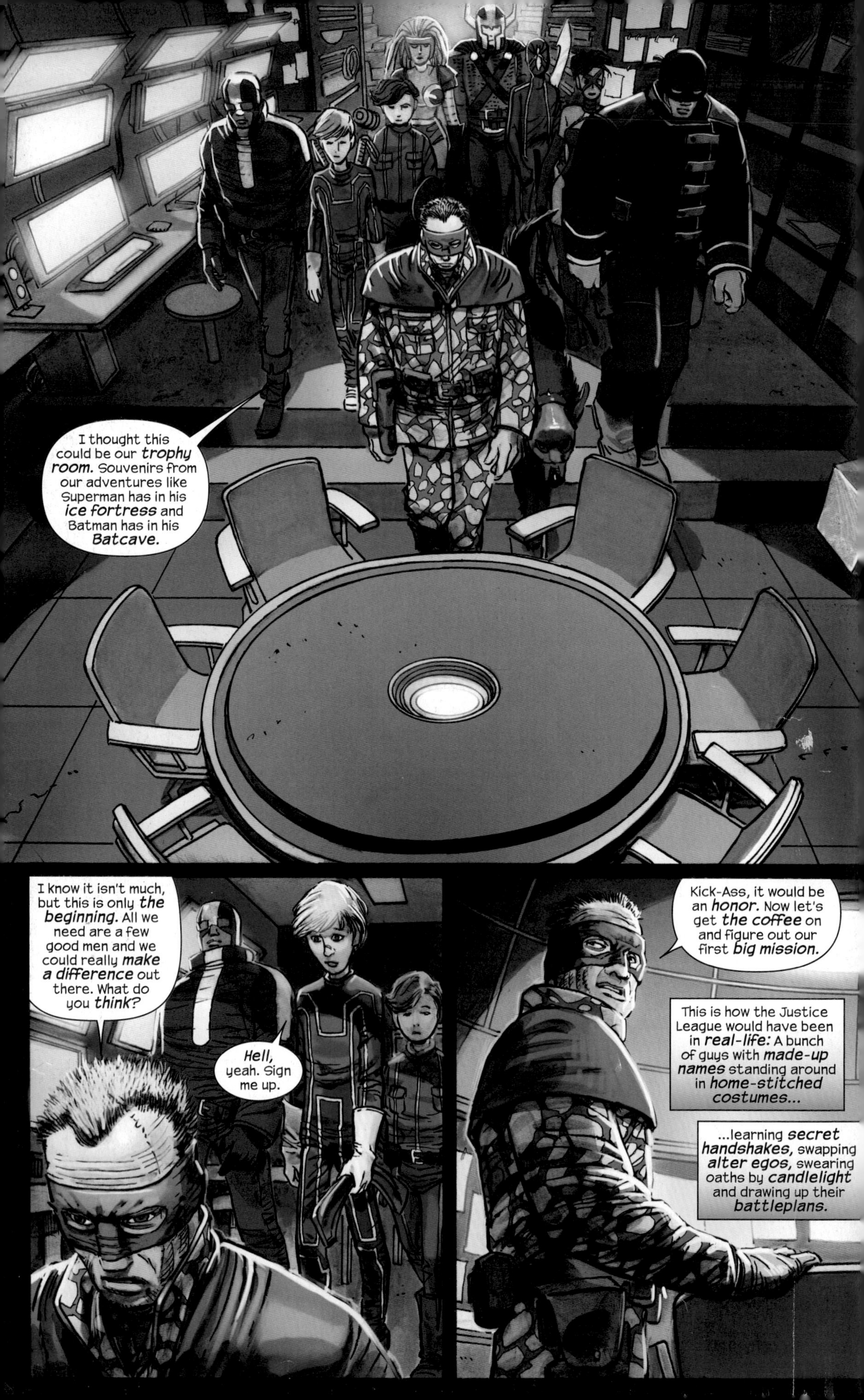

I thought this could be our trophy room. Souvenirs from our adventures like Superman has in his ice fortress and Batman has in his Batcave.
I know it isn't much, but this is only the beginning. All we need are a few good men and we could really make a difference out there. What do you think?
Hell, yeah. Sign me up.
Kick-Ass, it would be an honor. Now let's get the coffee on and figure out our first big mission.
This is how the Justice League would have been in real-life: A bunch of guys with made-up names standing around in home-stitched costumes...
...learning secret handshakes, swapping alter egos, swearing oaths by candlelight and drawing up their battleplans.

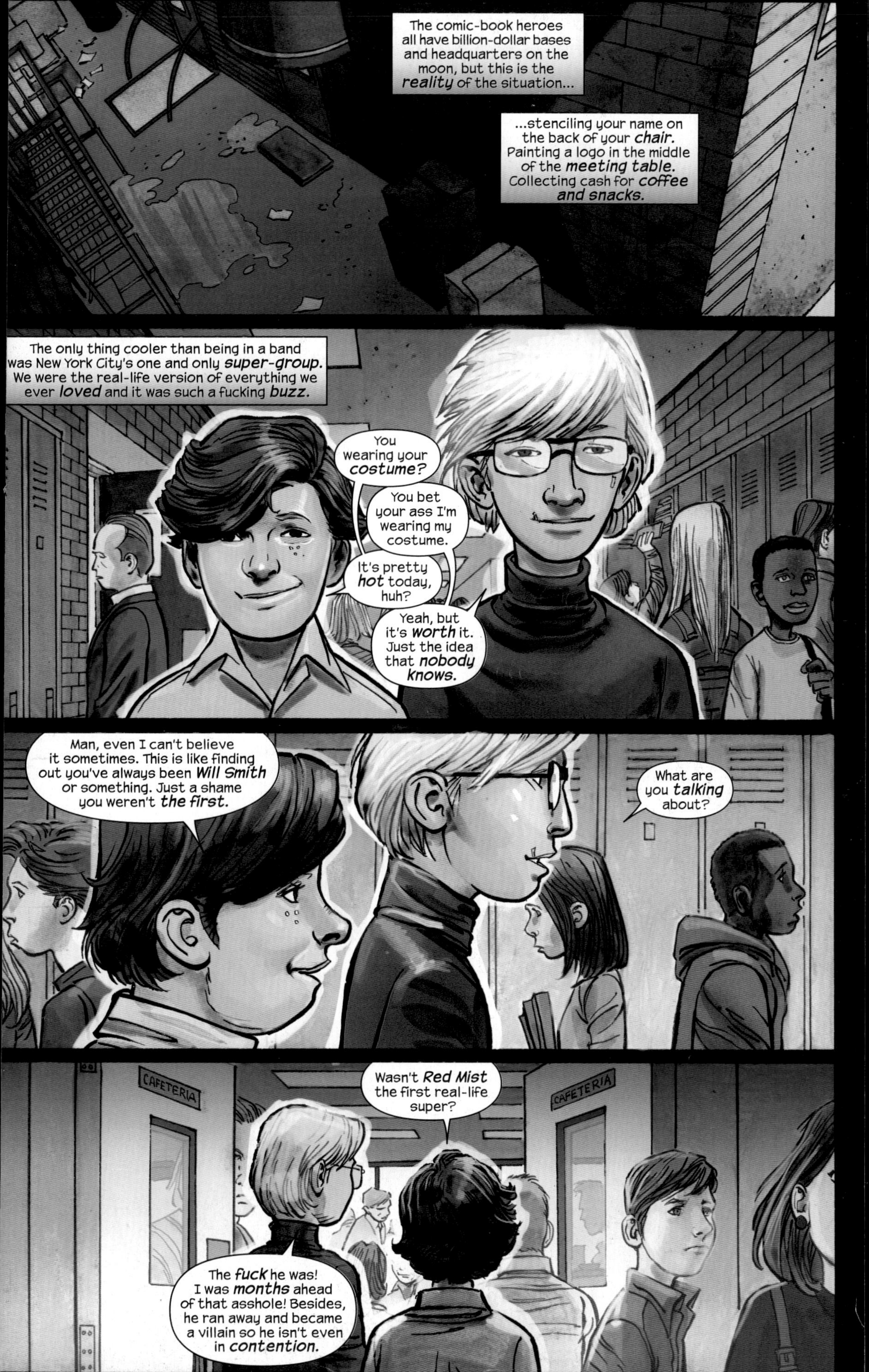
The comic-book heroes all have billion-dollar bases and headquarters on the moon, but this is the *reality* of the situation...
...stenciling your name on the back of your *chair.* Painting a logo in the middle of the *meeting table.* Collecting cash for *coffee and snacks.*
The only thing cooler than being in a band was New York City's one and only *super-group.* We were the real-life version of everything we ever *loved* and it was such a fucking *buzz.*
You wearing your *costume?*
You bet your ass I'm wearing my costume.
It's pretty *hot* today, huh?
Yeah, but it's *worth* it. Just the idea that *nobody knows.*
Man, even I can't believe it sometimes. This is like finding out you've always been *Will Smith* or something. Just a shame you weren't *the first.*
What are you *talking* about?
CAFETERIA
CAFETERIA
Wasn't *Red Mist* the first real-life super?
The *fuck* he was! I was *months* ahead of that asshole! Besides, he ran away and became a villain so he isn't even in *contention.*

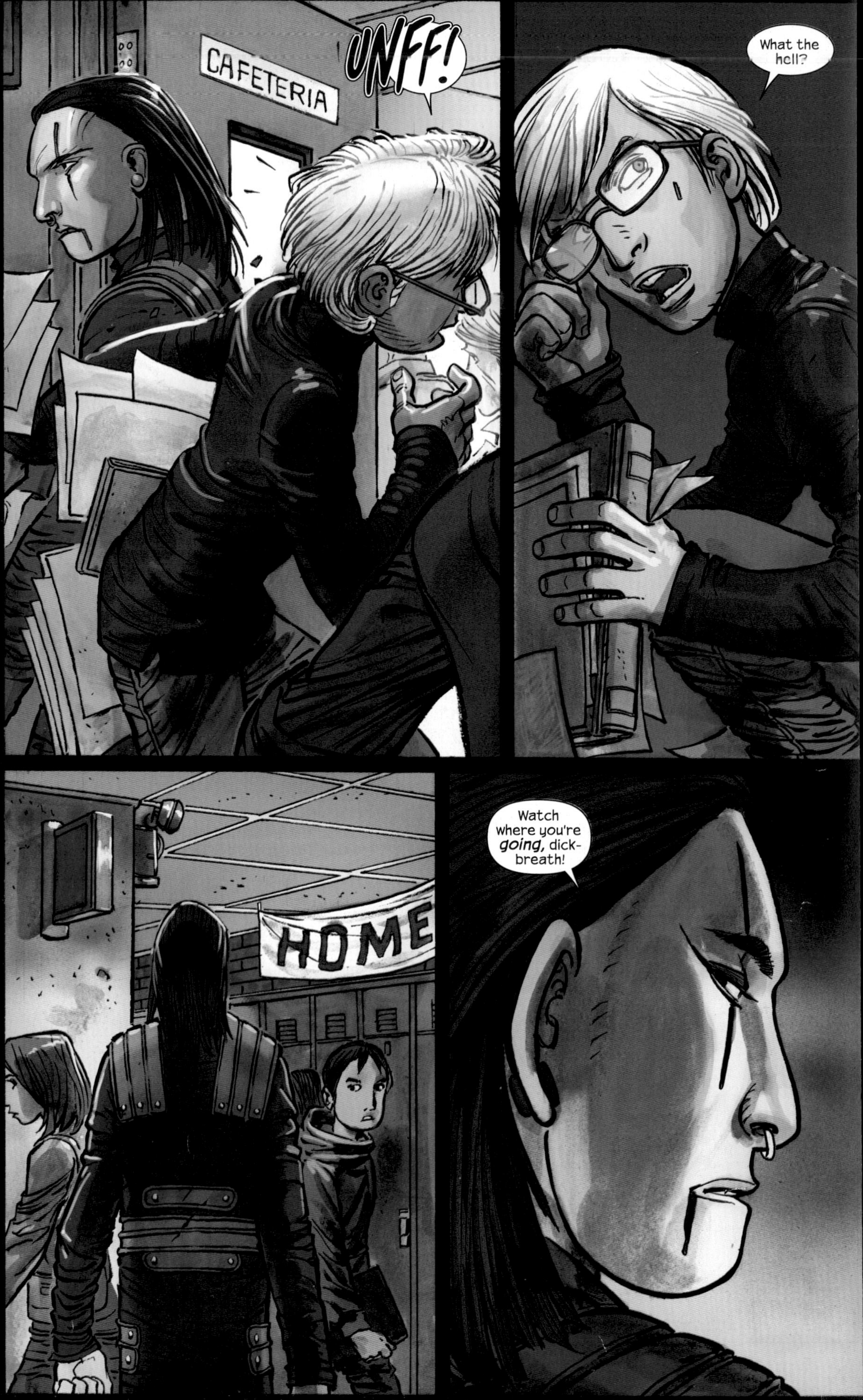
CAFETERIA
UNFF!
What the hell?
HOME
Watch where you're *going,* dick-breath!

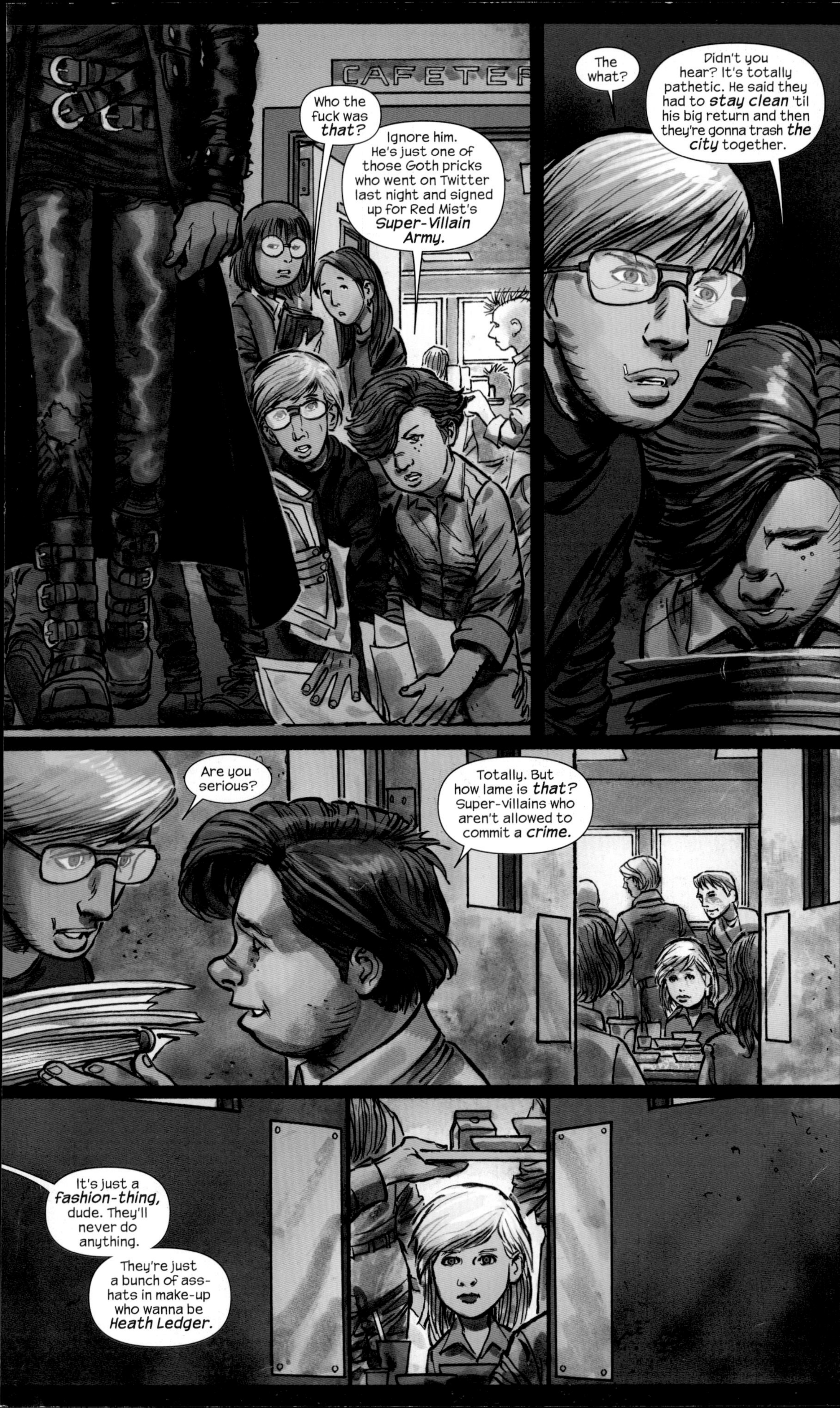
CAFETER
Who the fuck was that?
Ignore him. He's just one of those Goth pricks who went on Twitter last night and signed up for Red Mist's Super-Villain Army.
The what?
Didn't you hear? It's totally pathetic. He said they had to stay clean 'til his big return and then they're gonna trash the city together.
Are you serious?
Totally. But how lame is that? Super-villains who aren't allowed to commit a crime.
It's just a fashion-thing, dude. They'll never do anything.
They're just a bunch of ass-hats in make-up who wanna be Heath Ledger.

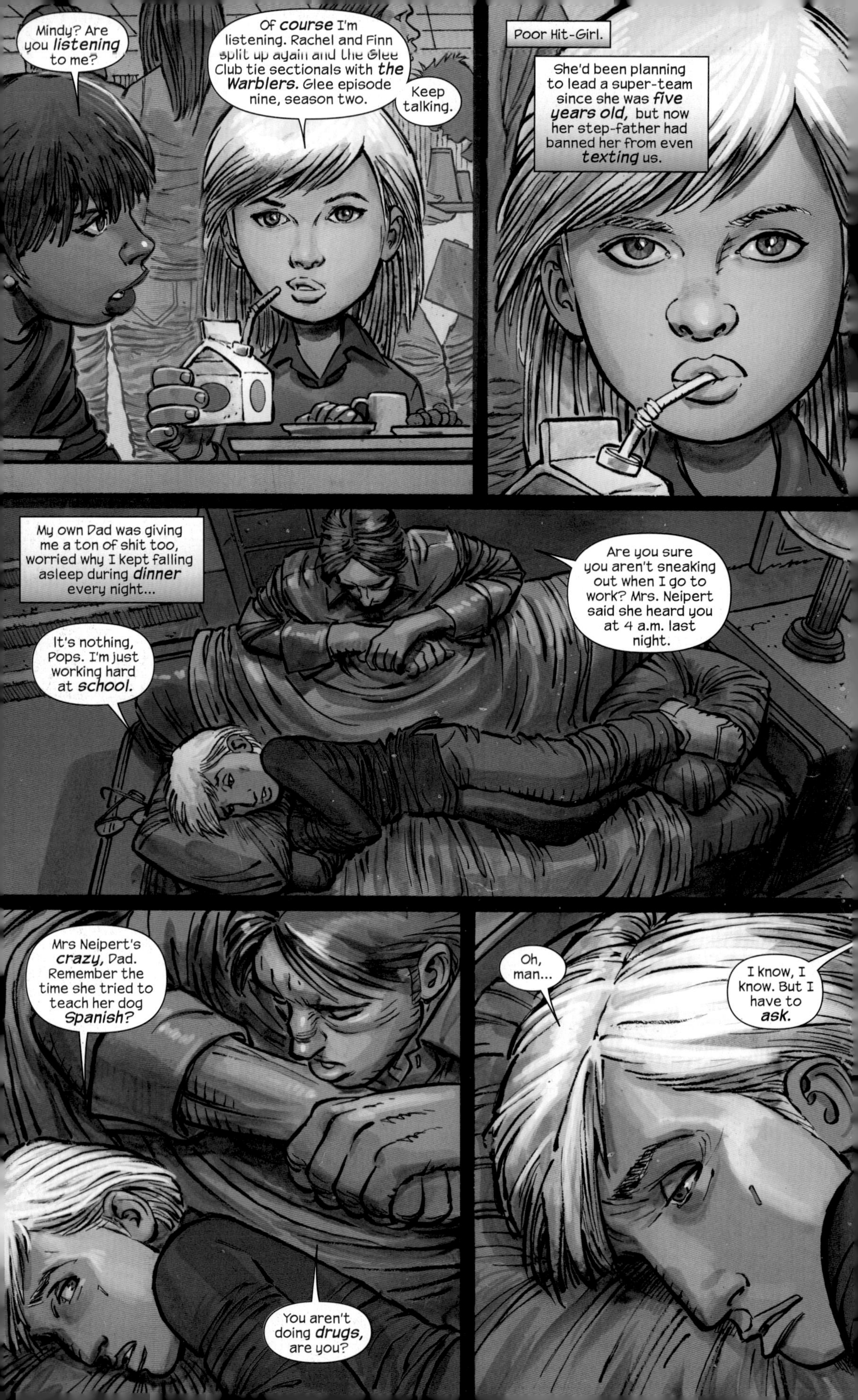
Mindy? Are you *listening* to me?
Of *course* I'm listening. Rachel and Finn split up again and the Glee Club tie sectionals with *the Warblers.* Glee episode nine, season two.
Keep talking.
Poor Hit-Girl.
She'd been planning to lead a super-team since she was *five years old,* but now her step-father had banned her from even *texting* us.
My own Dad was giving me a ton of shit too, worried why I kept falling asleep during *dinner* every night...
Are you sure you aren't sneaking out when I go to work? Mrs. Neipert said she heard you at 4 a.m. last night.
It's nothing, Pops. I'm just working hard at *school.*
Mrs Neipert's *crazy,* Dad. Remember the time she tried to teach her dog *Spanish?*
You aren't doing *drugs,* are you?
Oh, man...
I know, I know. But I have to *ask.*

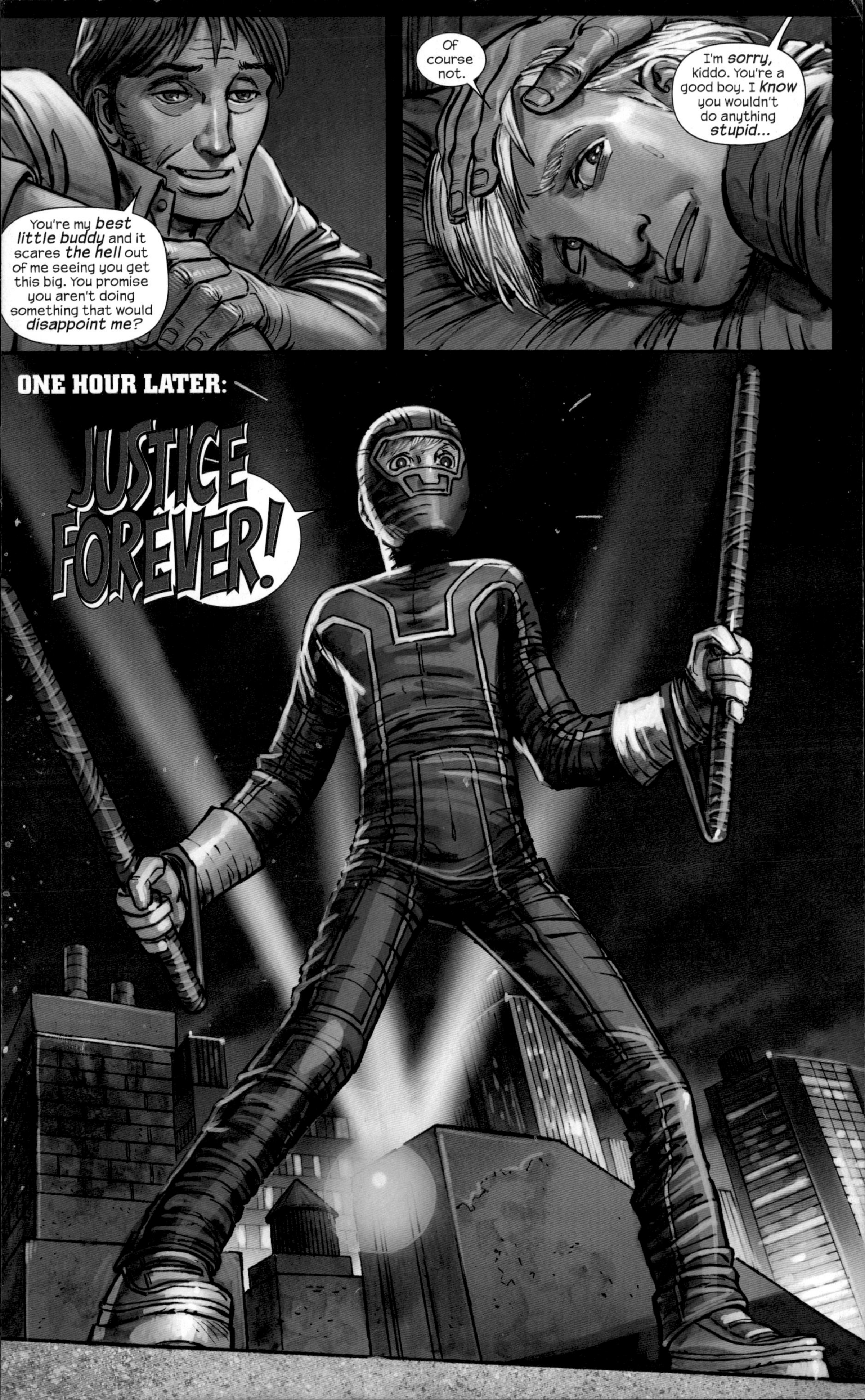

You're my best little buddy and it scares the hell out of me seeing you get this big. You promise you aren't doing something that would disappoint me?
Of course not.
I'm sorry, kiddo. You're a good boy. I know you wouldn't do anything stupid...
ONE HOUR LATER:
JUSTICE FOREVER!

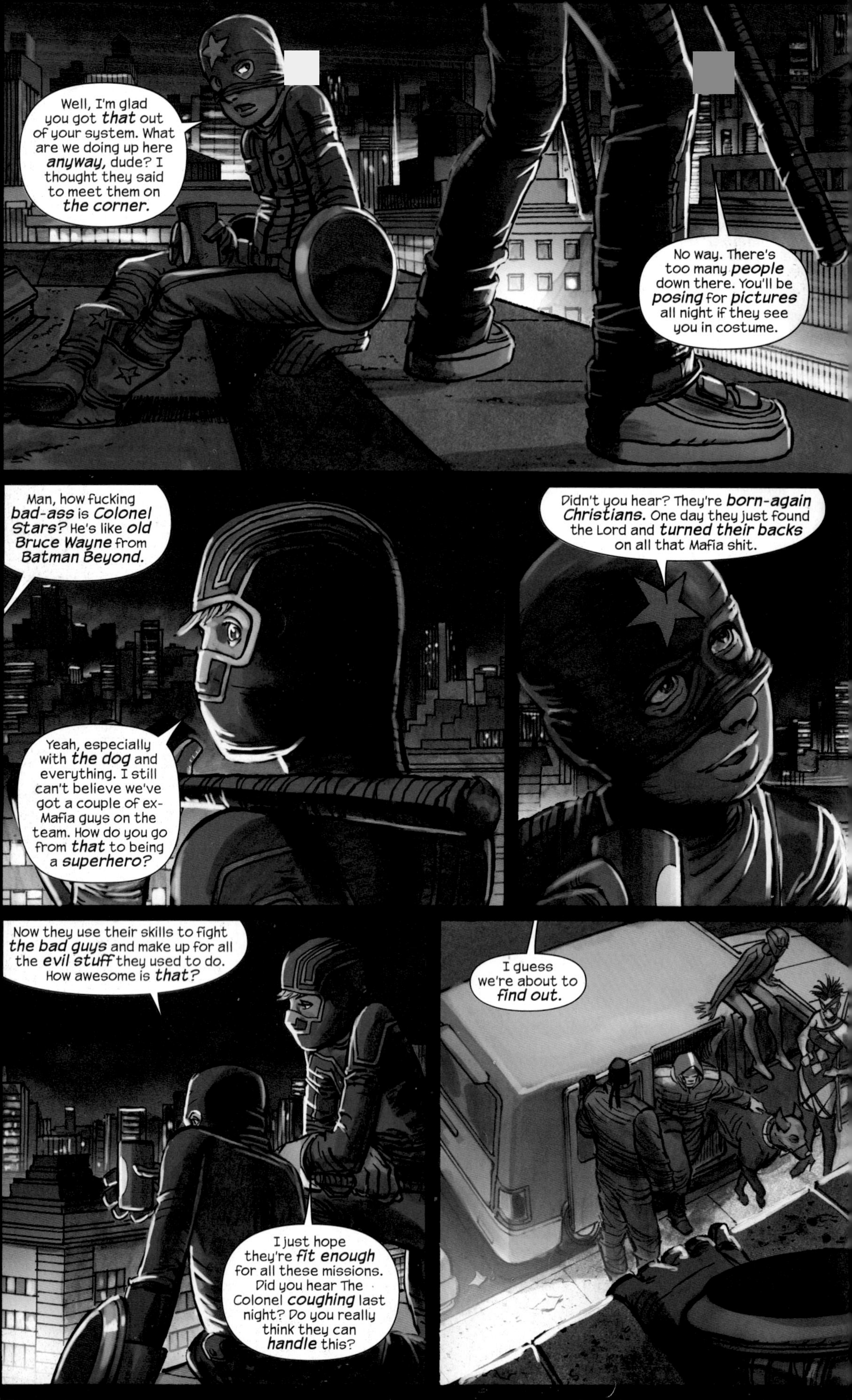

Well, I'm glad you got that out of your system. What are we doing up here anyway, dude? I thought they said to meet them on the corner.
No way. There's too many people down there. You'll be posing for pictures all night if they see you in costume.
Man, how fucking bad-ass is Colonel Stars? He's like old Bruce Wayne from Batman Beyond.
Yeah, especially with the dog and everything. I still can't believe we've got a couple of ex-Mafia guys on the team. How do you go from that to being a superhero?
Didn't you hear? They're born-again Christians. One day they just found the Lord and turned their backs on all that Mafia shit.
Now they use their skills to fight the bad guys and make up for all the evil stuff they used to do. How awesome is that?
I just hope they're fit enough for all these missions. Did you hear The Colonel coughing last night? Do you really think they can handle this?
I guess we're about to find out.

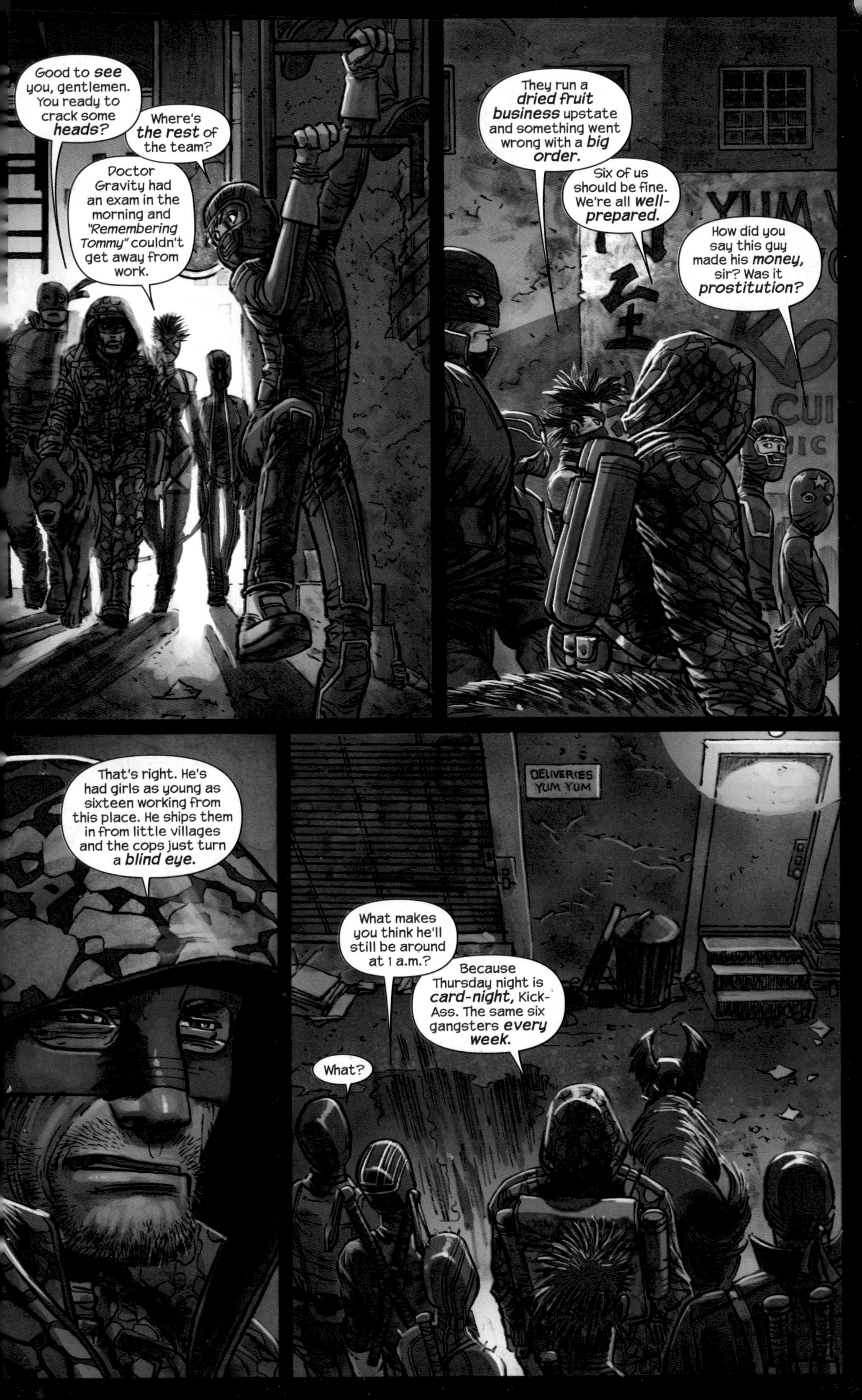
Good to see you, gentlemen. You ready to crack some heads?
Where's the rest of the team?
Doctor Gravity had an exam in the morning and "Remembering Tommy" couldn't get away from work.
They run a dried fruit business upstate and something went wrong with a big order.
Six of us should be fine. We're all well-prepared.
How did you say this guy made his money, sir? Was it prostitution?
That's right. He's had girls as young as sixteen working from this place. He ships them in from little villages and the cops just turn a blind eye.
DELIVERIES YUM YUM
What makes you think he'll still be around at 1 a.m.?
Because Thursday night is card-night, Kick-Ass. The same six gangsters every week.
What?

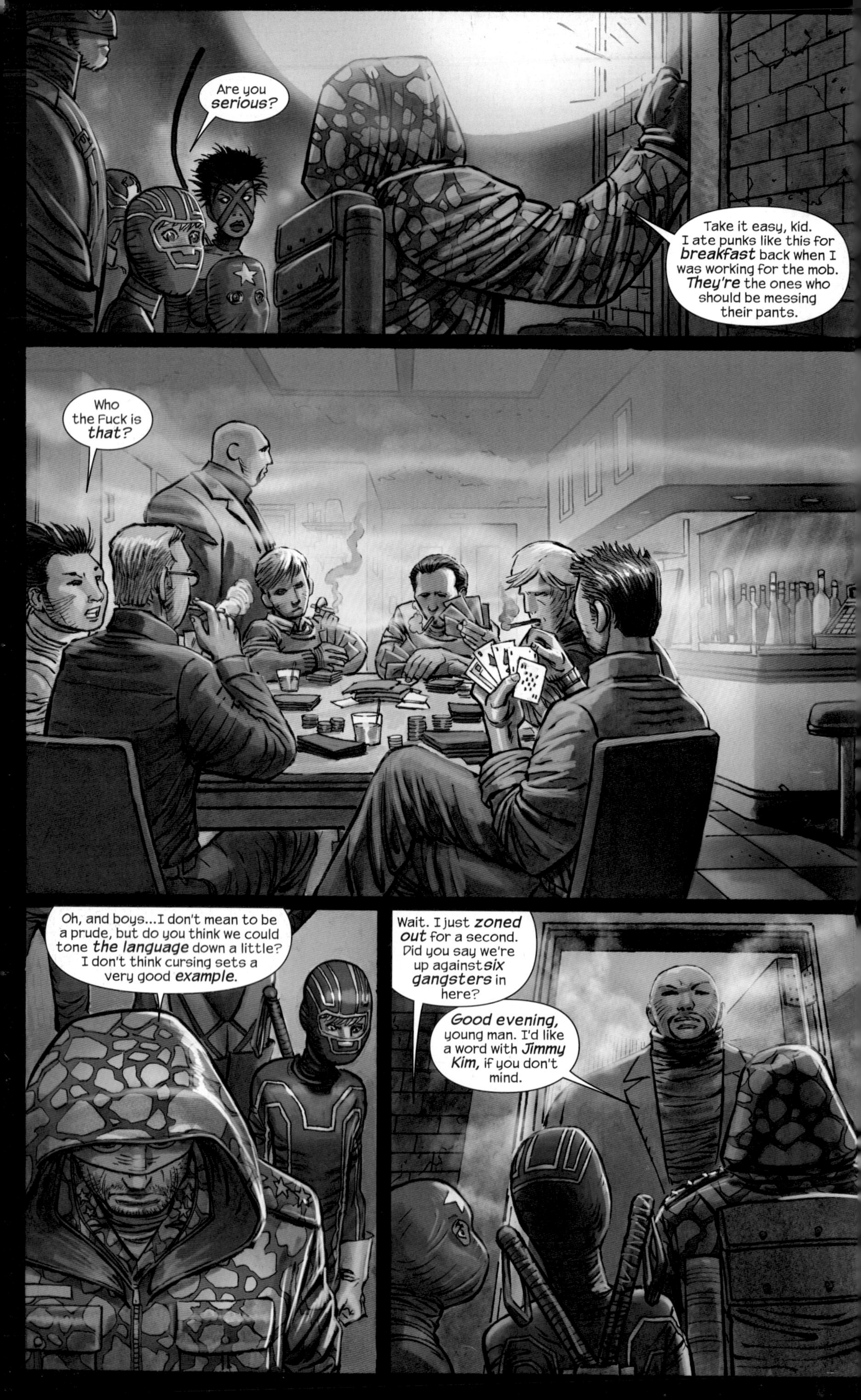
Are you serious?
Take it easy, kid. I ate punks like this for breakfast back when I was working for the mob. They're the ones who should be messing their pants.
Who the Fuck is that?
Oh, and boys...I don't mean to be a prude, but do you think we could tone the language down a little? I don't think cursing sets a very good example.
Wait. I just zoned out for a second. Did you say we're up against six gangsters in here?
Good evening, young man. I'd like a word with Jimmy Kim, if you don't mind.

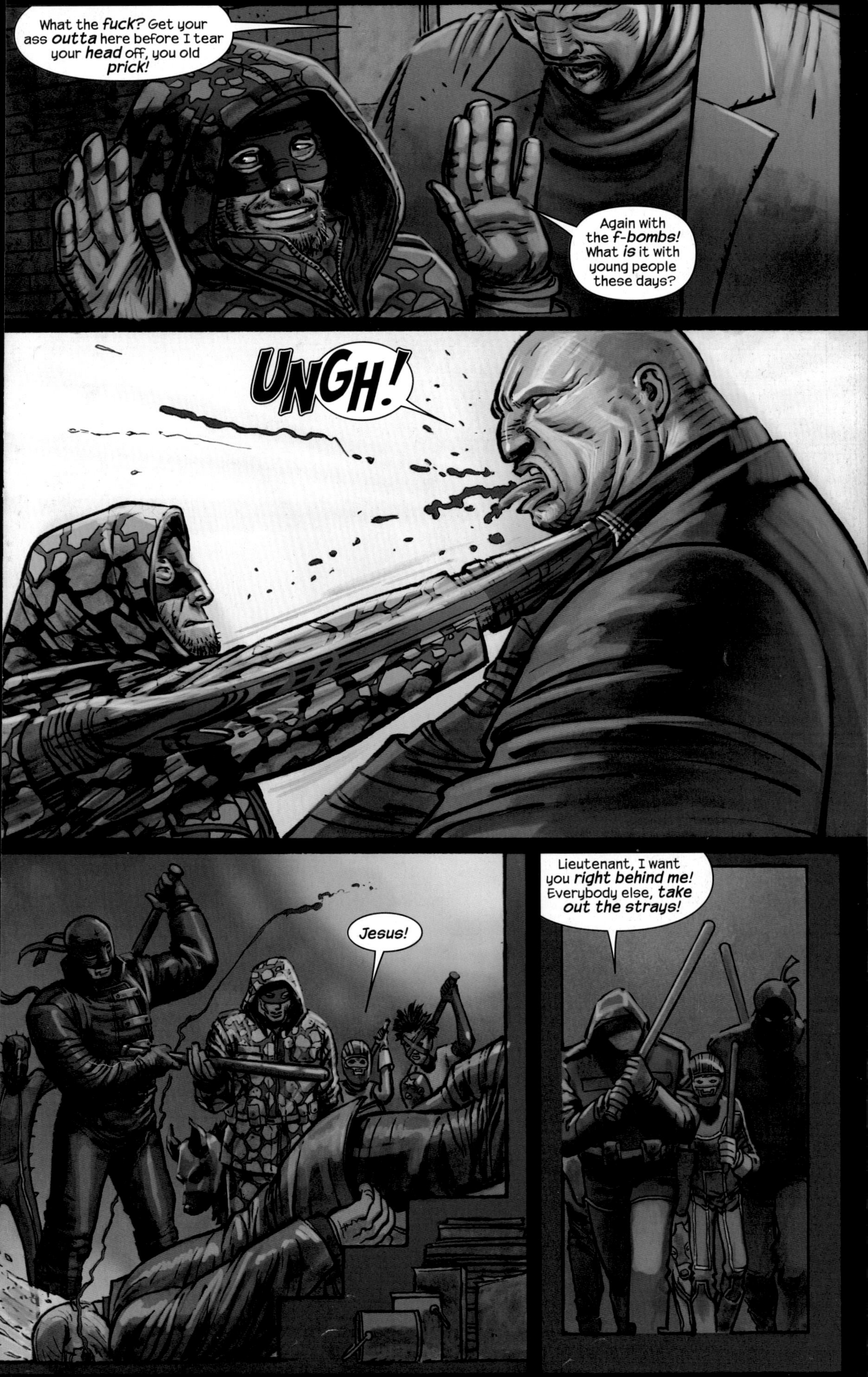
What the *fuck*? Get your ass *outta* here before I tear your *head* off, you old *prick!*
Again with the *f-bombs!* What *is* it with young people these days?
UNGH!
Jesus!
Lieutenant, I want you *right behind me!* Everybody else, *take out the strays!*

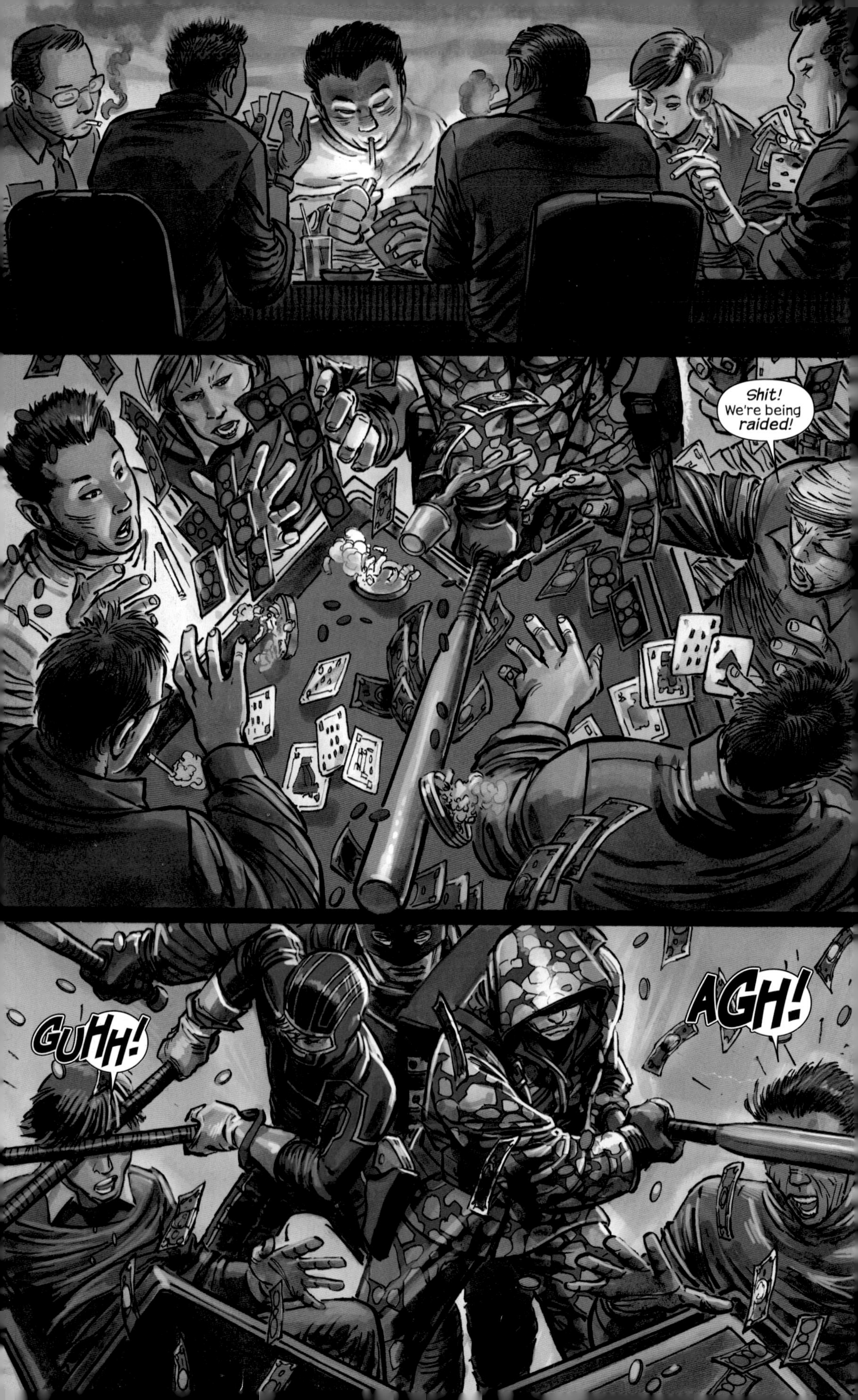
Shit! We're being raided!
GUHH!
AGH!

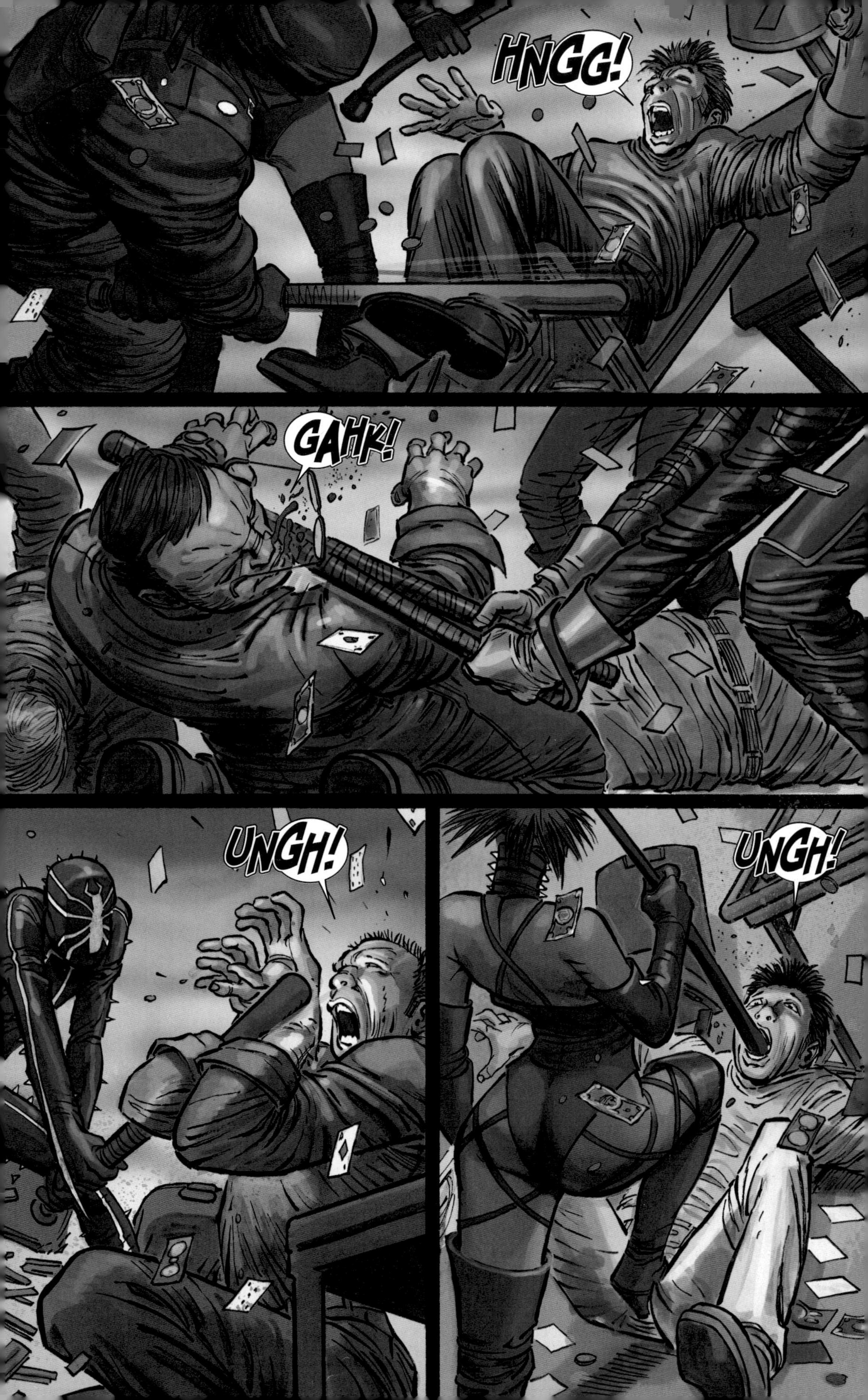
HNGG!
GAHK!
UNGH!
UNGH!

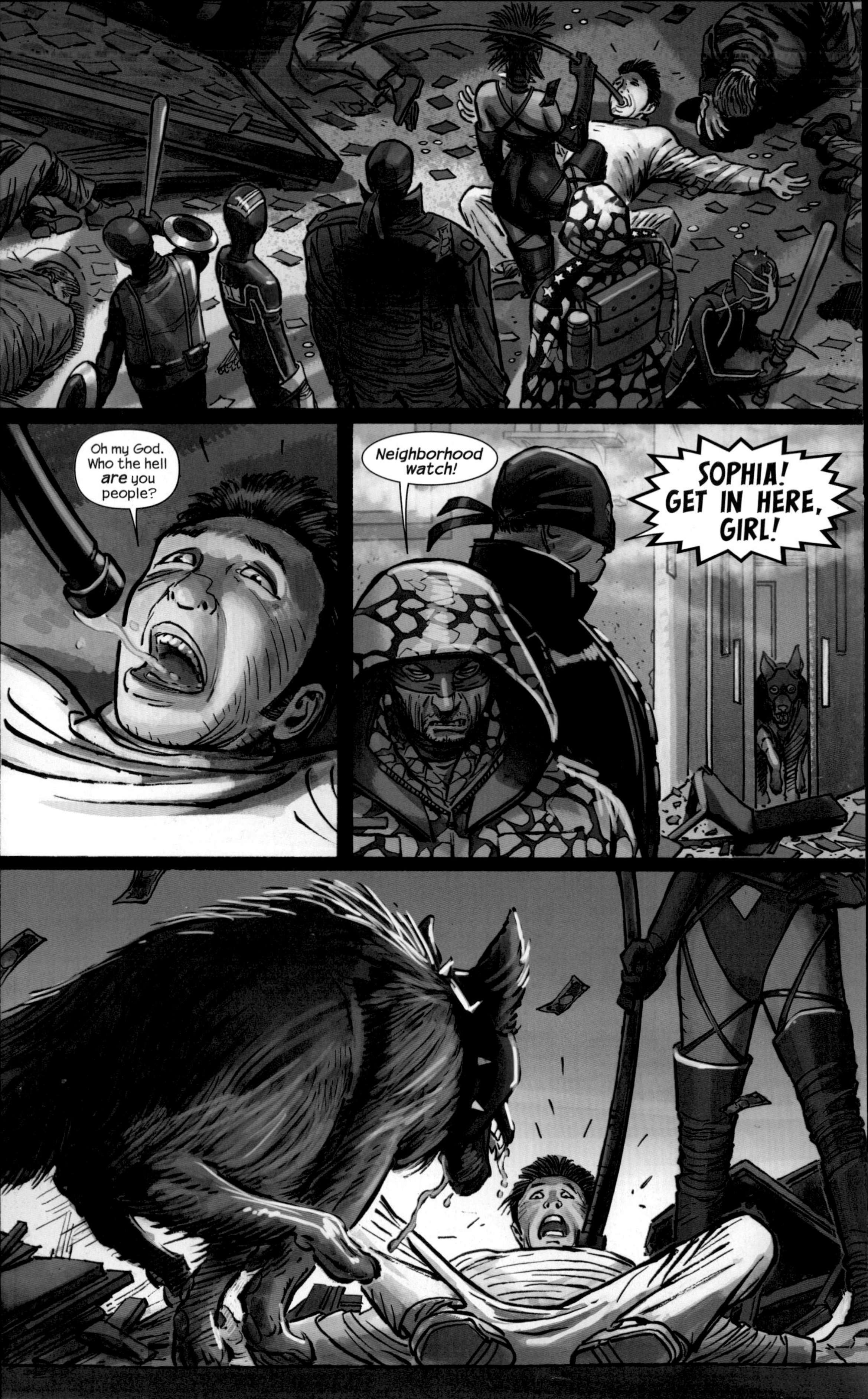
Oh my God. Who the hell *are* you people?
Neighborhood watch!
SOPHIA! GET IN HERE, GIRL!

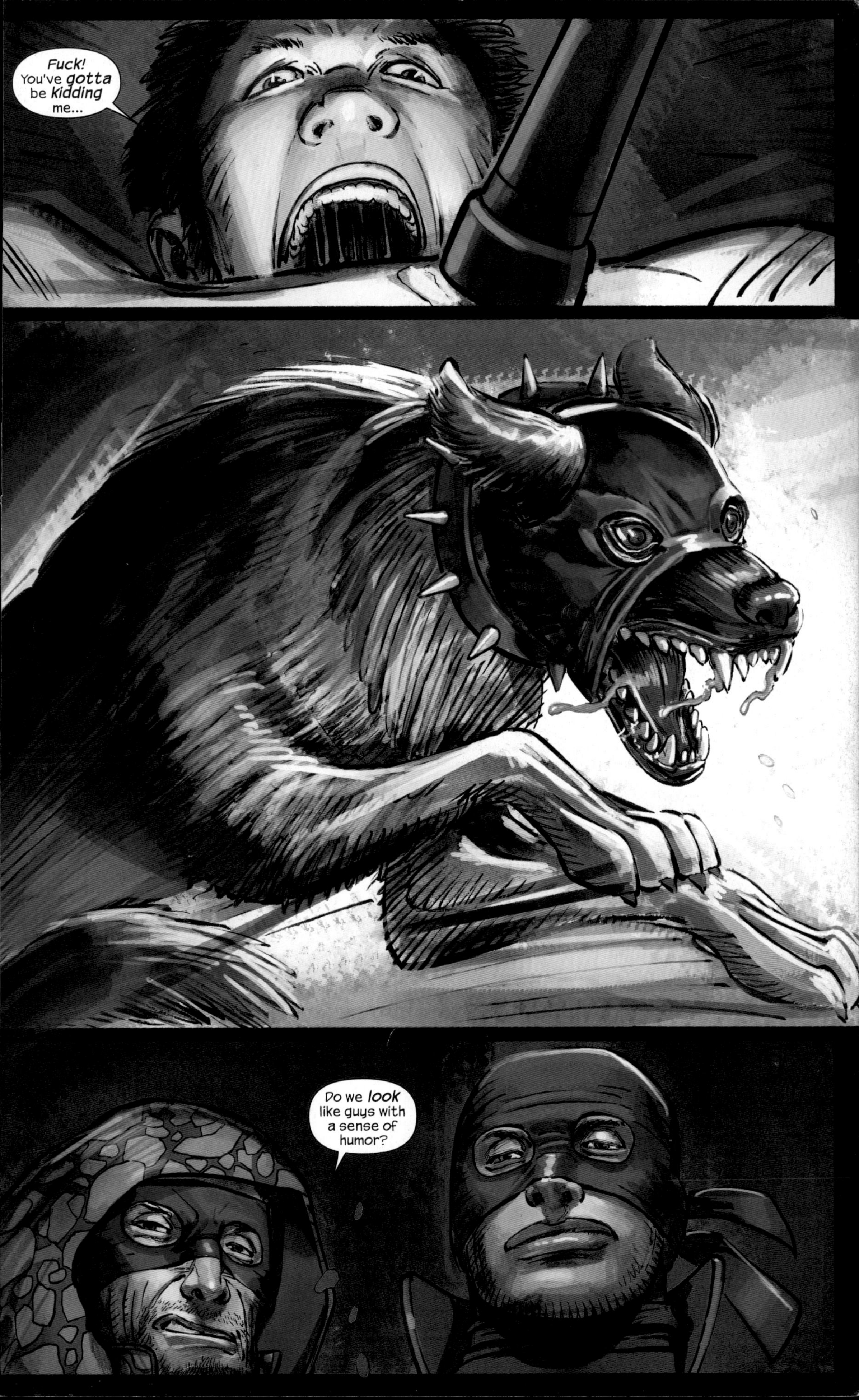
Fuck! You've gotta be kidding me...
Do we look like guys with a sense of humor?

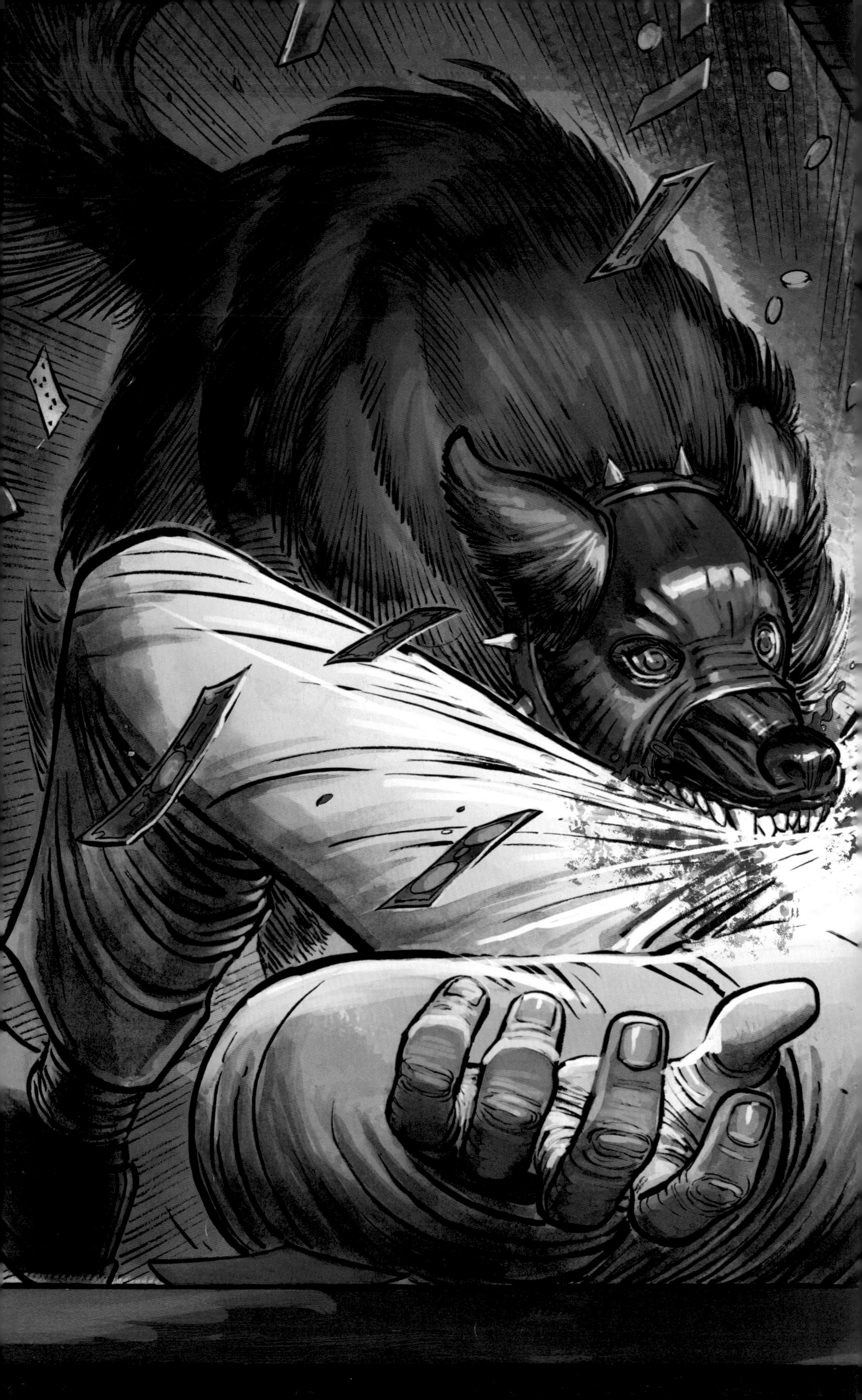

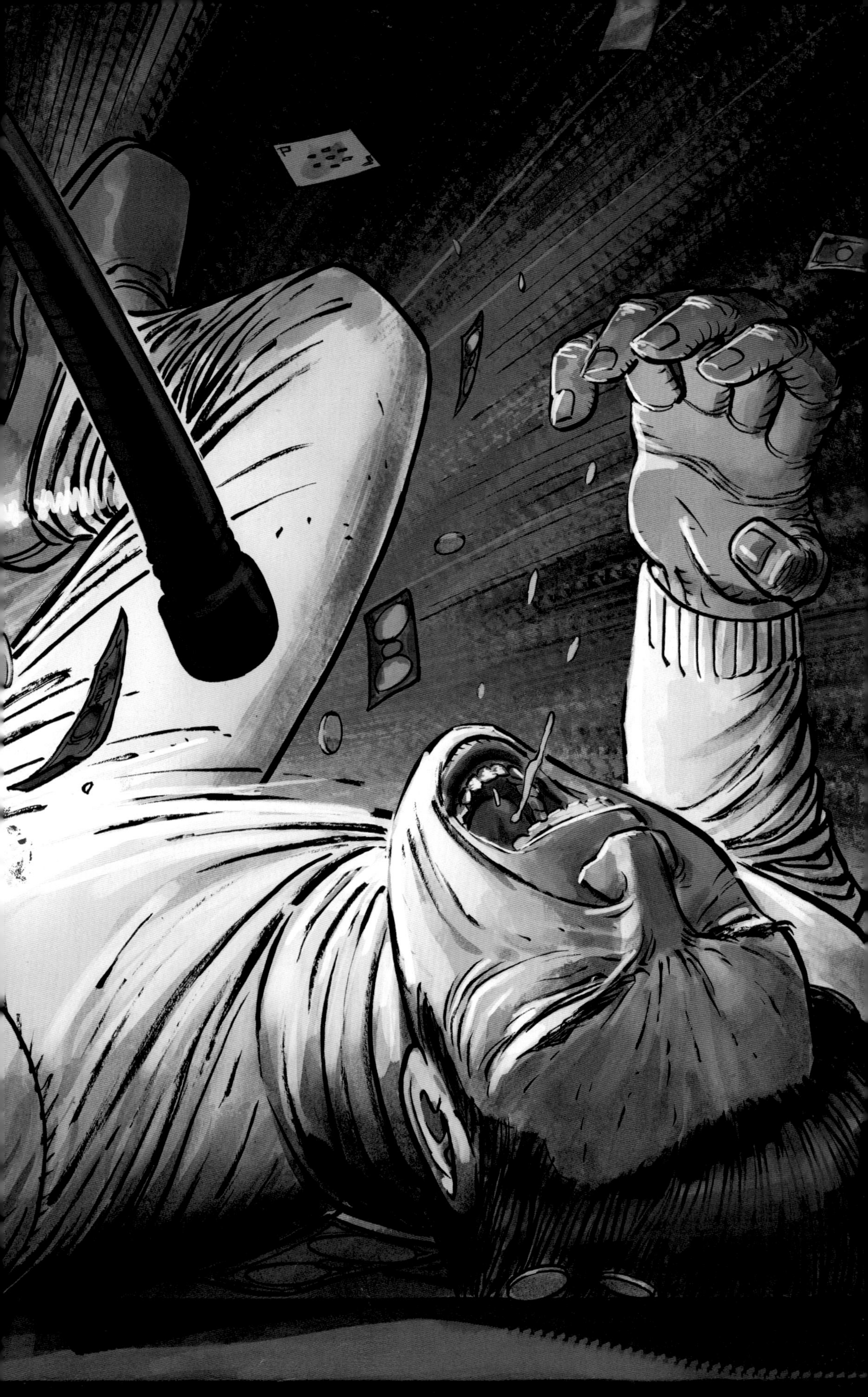

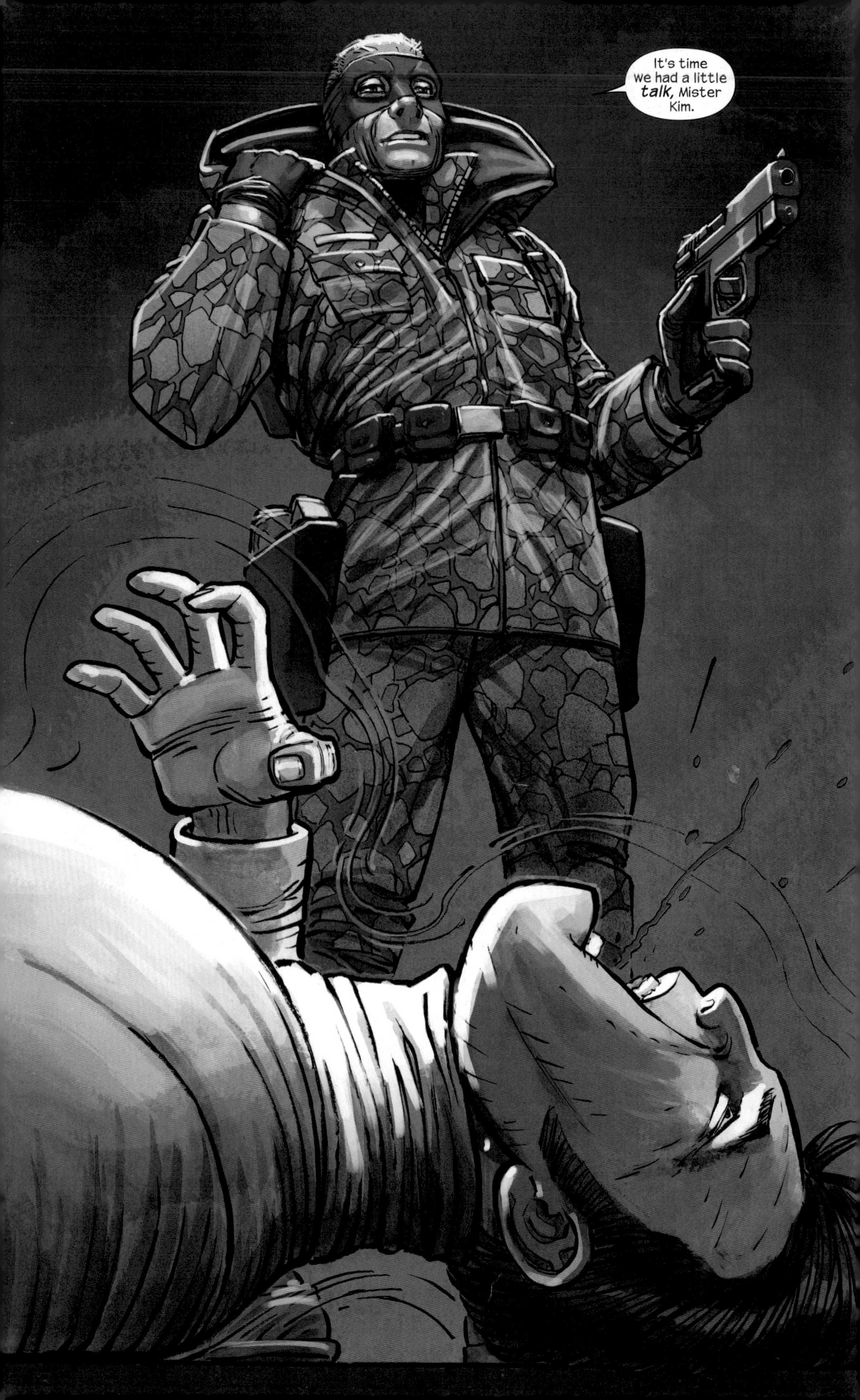
It's time we had a little *talk,* Mister Kim.

THREE

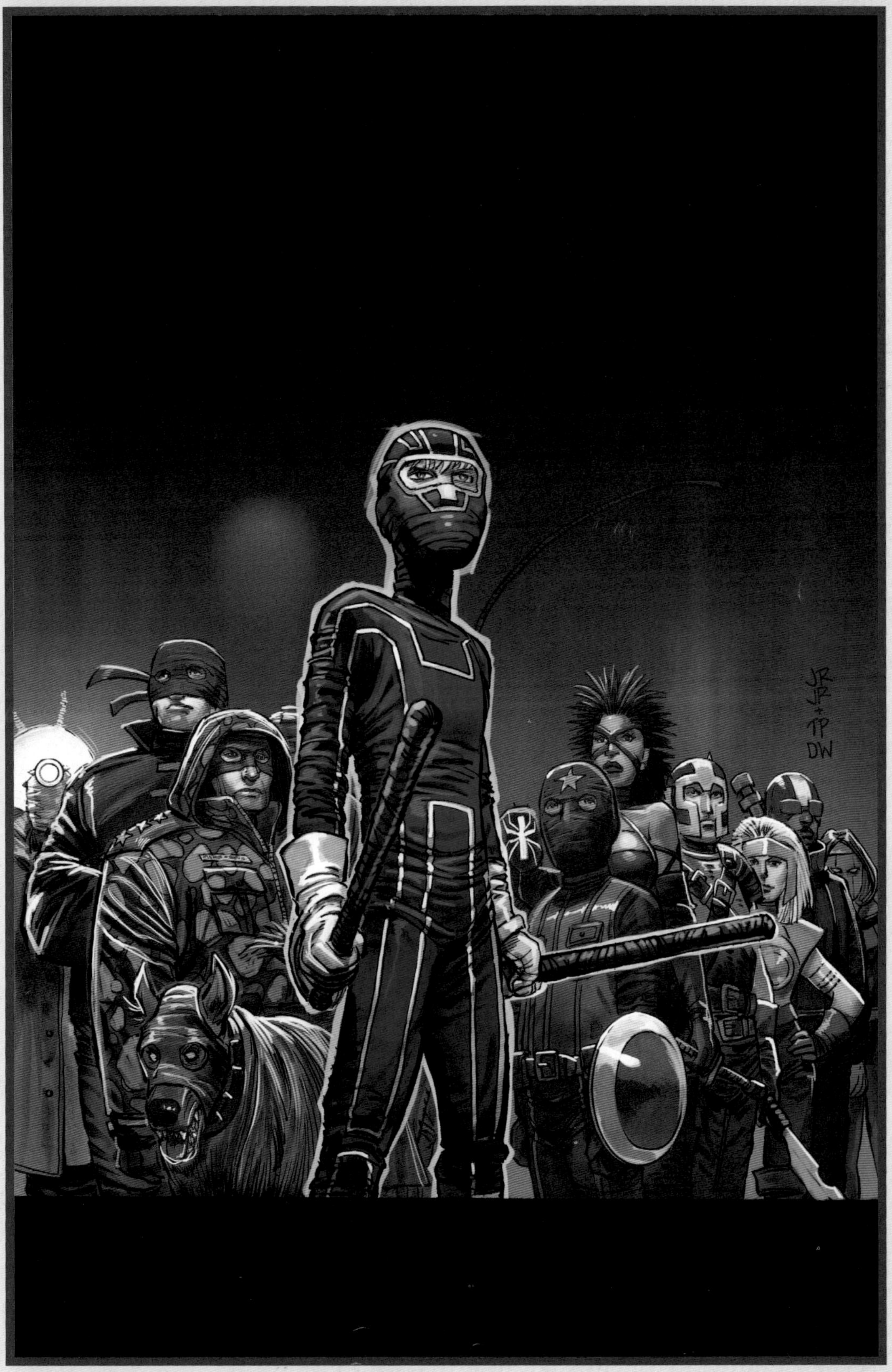
JR JR + TP DW

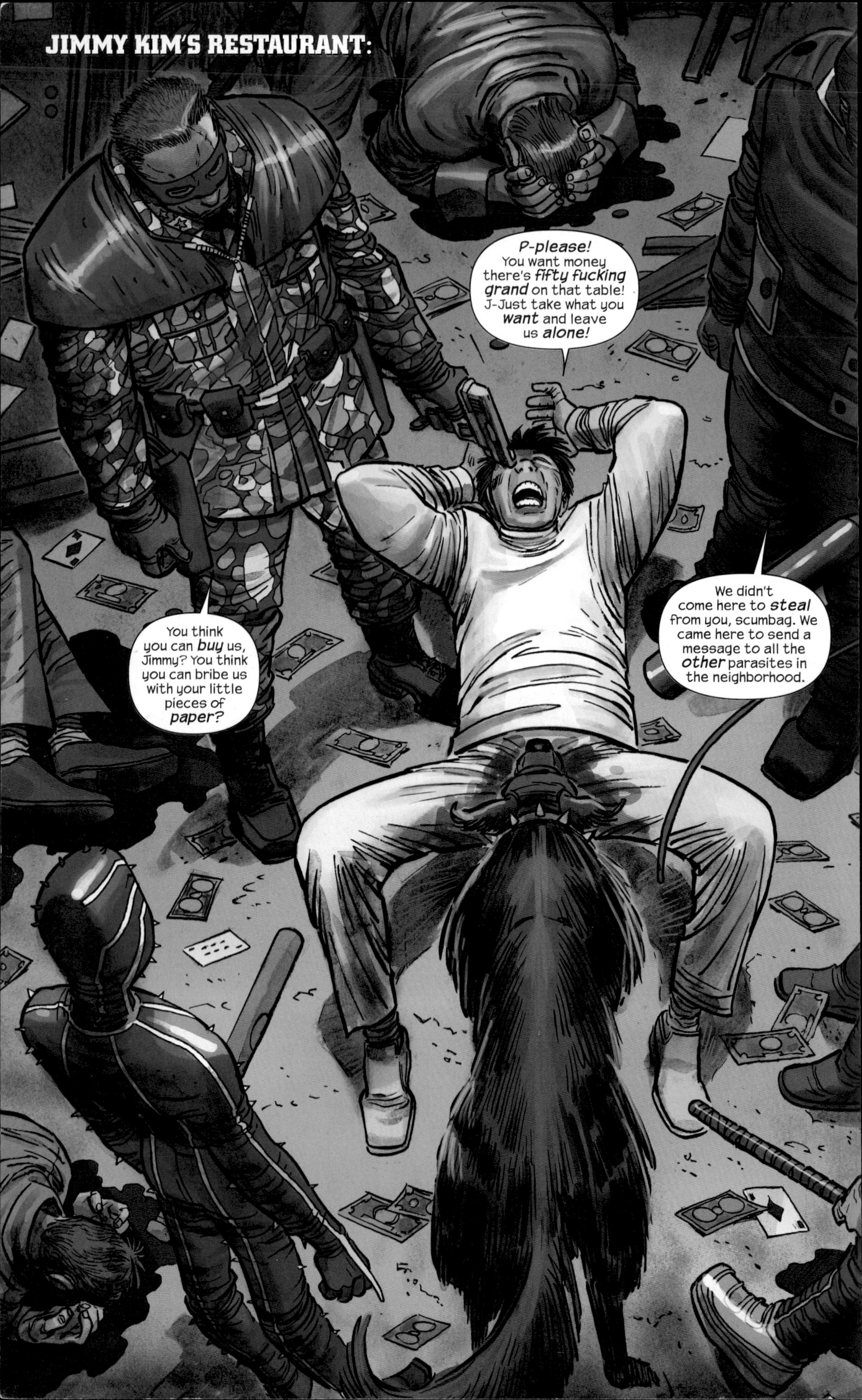
JIMMY KIM'S RESTAURANT:
P-please! You want money there's fifty fucking grand on that table! J-Just take what you want and leave us alone!
You think you can buy us, Jimmy? You think you can bribe us with your little pieces of paper?
We didn't come here to steal from you, scumbag. We came here to send a message to all the other parasites in the neighborhood.

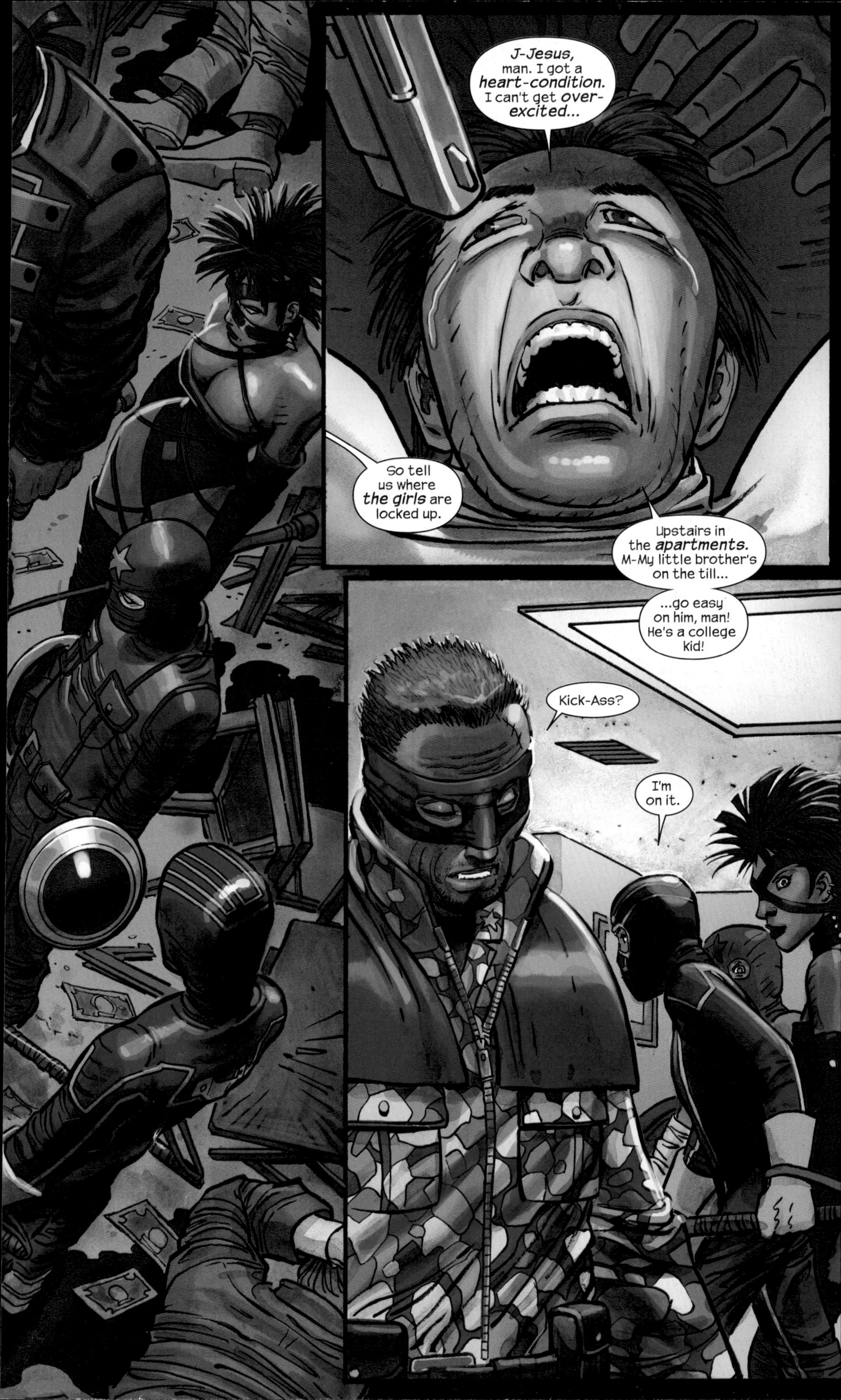
J-Jesus, man. I got a heart-condition. I can't get over-excited...
So tell us where the girls are locked up.
Upstairs in the apartments. M-My little brother's on the till...
...go easy on him, man! He's a college kid!
Kick-Ass?
I'm on it.

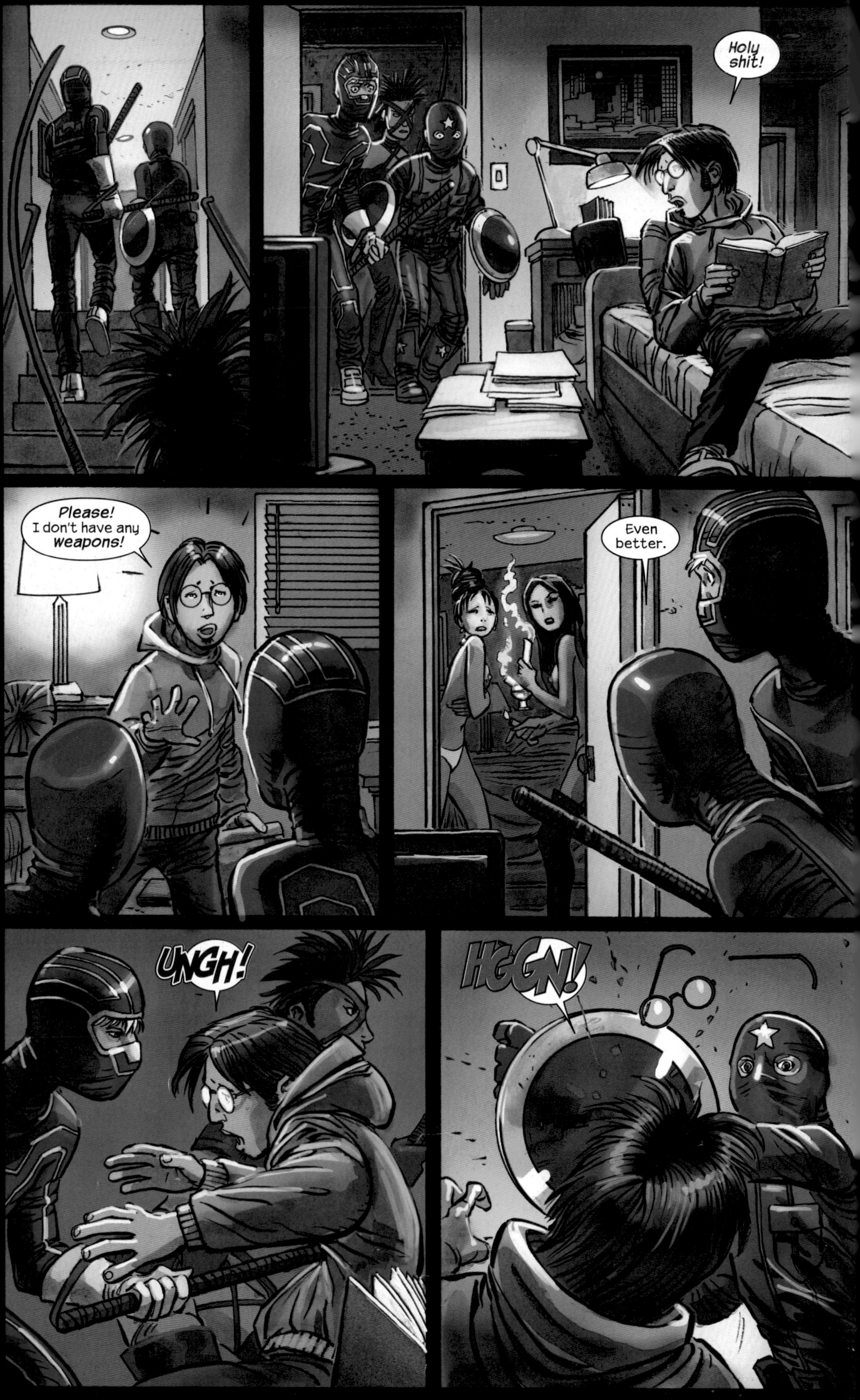
Holy shit!
Please! I don't have any weapons!
Even better.
UNGH!
HGGN!

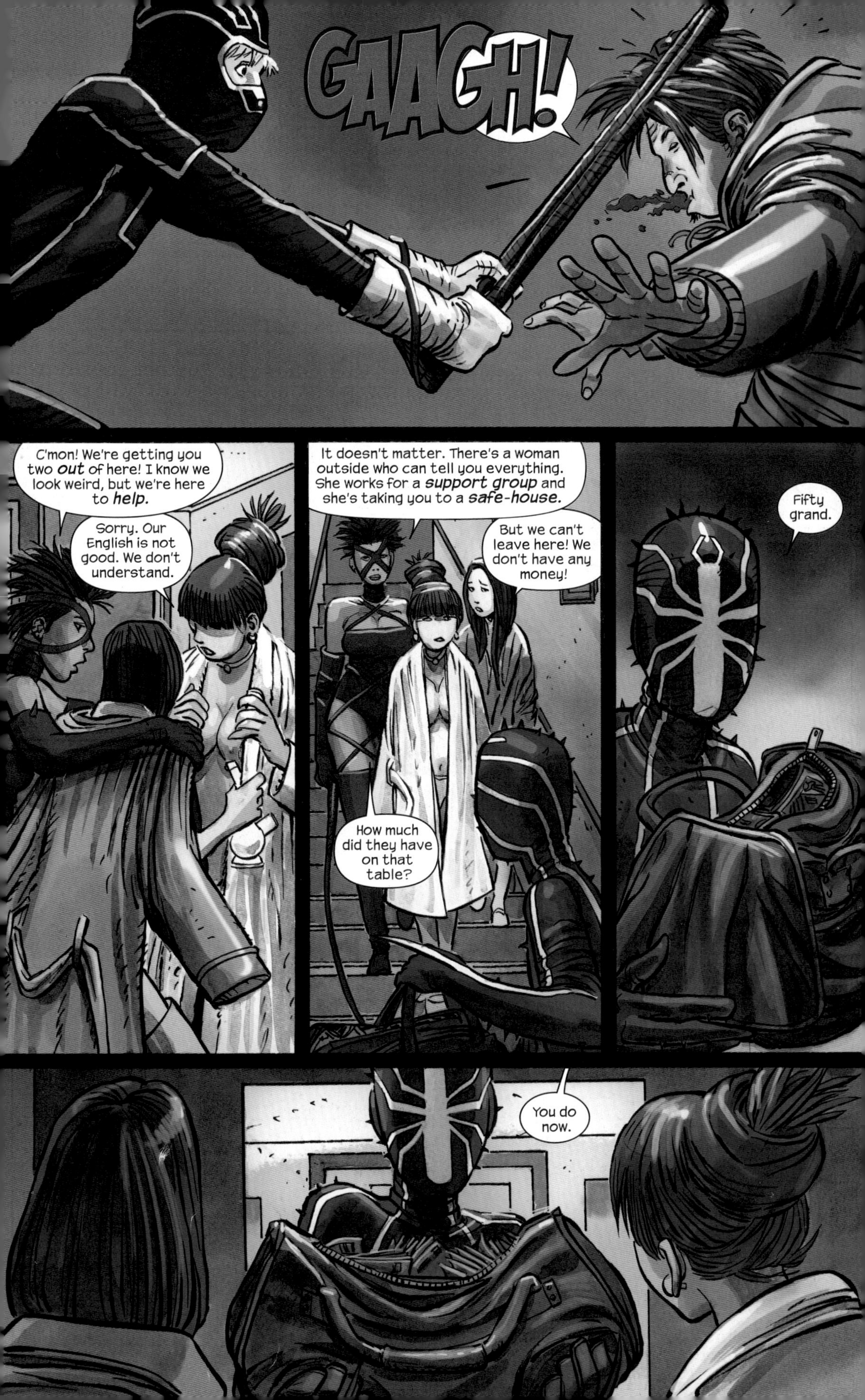
GAAGH!
C'mon! We're getting you two out of here! I know we look weird, but we're here to help.
...
Sorry. Our English is not good. We don't understand.
It doesn't matter. There's a woman outside who can tell you everything. She works for a support group and she's taking you to a safe-house.
But we can't leave here! We don't have any money!
How much did they have on that table?
Fifty grand.
You do now.

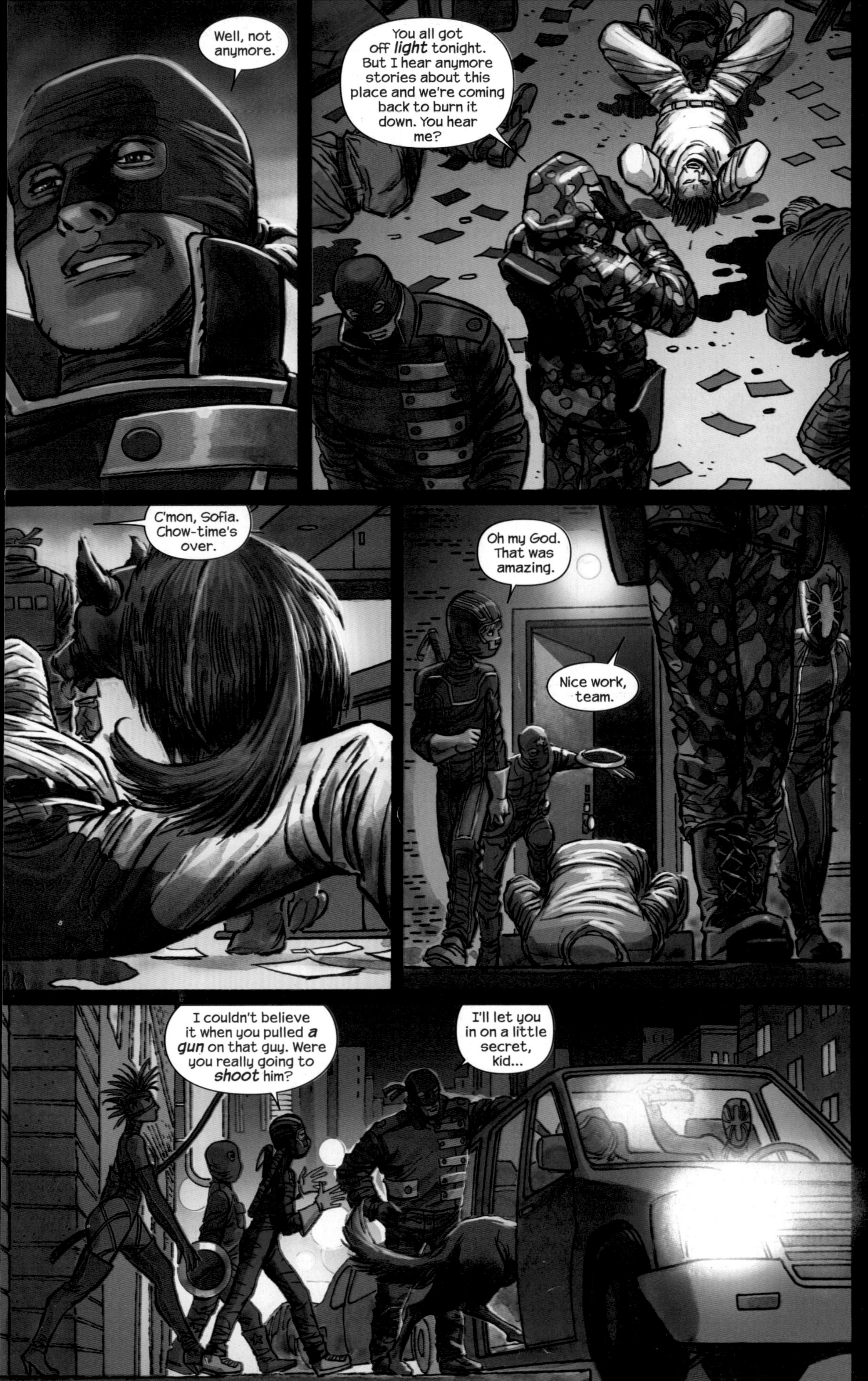

Well, not anymore.
You all got off *light* tonight. But I hear anymore stories about this place and we're coming back to burn it down. You hear me?
C'mon, Sofia. Chow-time's over.
Oh my God. That was amazing.
Nice work, team.
I couldn't believe it when you pulled *a gun* on that guy. Were you really going to *shoot* him?
I'll let you in on a little secret, kid...

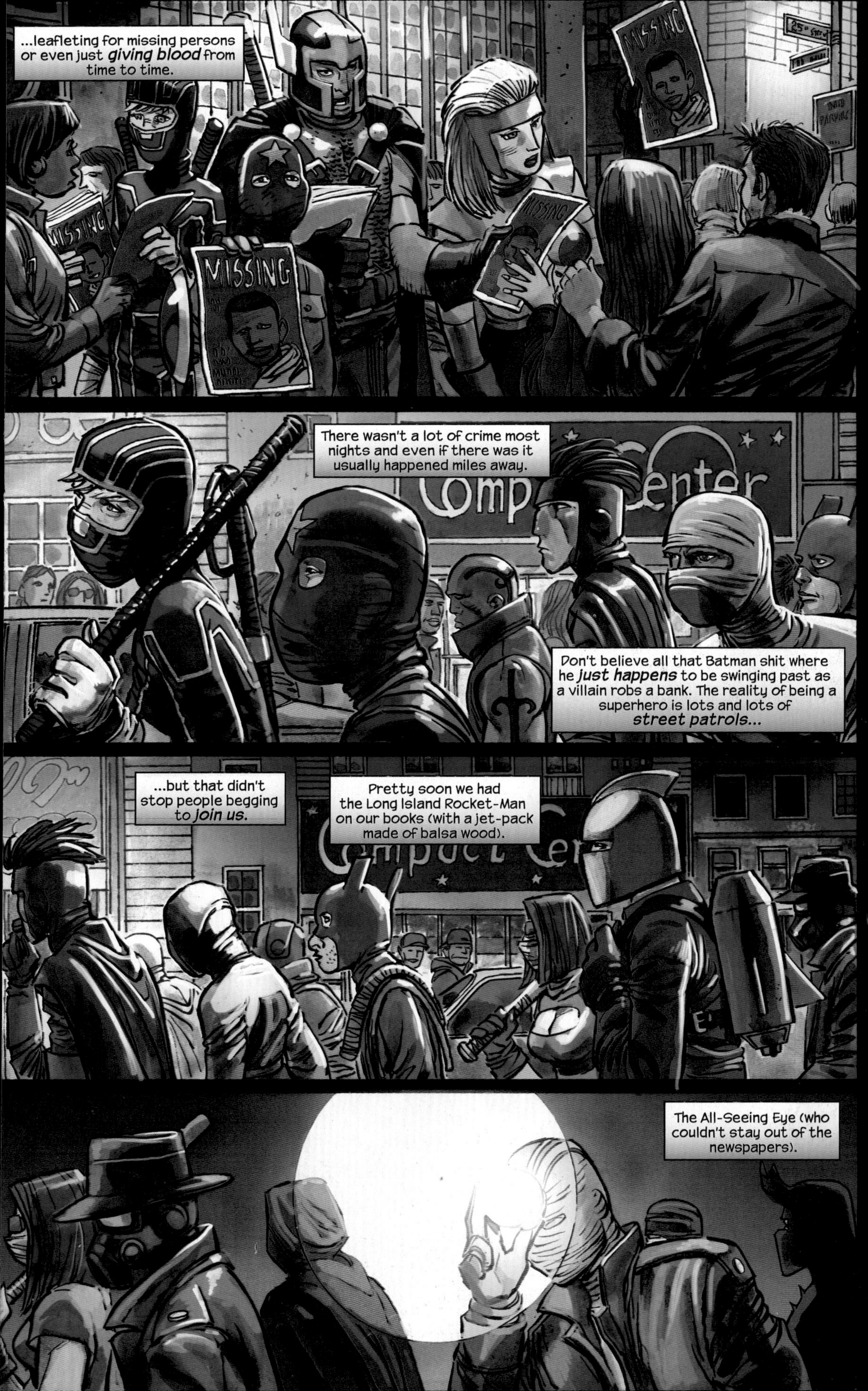

...leafleting for missing persons or even just *giving blood* from time to time.
MISSING
MISSING
MISSING
MISSING
There wasn't a lot of crime most nights and even if there was it usually happened miles away.
Don't believe all that Batman shit where he *just happens* to be swinging past as a villain robs a bank. The reality of being a superhero is lots and lots of *street patrols...*
...but that didn't stop people begging to *join us.*
Pretty soon we had the Long Island Rocket-Man on our books (with a jet-pack made of balsa wood).
The All-Seeing Eye (who couldn't stay out of the newspapers).

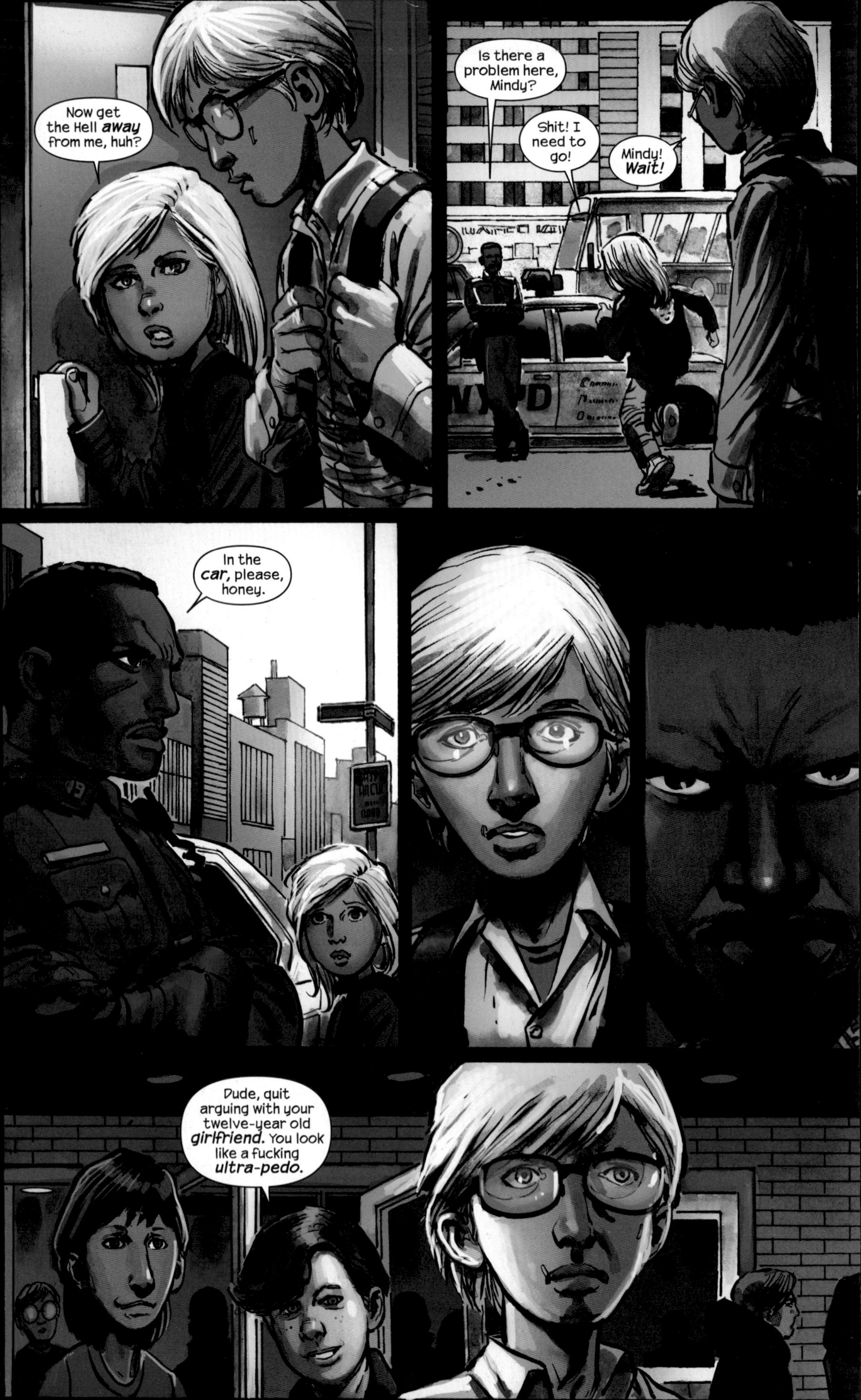
Now get the Hell away from me, huh?
Is there a problem here, Mindy?
Shit! I need to go!
Mindy! Wait!
NYPD
In the car, please, honey.
Dude, quit arguing with your twelve-year old girlfriend. You look like a fucking ultra-pedo.

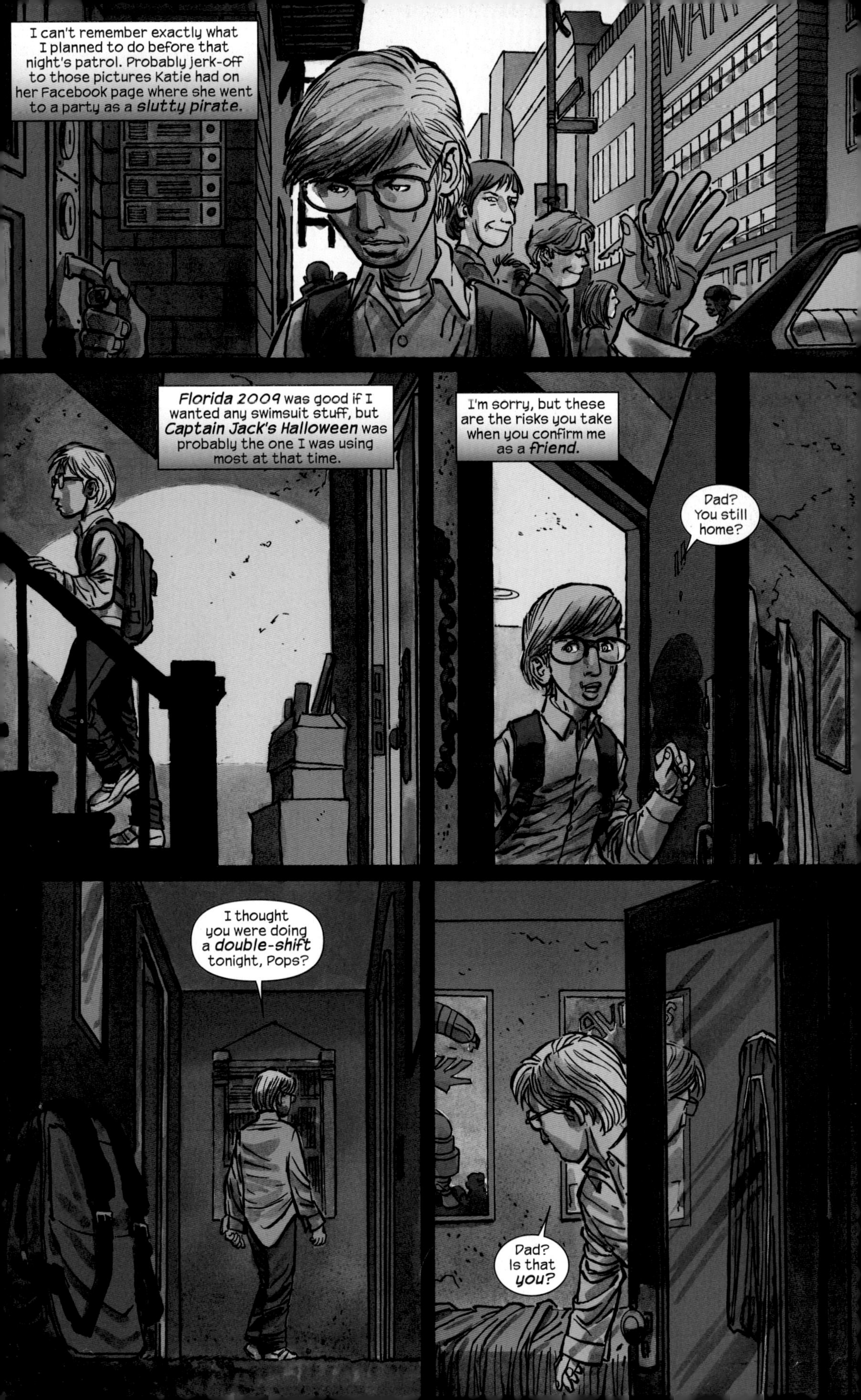
I can't remember exactly what I planned to do before that night's patrol. Probably jerk-off to those pictures Katie had on her Facebook page where she went to a party as a *slutty pirate*.
Florida 2009 was good if I wanted any swimsuit stuff, but *Captain Jack's Halloween* was probably the one I was using most at that time.
I'm sorry, but these are the risks you take when you confirm me as a *friend*.
Dad? You still home?
I thought you were doing a *double-shift* tonight, Pops?
Dad? Is that *you*?

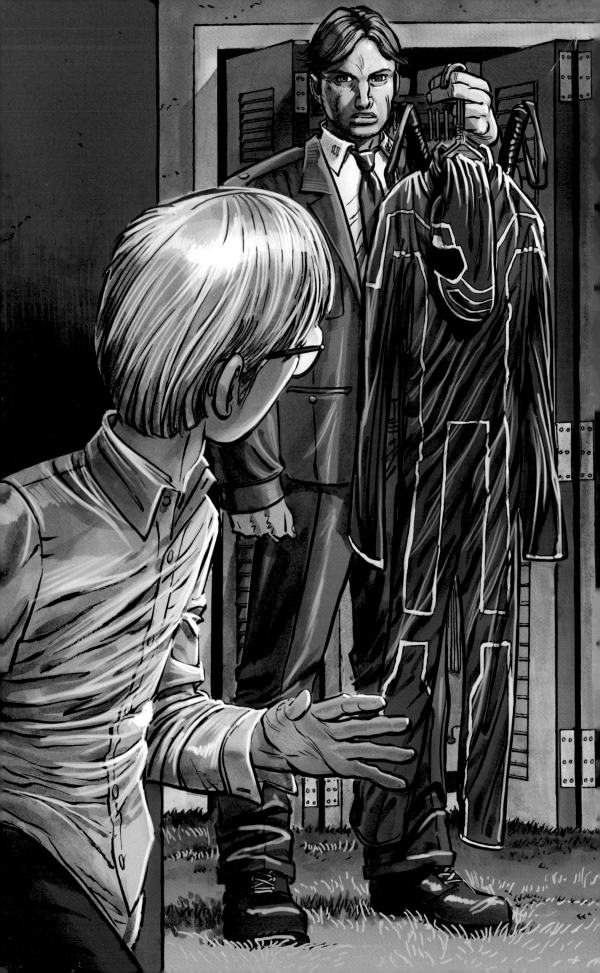

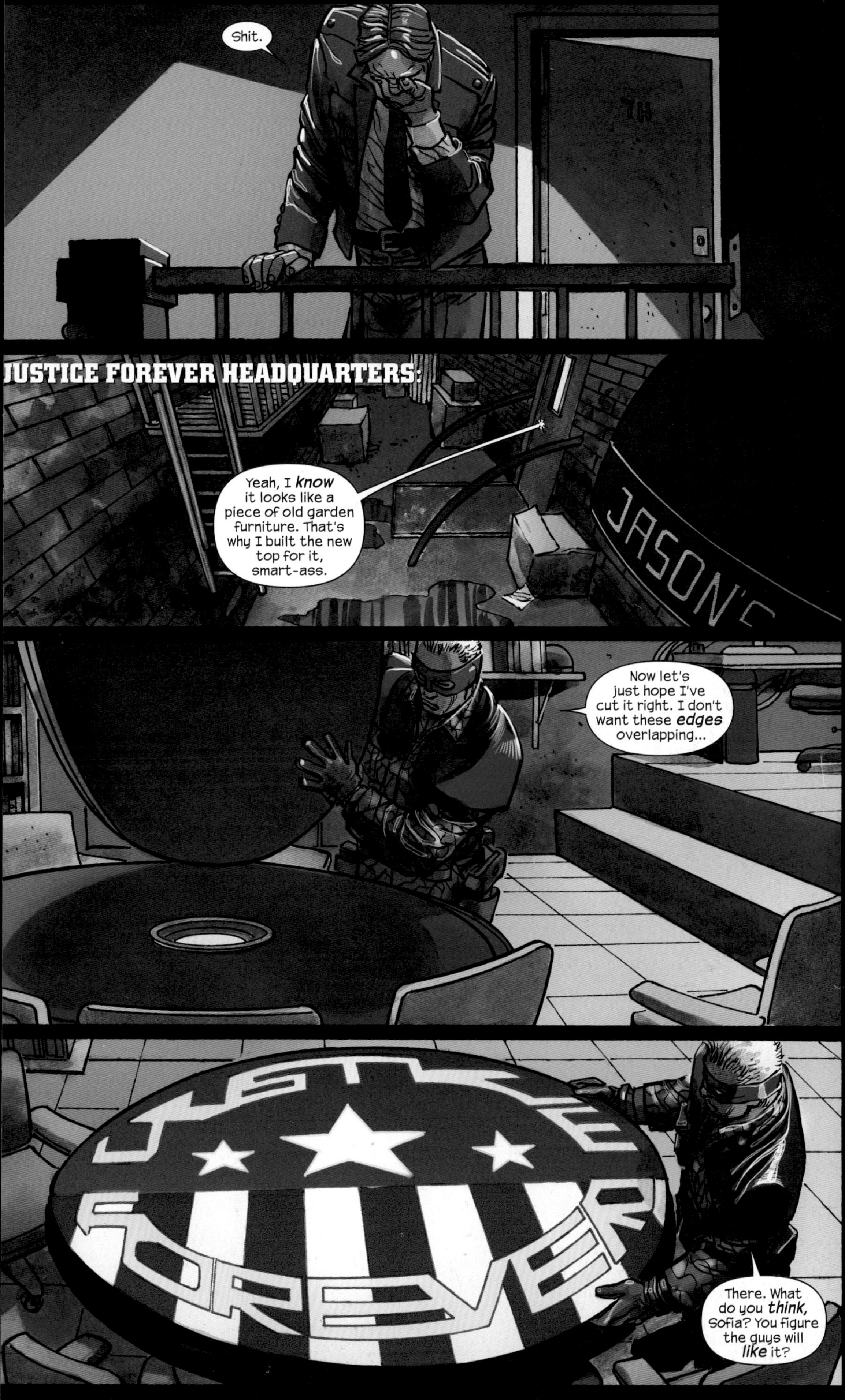

Shit.
JUSTICE FOREVER HEADQUARTERS:
Yeah, I **know** it looks like a piece of old garden furniture. That's why I built the new top for it, smart-ass.
JASON'S
Now let's just hope I've cut it right. I don't want these **edges** overlapping...
JUSTICE FOREVER
There. What do you **think,** Sofia? You figure the guys will **like** it?

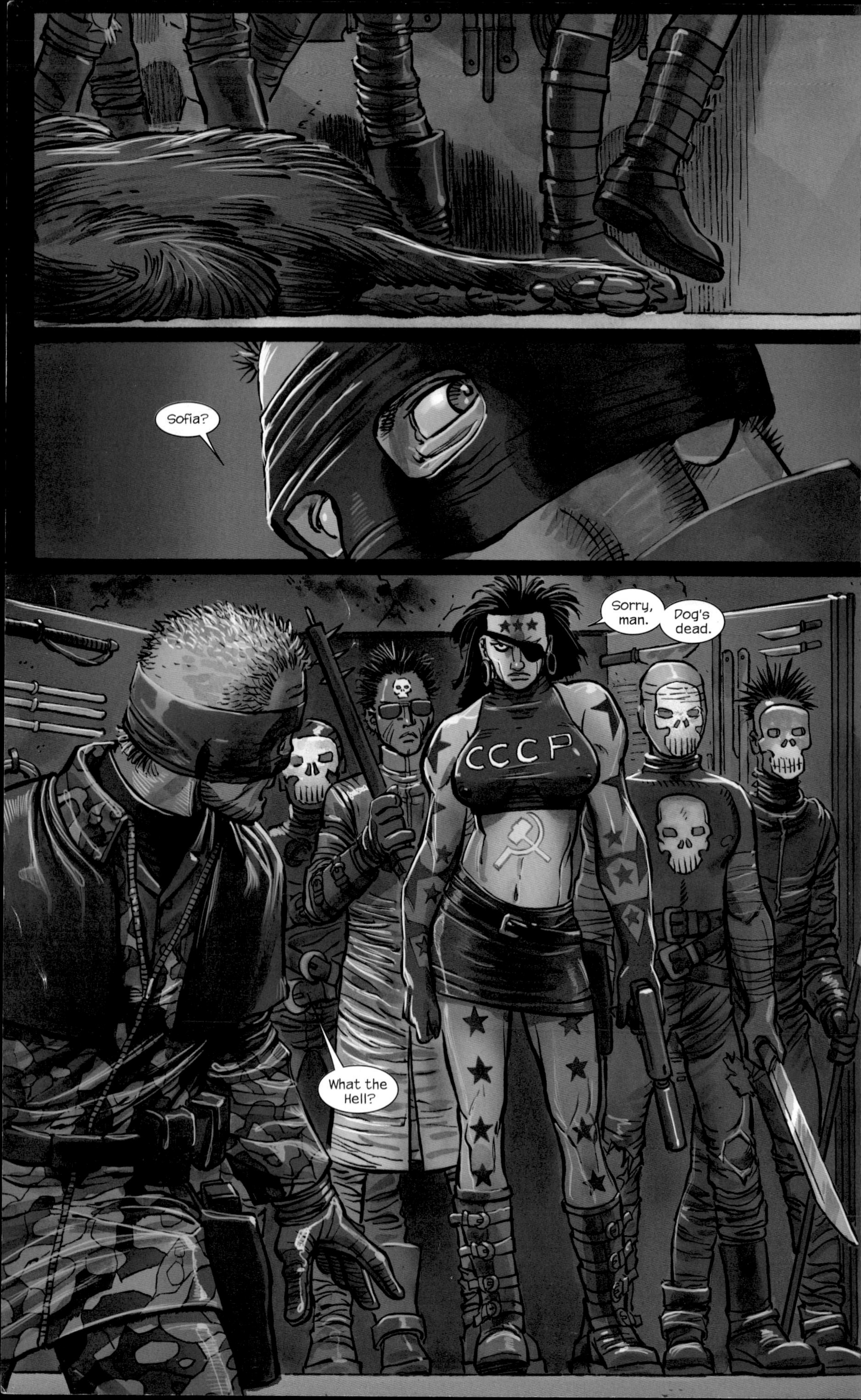
Sofia?
Sorry, man.
Dog's dead.
What the Hell?

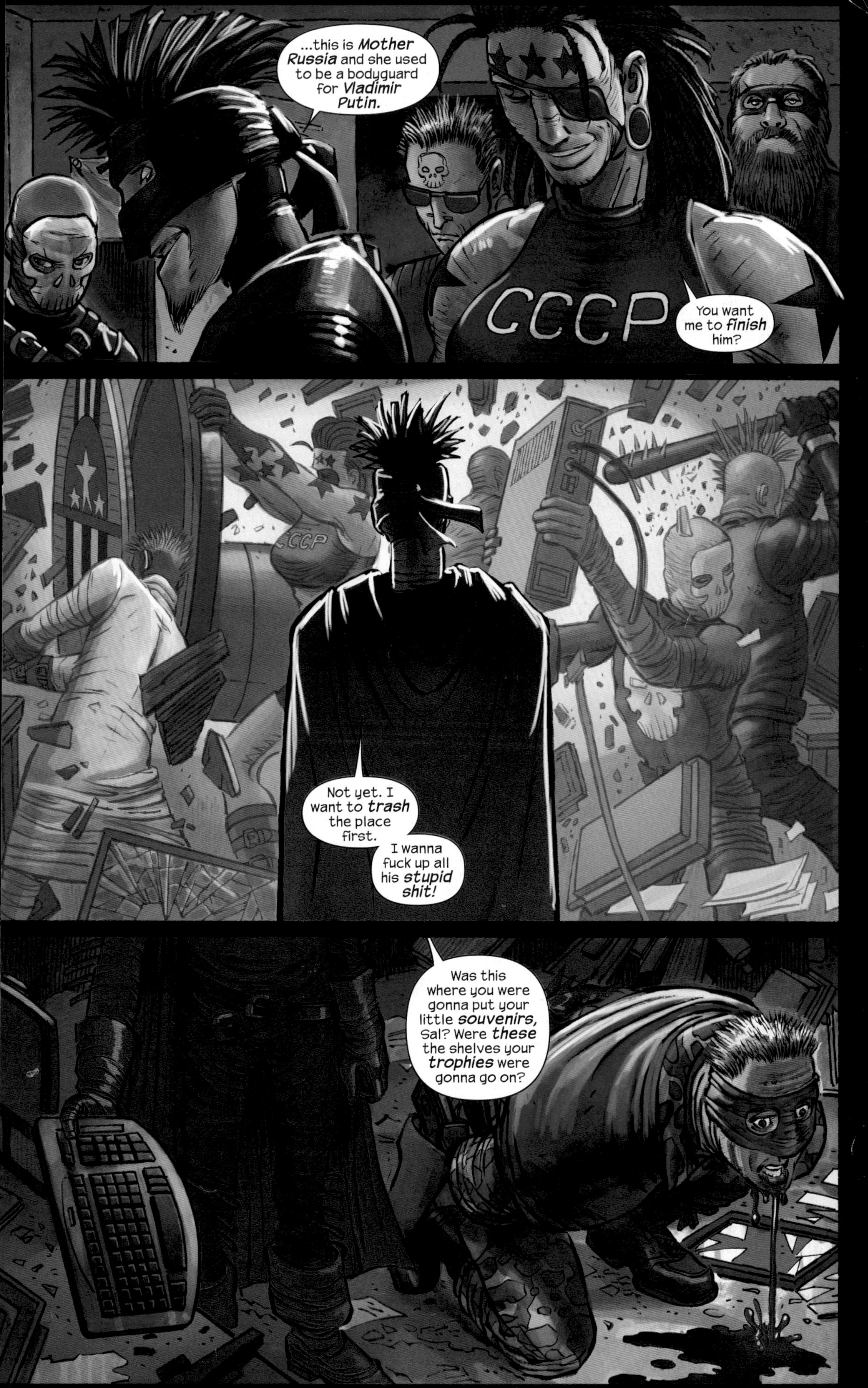
...this is *Mother Russia* and she used to be a bodyguard for *Vladimir Putin.*
CCCP
You want me to *finish* him?
Not yet. I want to *trash* the place first.
I wanna fuck up all his *stupid shit!*
Was this where you were gonna put your little *souvenirs,* Sal? Were *these* the shelves your *trophies* were gonna go on?

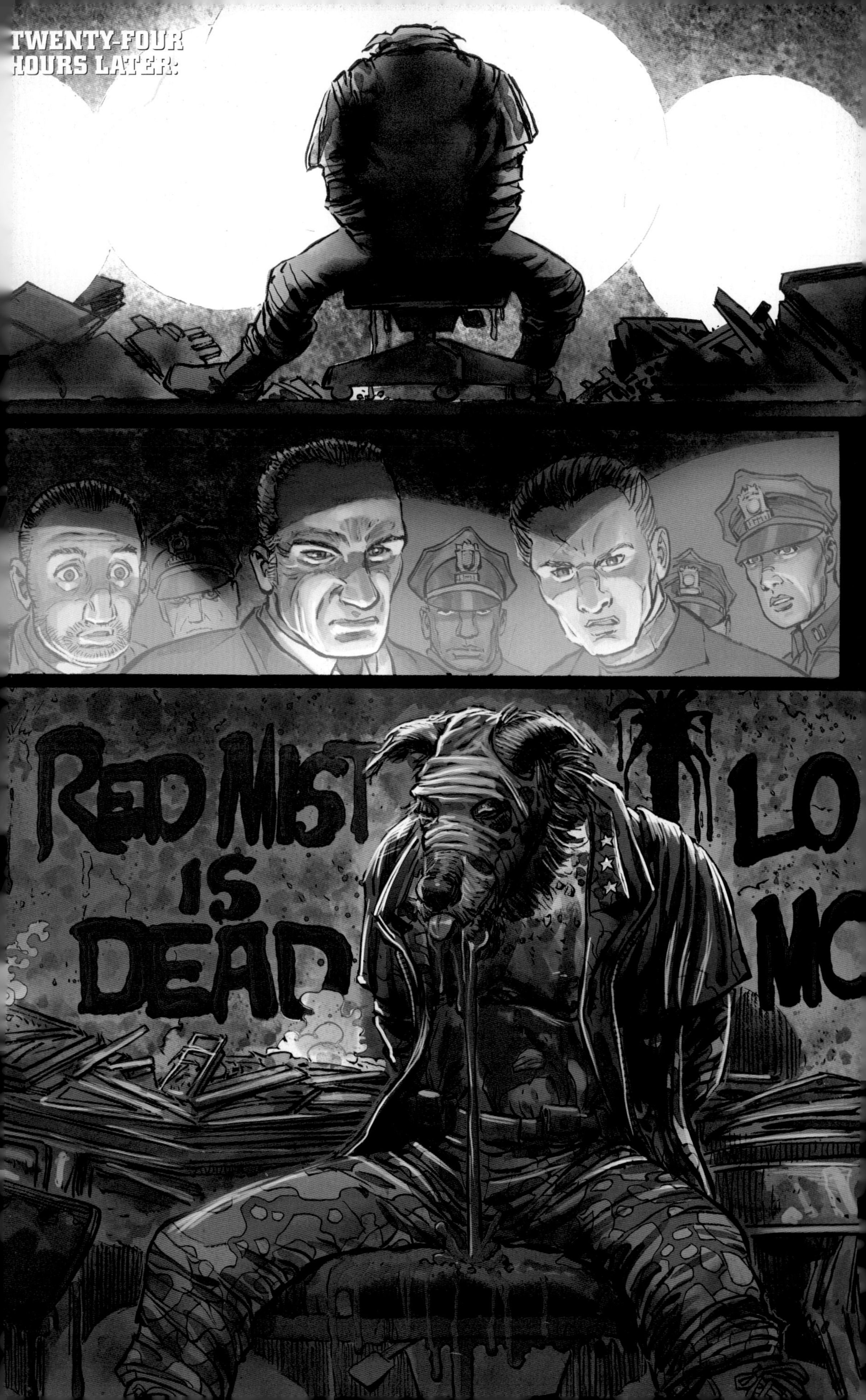
TWENTY-FOUR HOURS LATER:
RED MIST IS DEAD
LO
MO

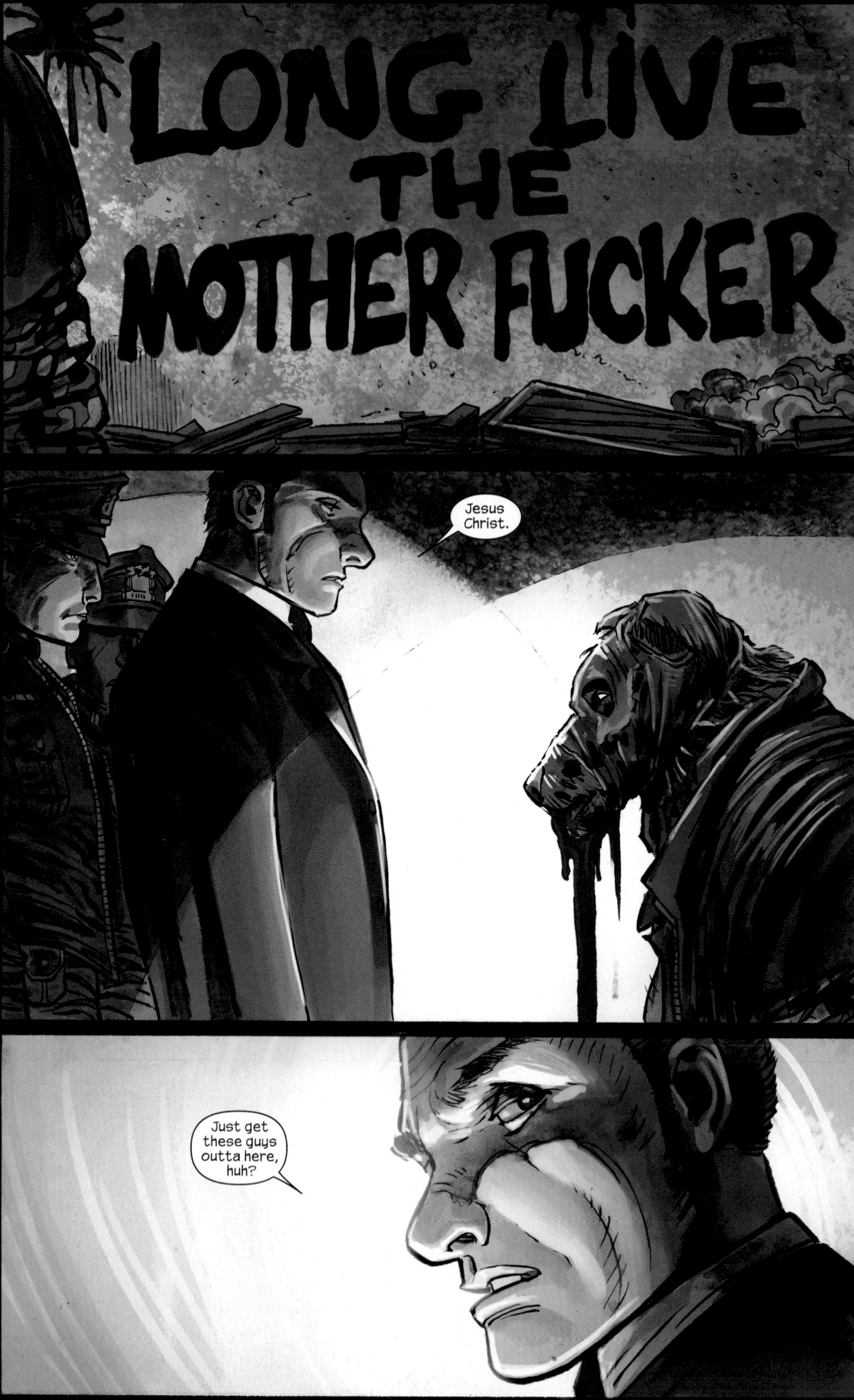
LONG LIVE THE MOTHER FUCKER
Jesus Christ.
Just get these guys outta here, huh?

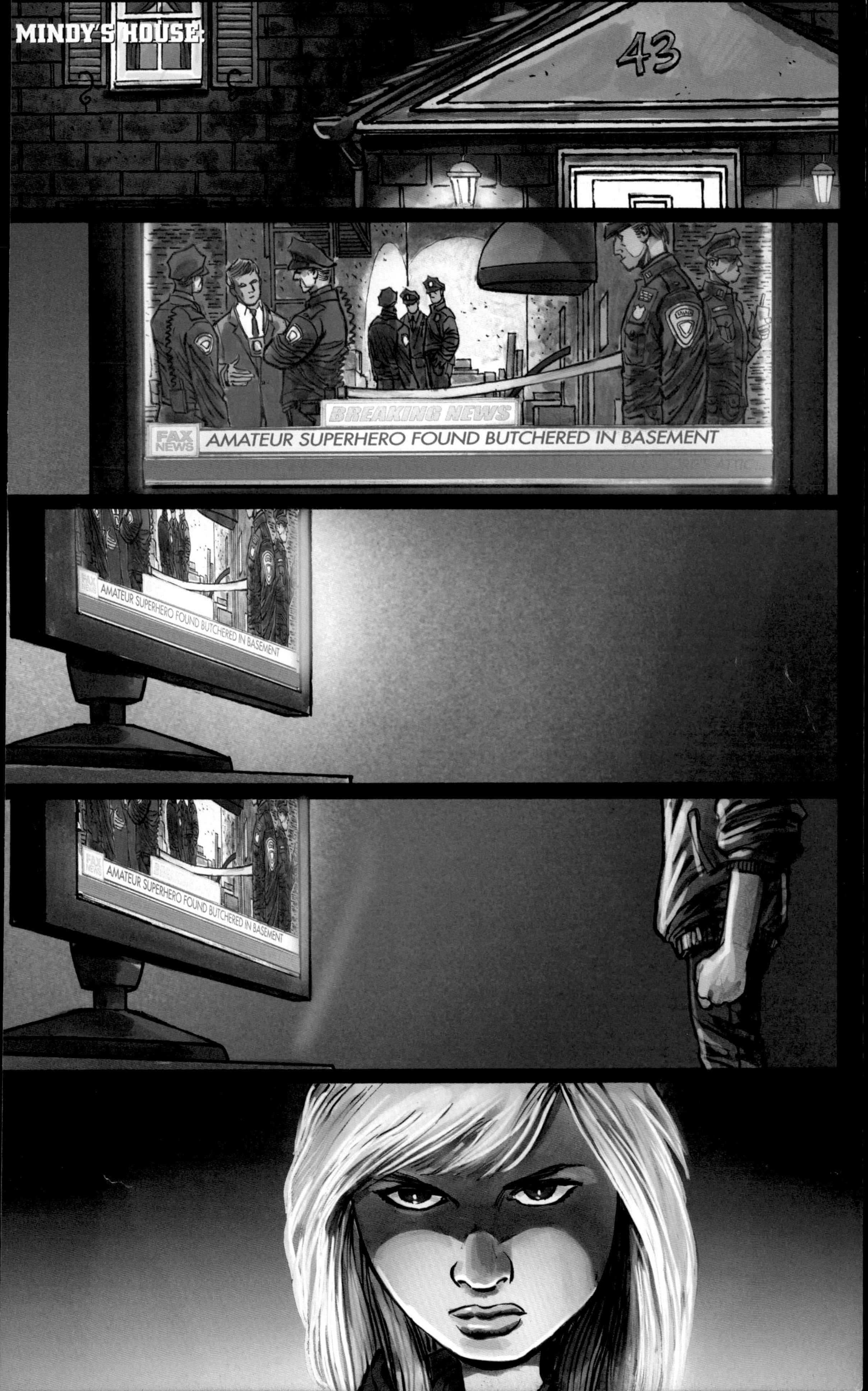
MINDY'S HOUSE:
43
BREAKING NEWS
FAX NEWS
AMATEUR SUPERHERO FOUND BUTCHERED IN BASEMENT
FAX NEWS
AMATEUR SUPERHERO FOUND BUTCHERED IN BASEMENT
FAX NEWS
AMATEUR SUPERHERO FOUND BUTCHERED IN BASEMENT

FOUR

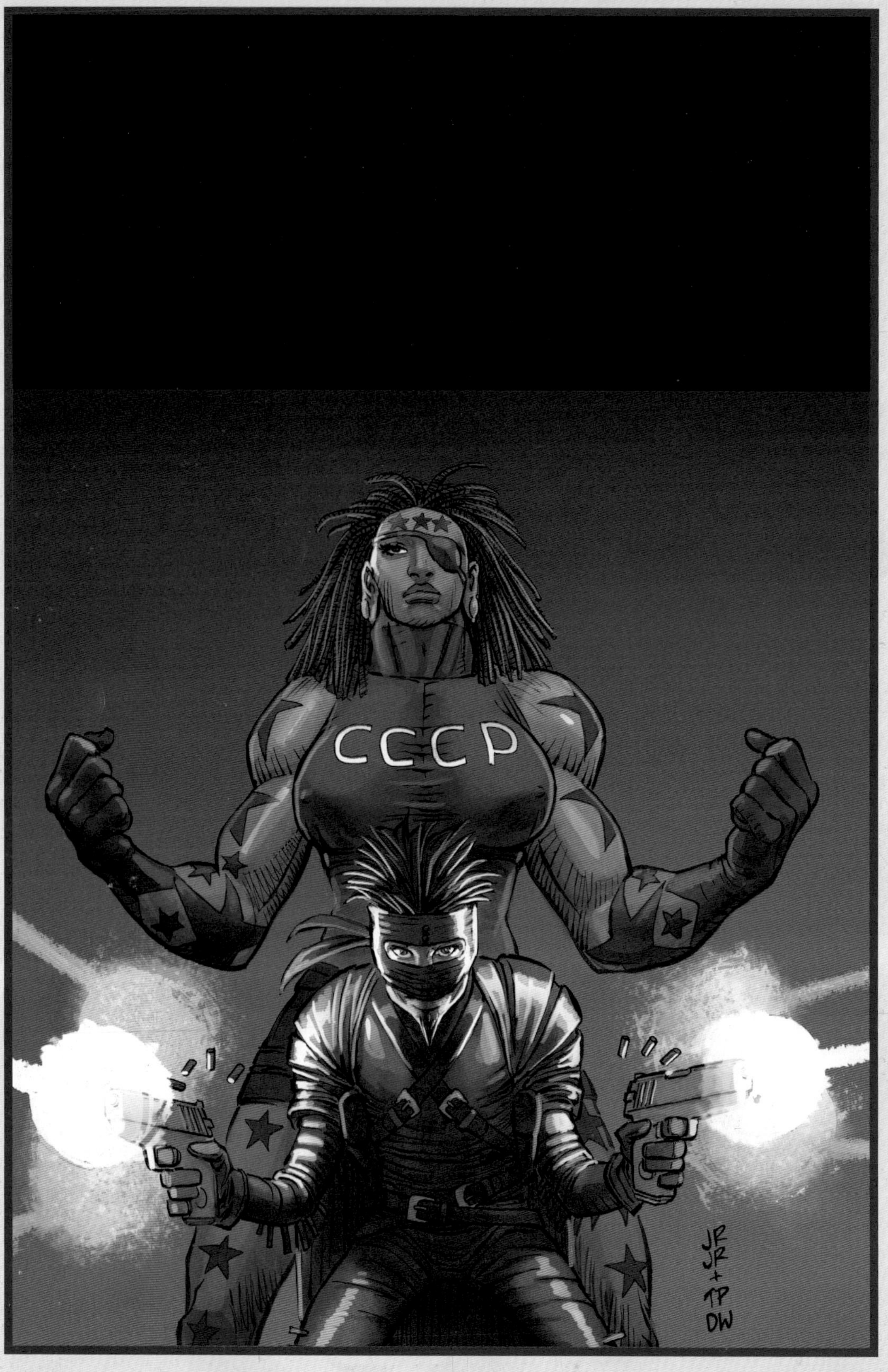
CCCP

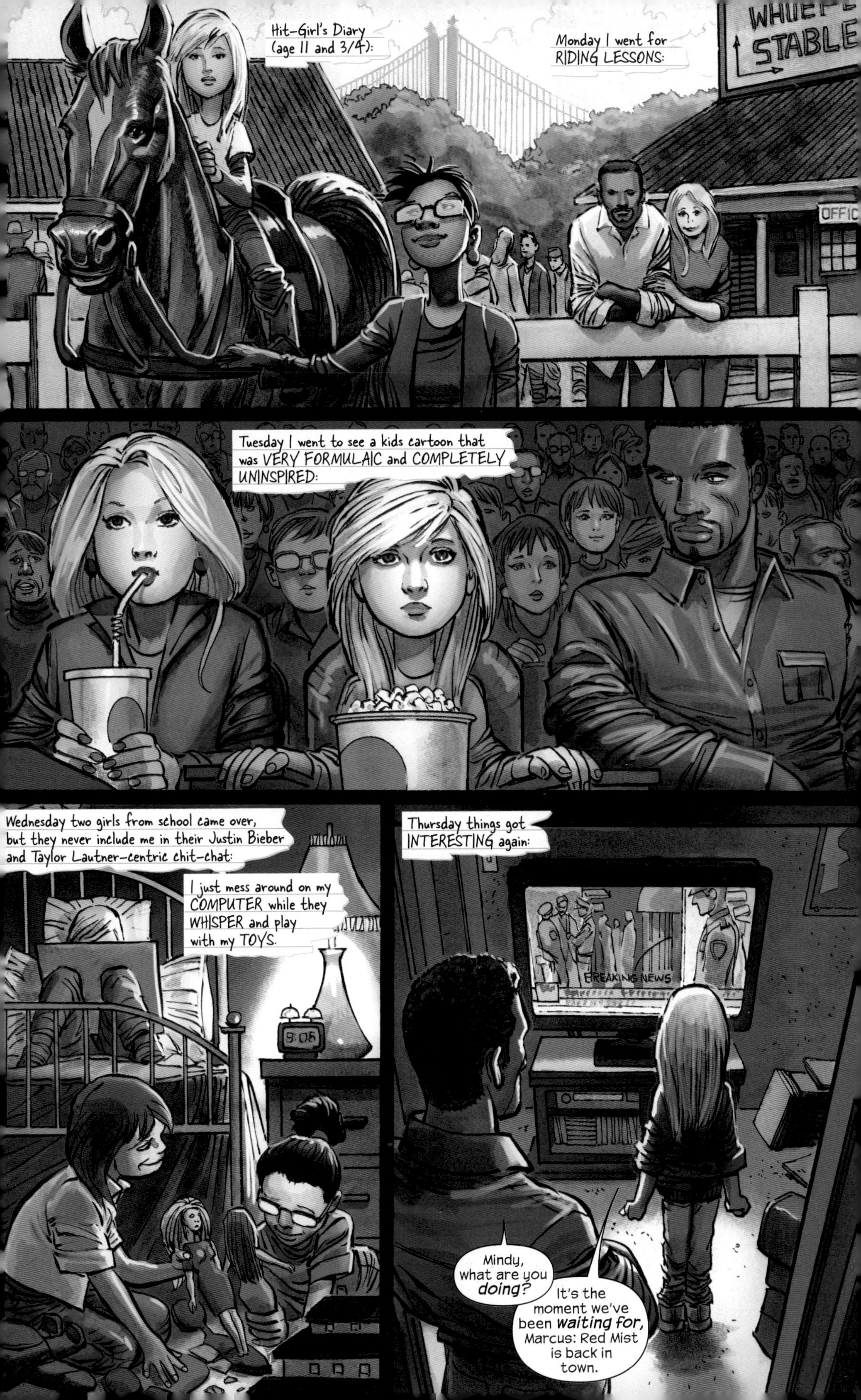

WHIFFL
STABLE
Hit-Girl's Diary (age 11 and 3/4):
Monday I went for RIDING LESSONS:
OFFIC
Tuesday I went to see a kids cartoon that was VERY FORMULAIC and COMPLETELY UNINSPIRED:
Wednesday two girls from school came over, but they never include me in their Justin Bieber and Taylor Lautner-centric chit-chat:
I just mess around on my COMPUTER while they WHISPER and play with my TOYS.
9:08
Thursday things got INTERESTING again:
BREAKING NEWS
Mindy, what are you doing?
It's the moment we've been waiting for, Marcus: Red Mist is back in town.

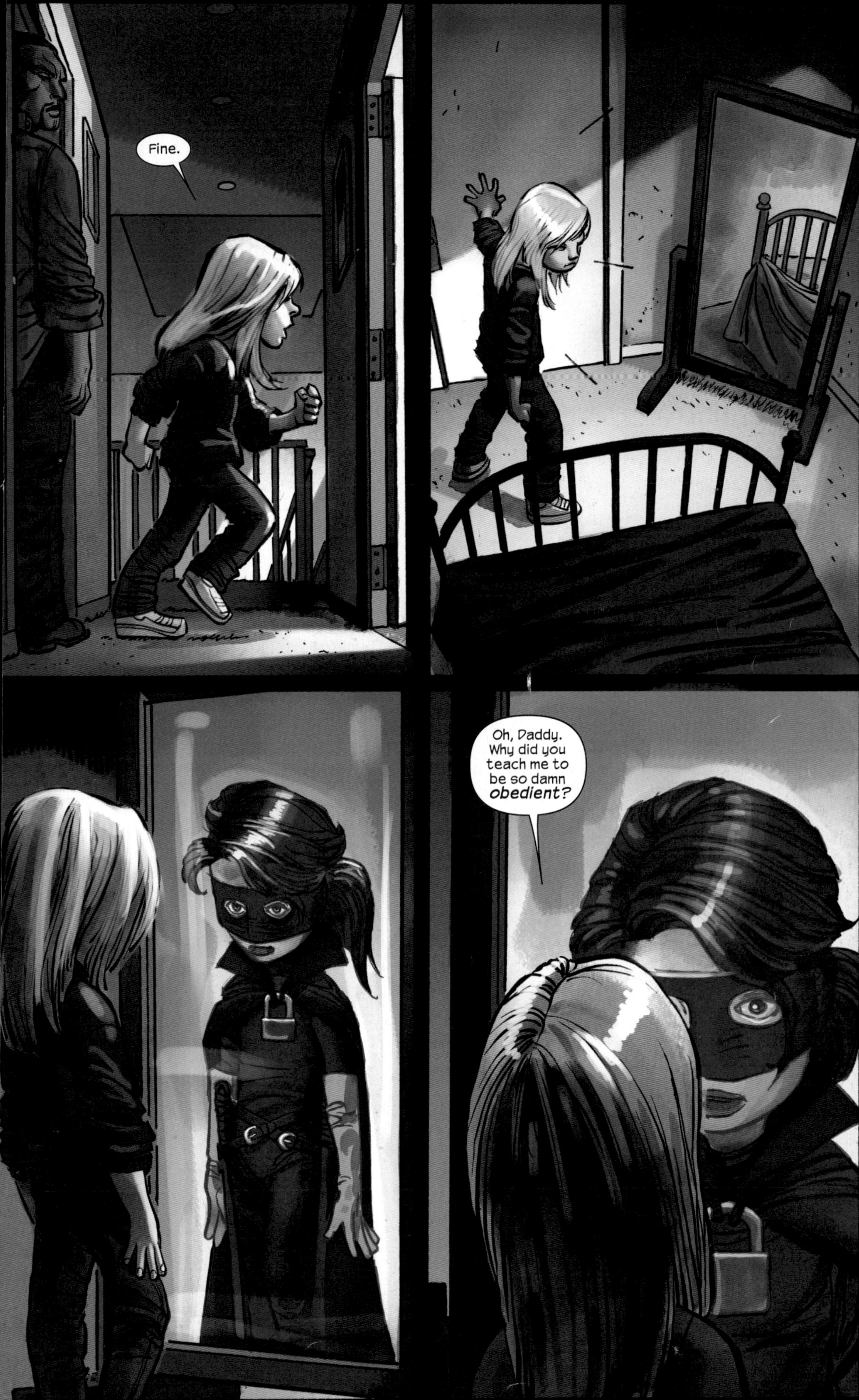
Fine.
Oh, Daddy. Why did you teach me to be so damn *obedient?*

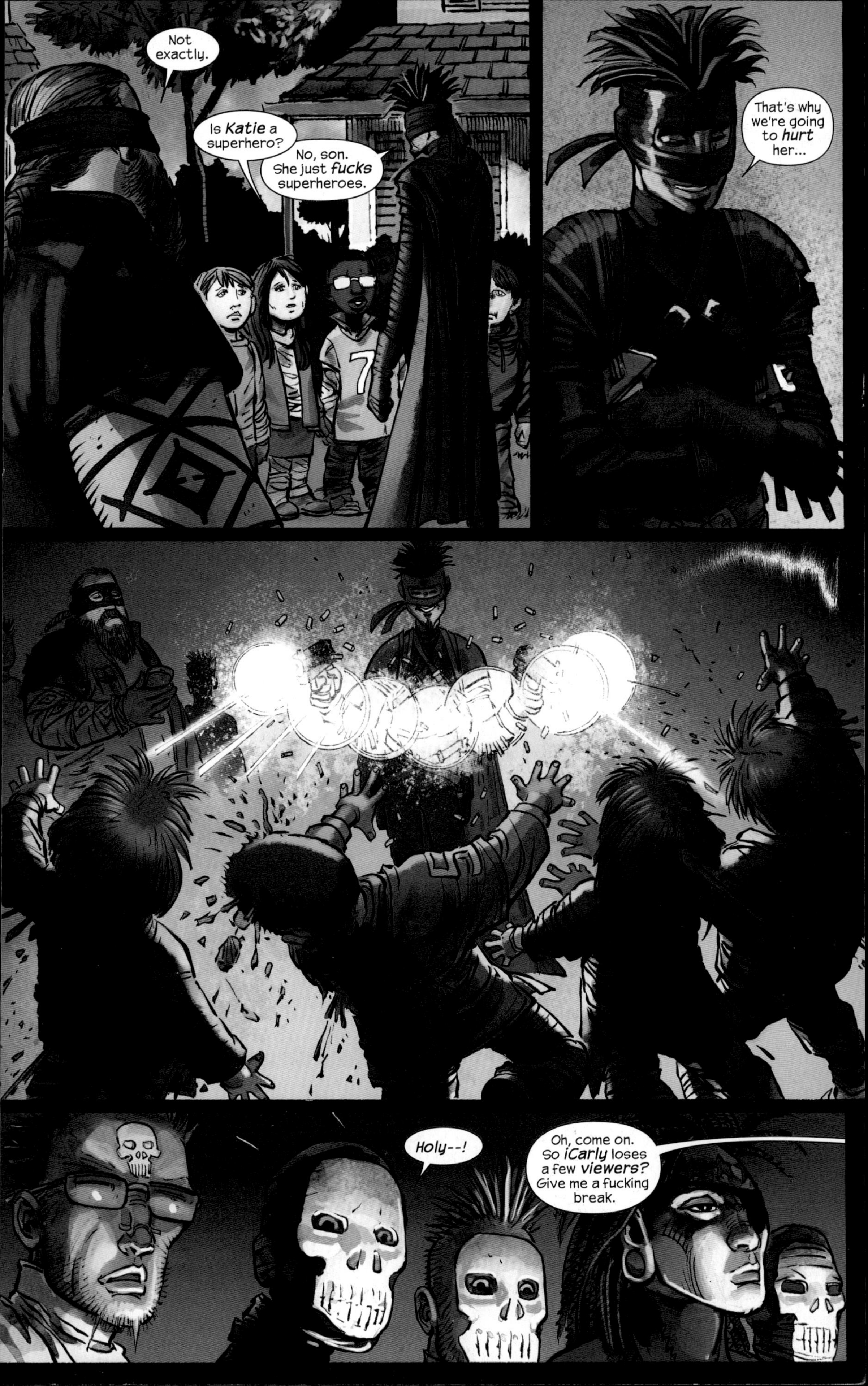
Not exactly.
Is *Katie* a superhero?
No, son. She just *fucks* superheroes.
That's why we're going to *hurt* her...
Holy--!
Oh, come on. So *iCarly* loses a few *viewers?* Give me a fucking break.

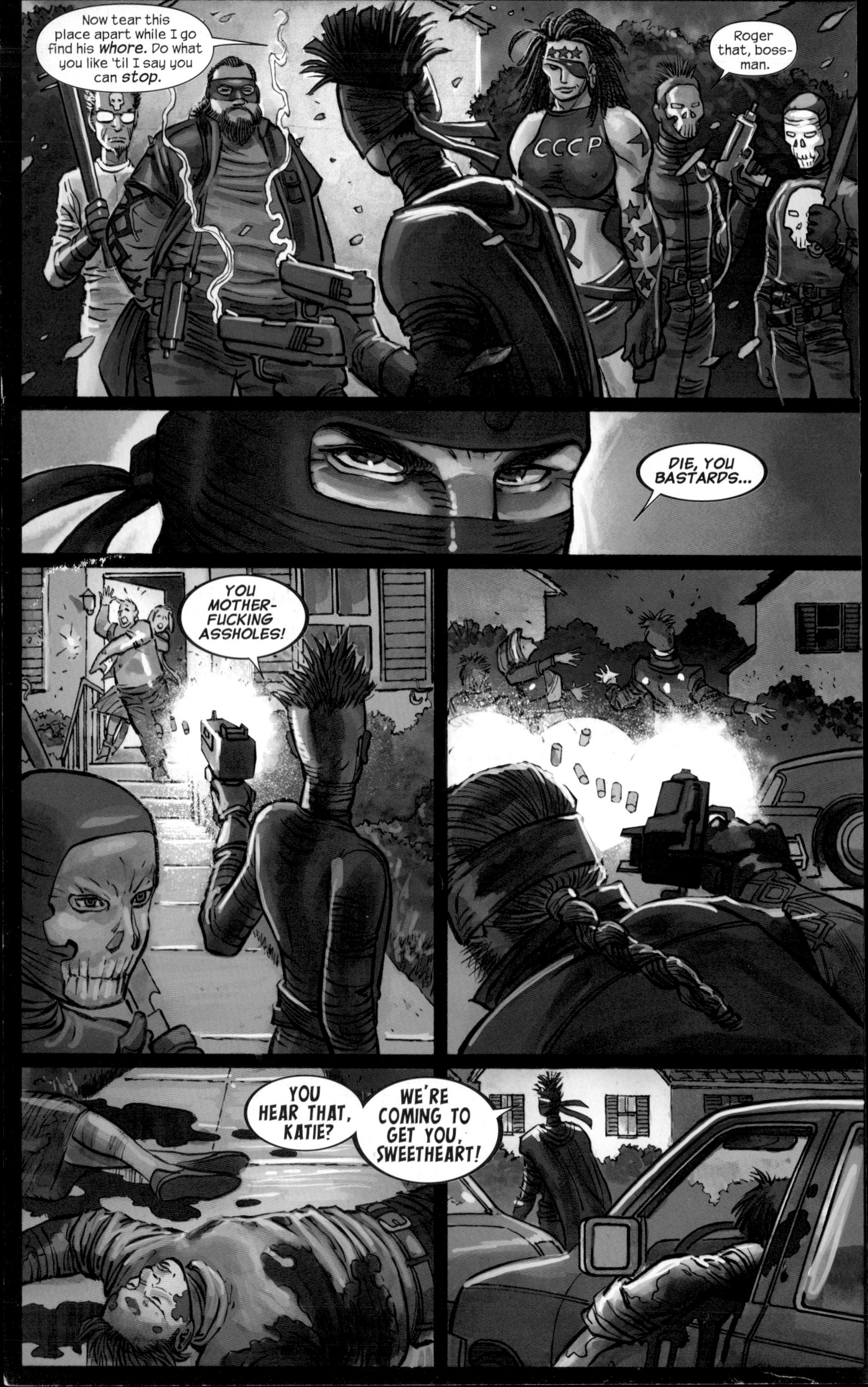
Now tear this place apart while I go find his *whore.* Do what you like 'til I say you can *stop.*
Roger that, boss-man.
DIE, YOU BASTARDS...
YOU MOTHER-FUCKING ASSHOLES!
YOU HEAR THAT, KATIE?
WE'RE COMING TO GET YOU, SWEETHEART!

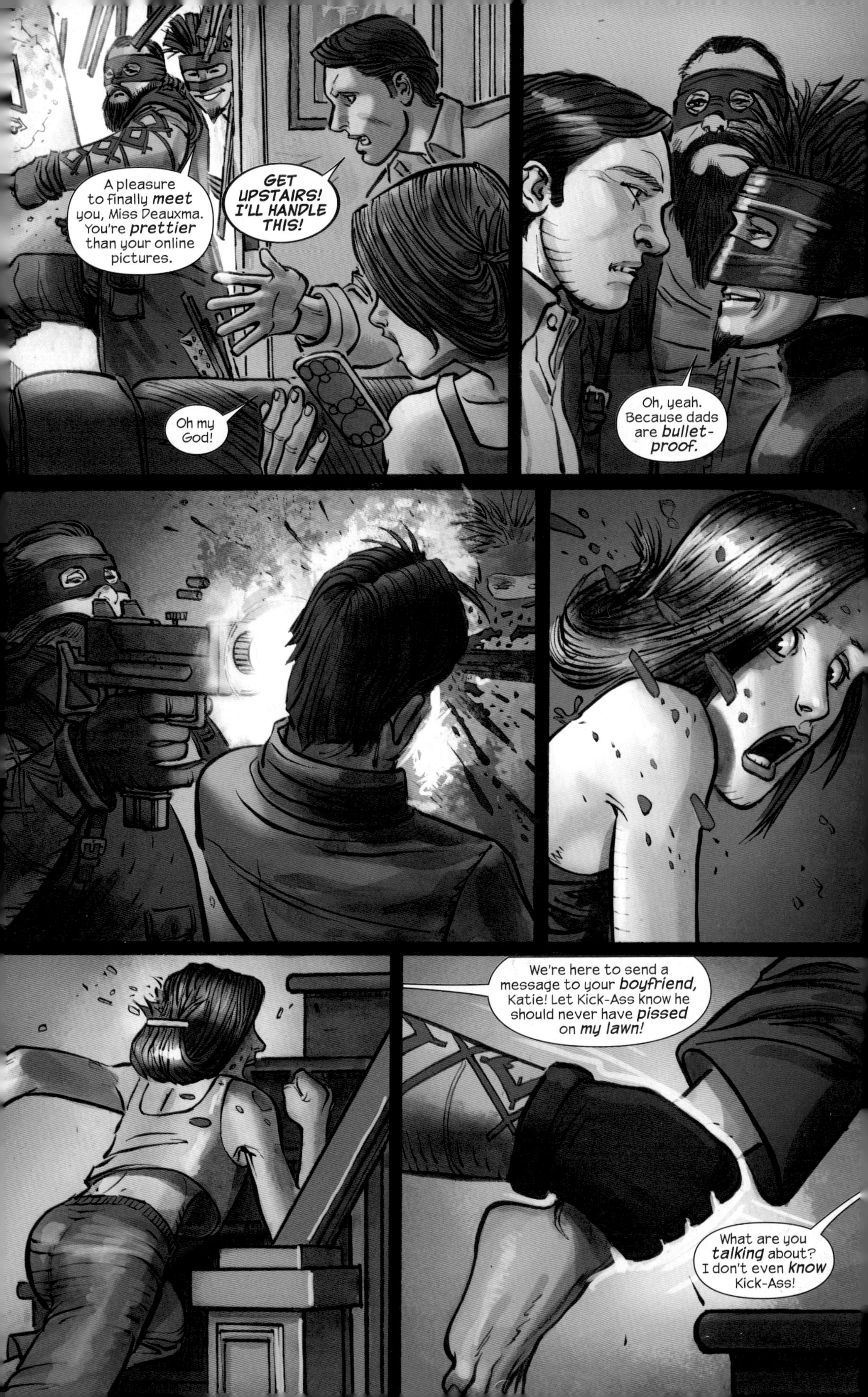
A pleasure to finally meet you, Miss Deauxma. You're prettier than your online pictures.
GET UPSTAIRS! I'LL HANDLE THIS!
Oh my God!
Oh, yeah. Because dads are bullet-proof.
We're here to send a message to your boyfriend, Katie! Let Kick-Ass know he should never have pissed on my lawn!
What are you talking about? I don't even know Kick-Ass!

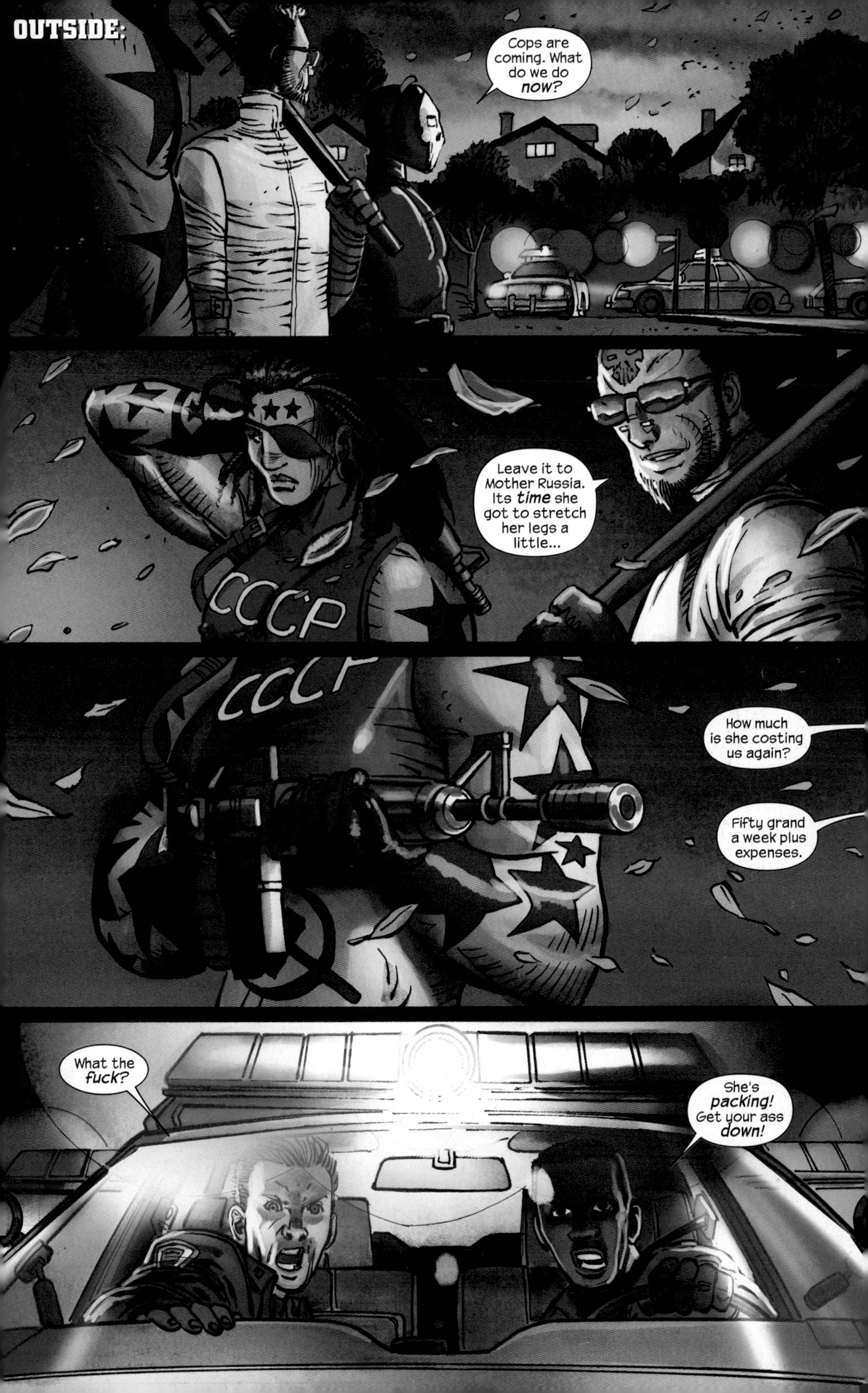
OUTSIDE:
Cops are coming. What do we do now?
Leave it to Mother Russia. Its time she got to stretch her legs a little...
CCCP
How much is she costing us again?
Fifty grand a week plus expenses.
What the fuck?
She's packing! Get your ass down!

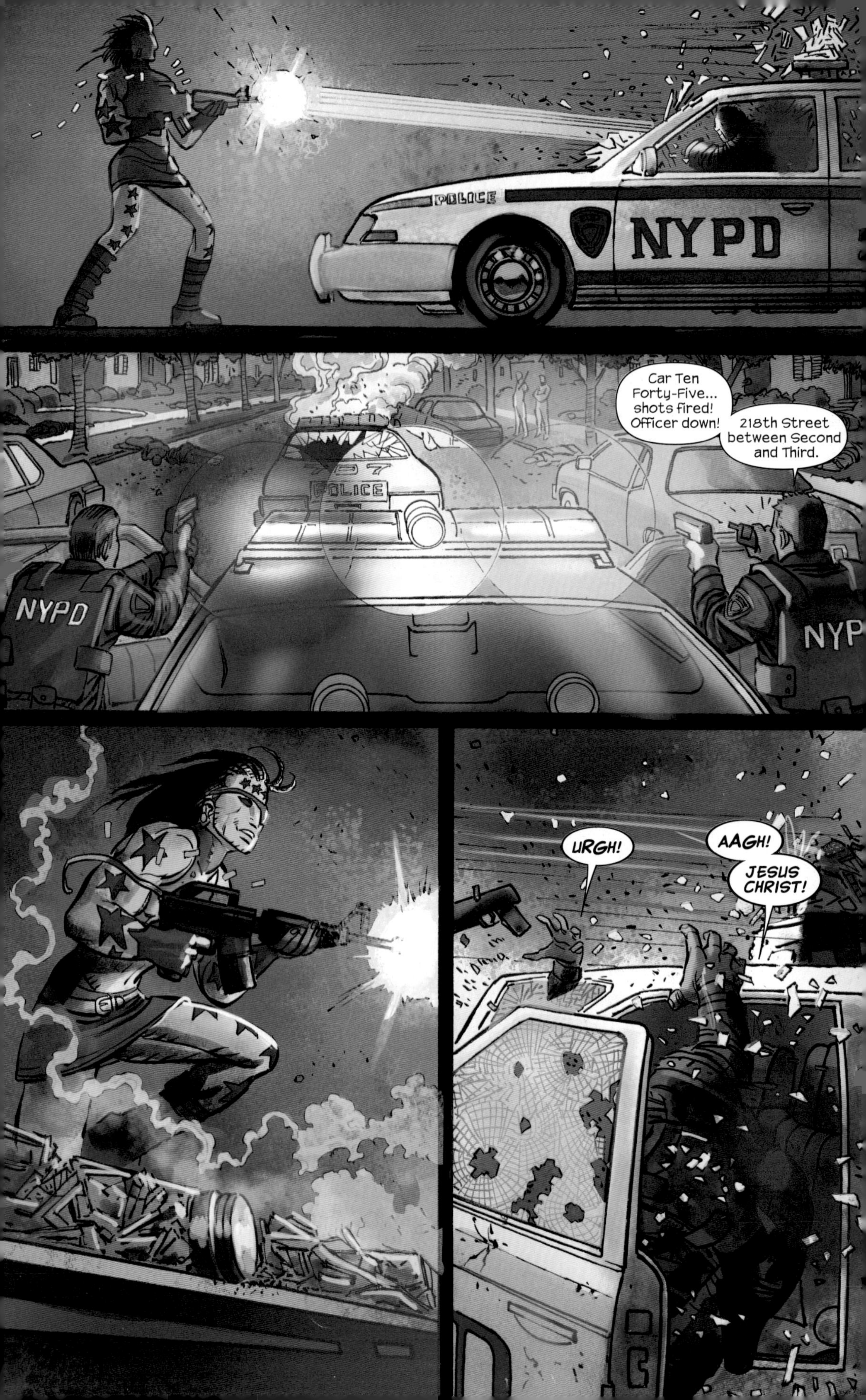
POLICE
NYPD
POLICE
NYPD
Car Ten Forty-Five... shots fired! Officer down!
218th Street between Second and Third.
NYP
URGH!
AAGH!
JESUS CHRIST!

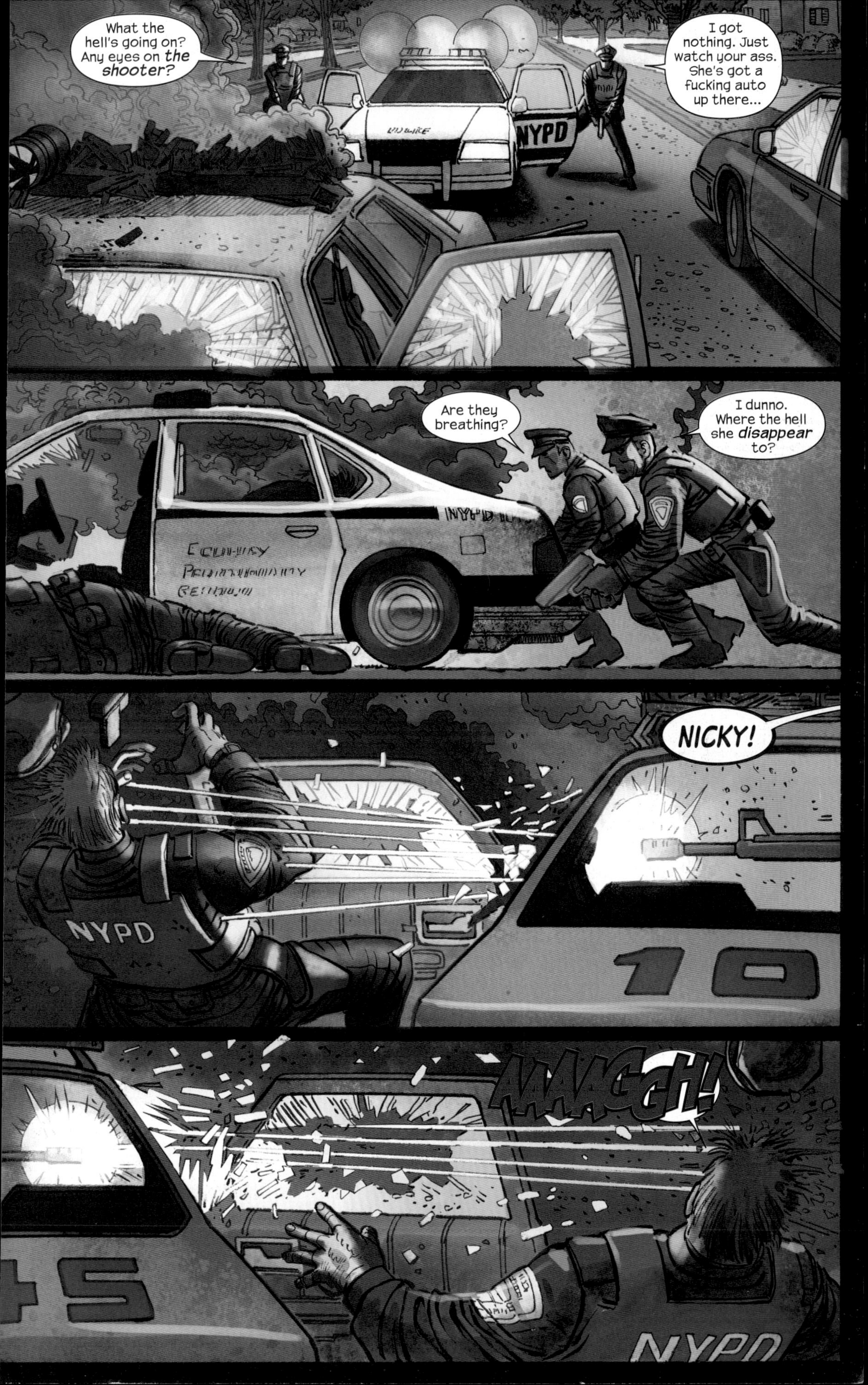
What the hell's going on? Any eyes on *the shooter*?
I got nothing. Just watch your ass. She's got a fucking auto up there...
NYPD
Are they breathing?
I dunno. Where the hell she *disappear* to?
NYPD
NICKY!
NYPD
10
AAAAGGH!
45
NYPD

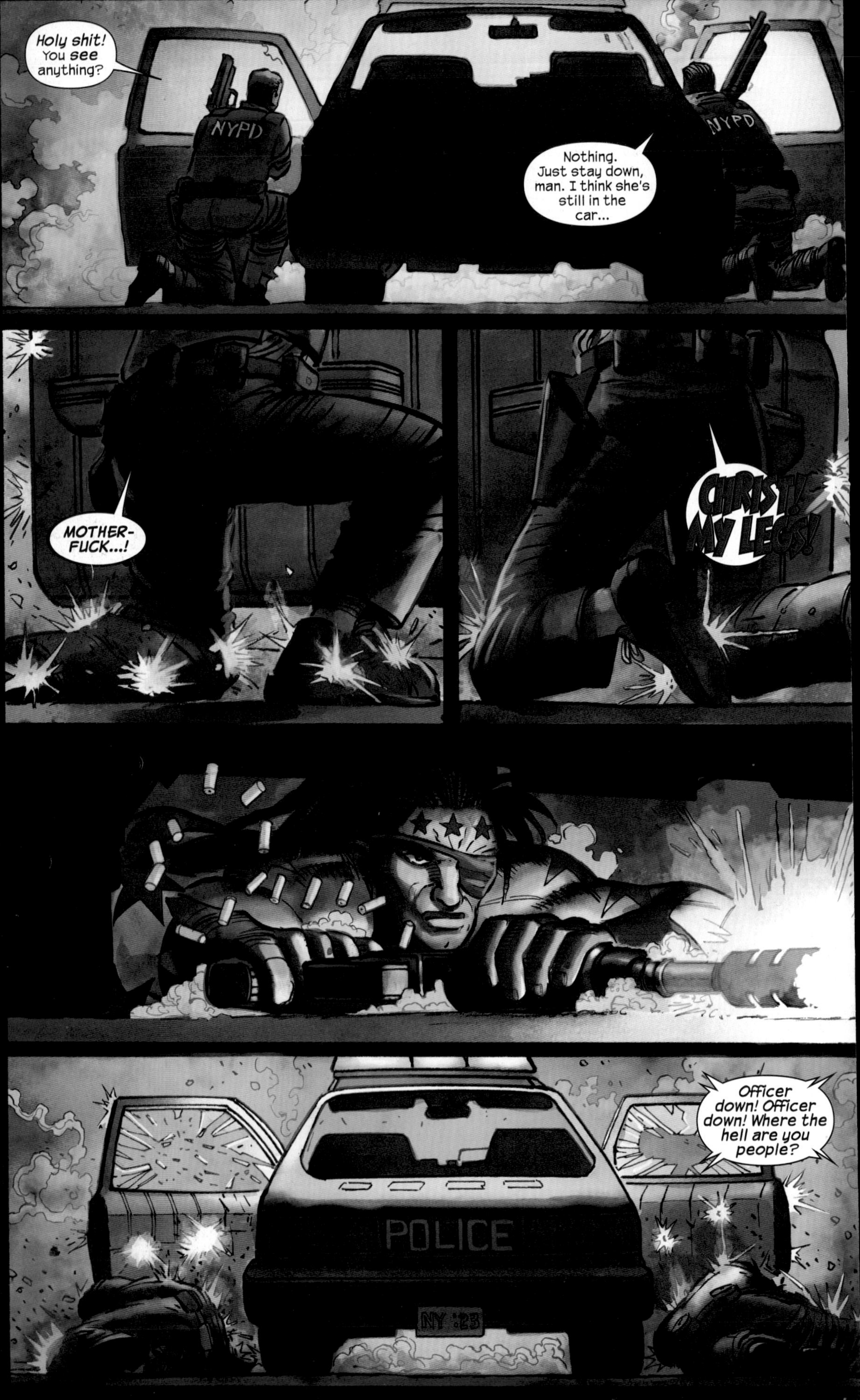
Holy shit! You see anything?
Nothing. Just stay down, man. I think she's still in the car...
MOTHER-FUCK...!
CHRIST! MY LEGS!
Officer down! Officer down! Where the hell are you people?
NYPD
NYPD
POLICE
NY '23

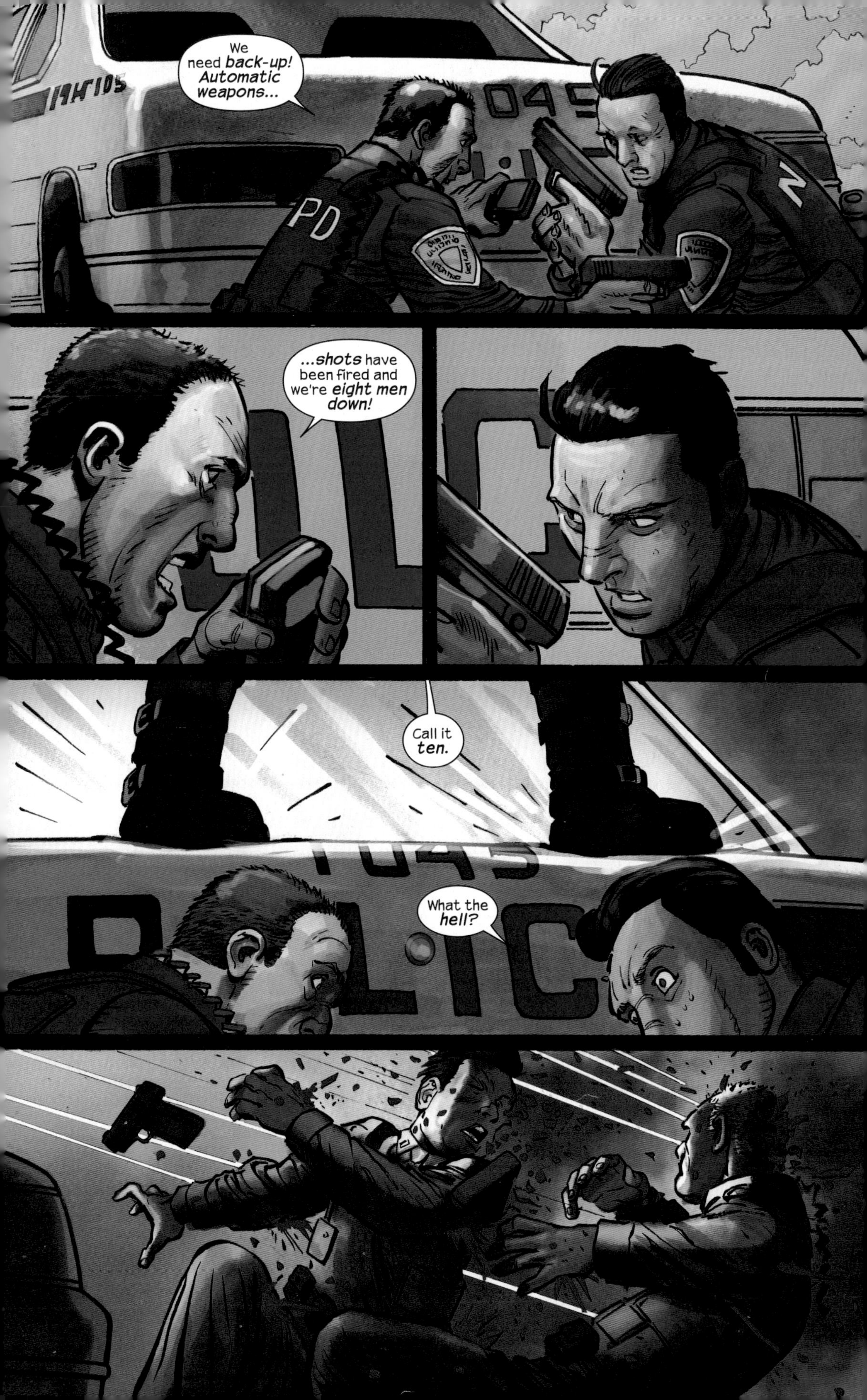
We need back-up! Automatic weapons...
...shots have been fired and we're eight men down!
Call it ten.
What the hell?

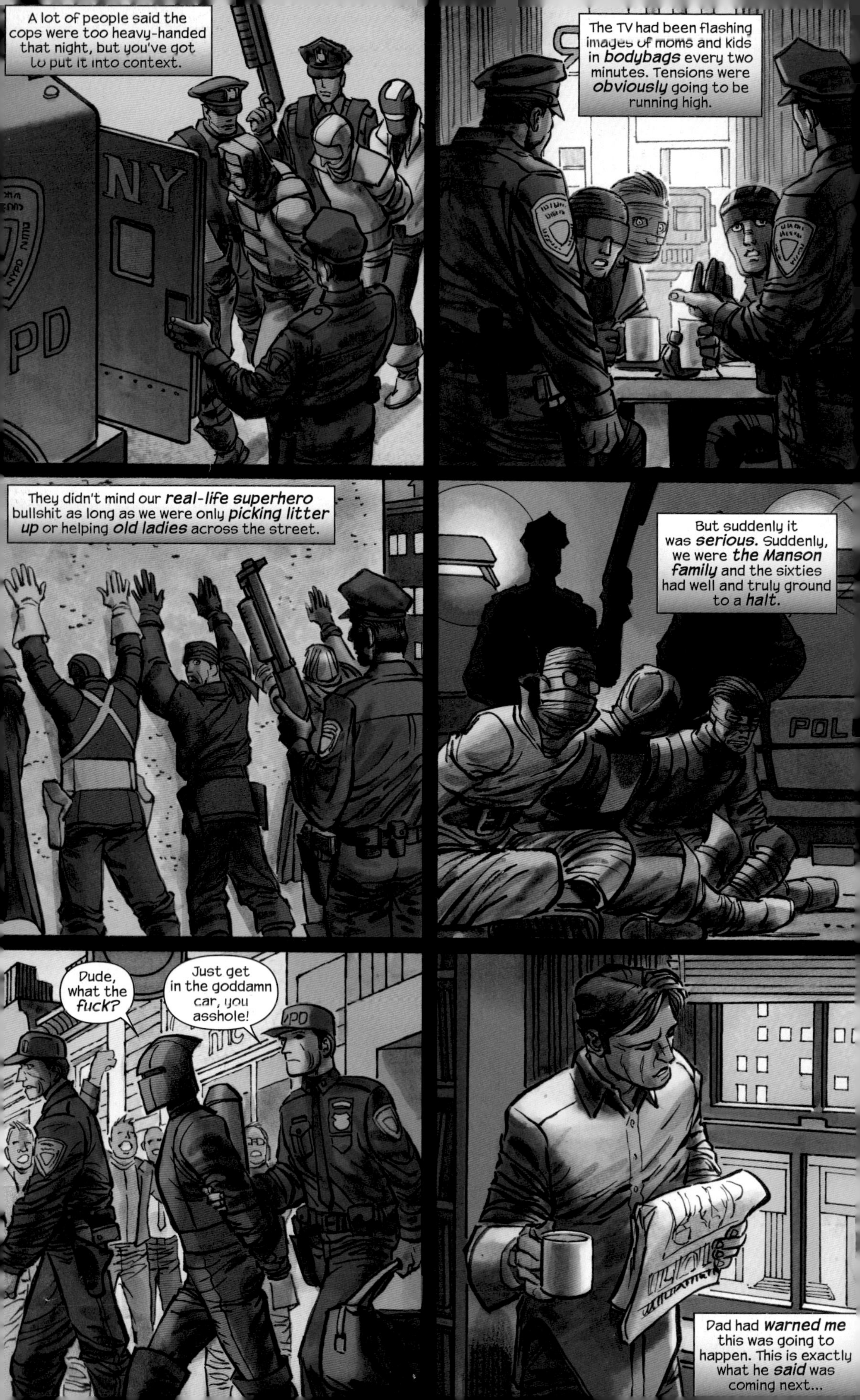
A lot of people said the cops were too heavy-handed that night, but you've got to put it into context.
NY
NYPD
The TV had been flashing images of moms and kids in *bodybags* every two minutes. Tensions were *obviously* going to be running high.
They didn't mind our *real-life superhero* bullshit as long as we were only *picking litter up* or helping *old ladies* across the street.
But suddenly it was *serious.* Suddenly, we were *the Manson family* and the sixties had well and truly ground to a *halt.*
POL
Dude, what the *fuck?*
Just get in the goddamn car, you asshole!
Dad had *warned me* this was going to happen. This is exactly what he *said* was coming next...

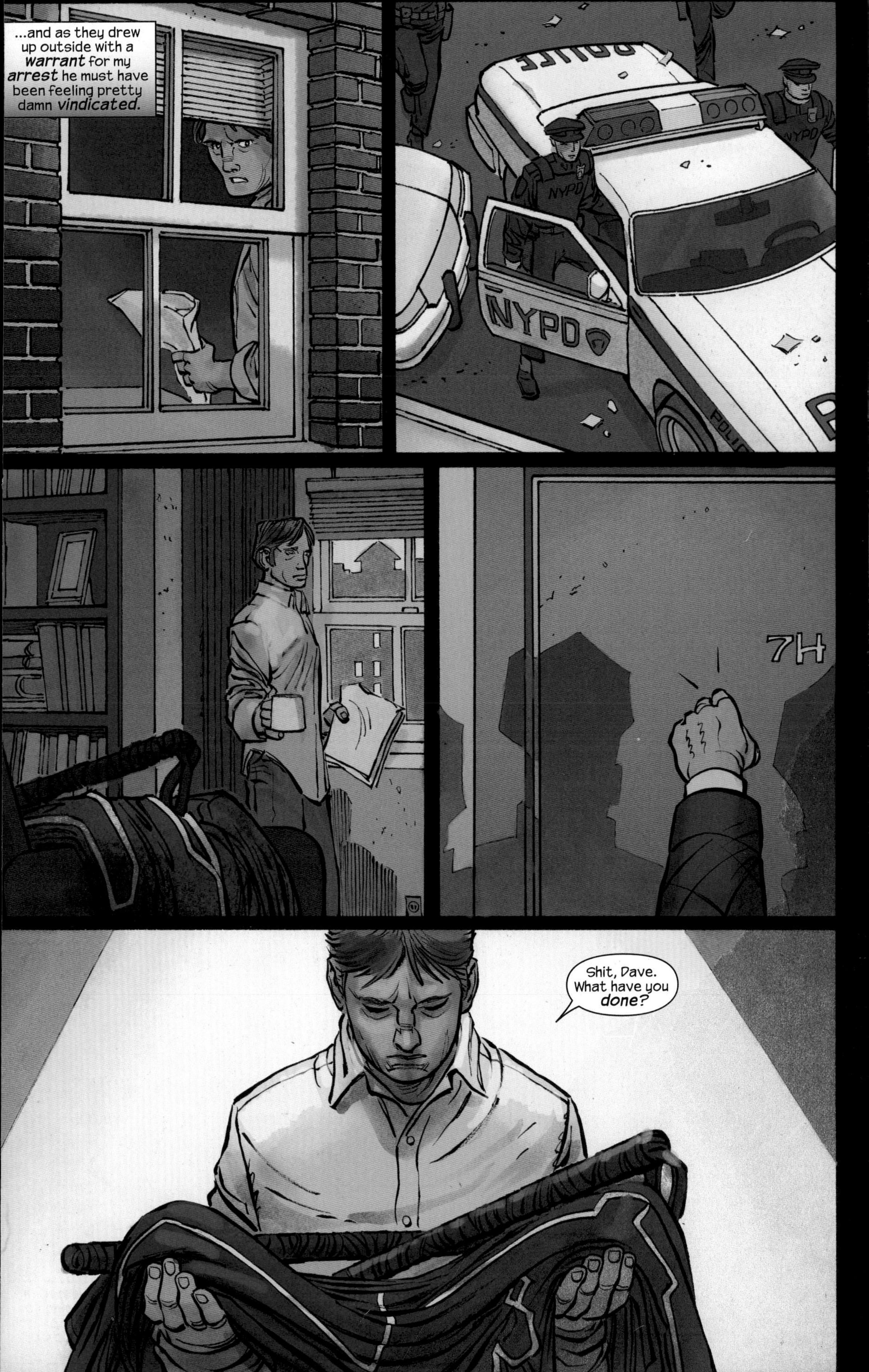

...and as they drew up outside with a *warrant* for my *arrest* he must have been feeling pretty damn *vindicated*.
NYPD
POLICE
NYPD
NYPD
7H
Shit, Dave. What have you *done*?

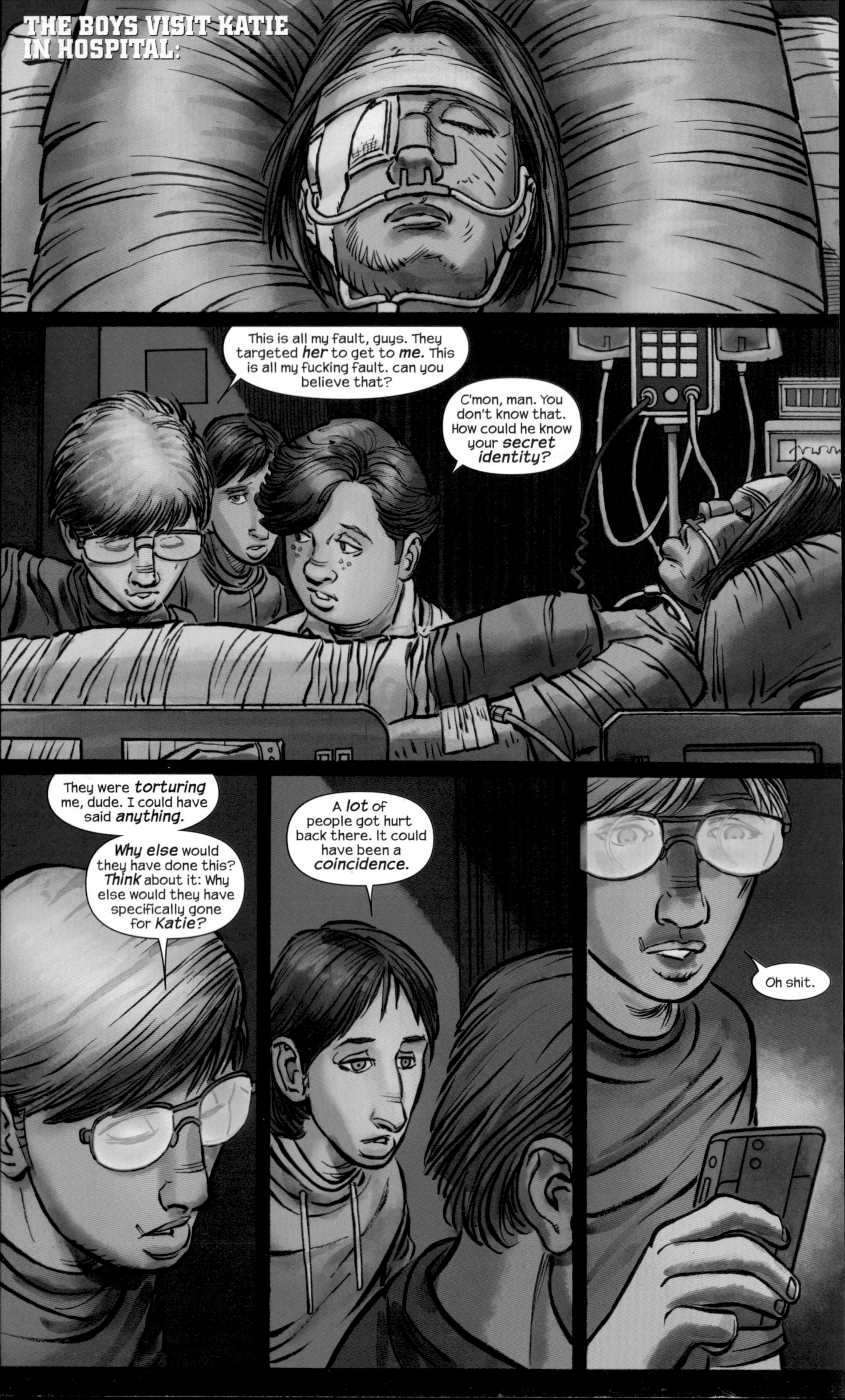
THE BOYS VISIT KATIE IN HOSPITAL:
This is all my fault, guys. They targeted her to get to me. This is all my fucking fault. can you believe that?
C'mon, man. You don't know that. How could he know your secret identity?
They were torturing me, dude. I could have said anything.
Why else would they have done this? Think about it: Why else would they have specifically gone for Katie?
A lot of people got hurt back there. It could have been a coincidence.
Oh shit.

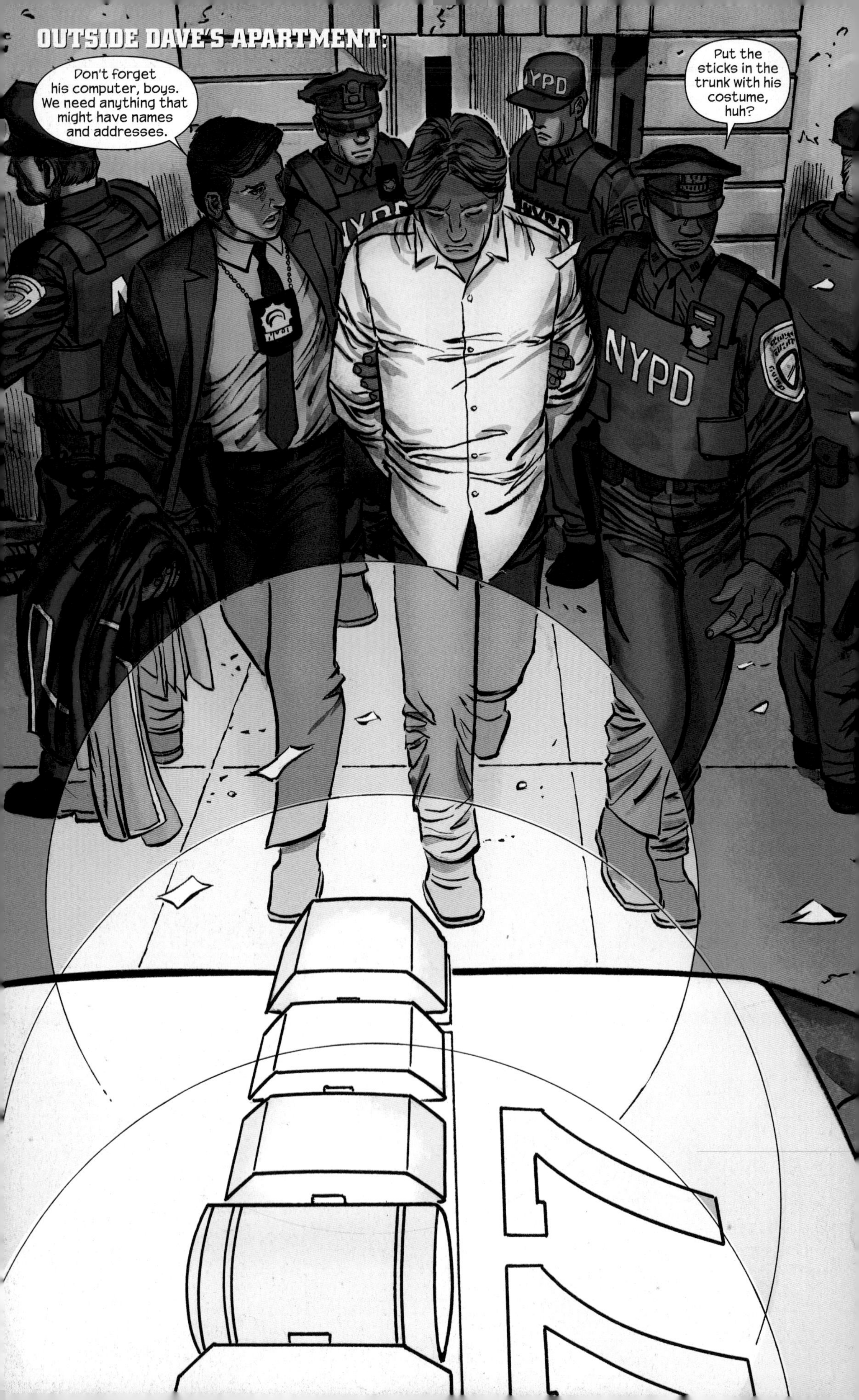
OUTSIDE DAVE'S APARTMENT:
Don't forget his computer, boys. We need anything that might have names and addresses.
Put the sticks in the trunk with his costume, huh?
NYPD
NYPD

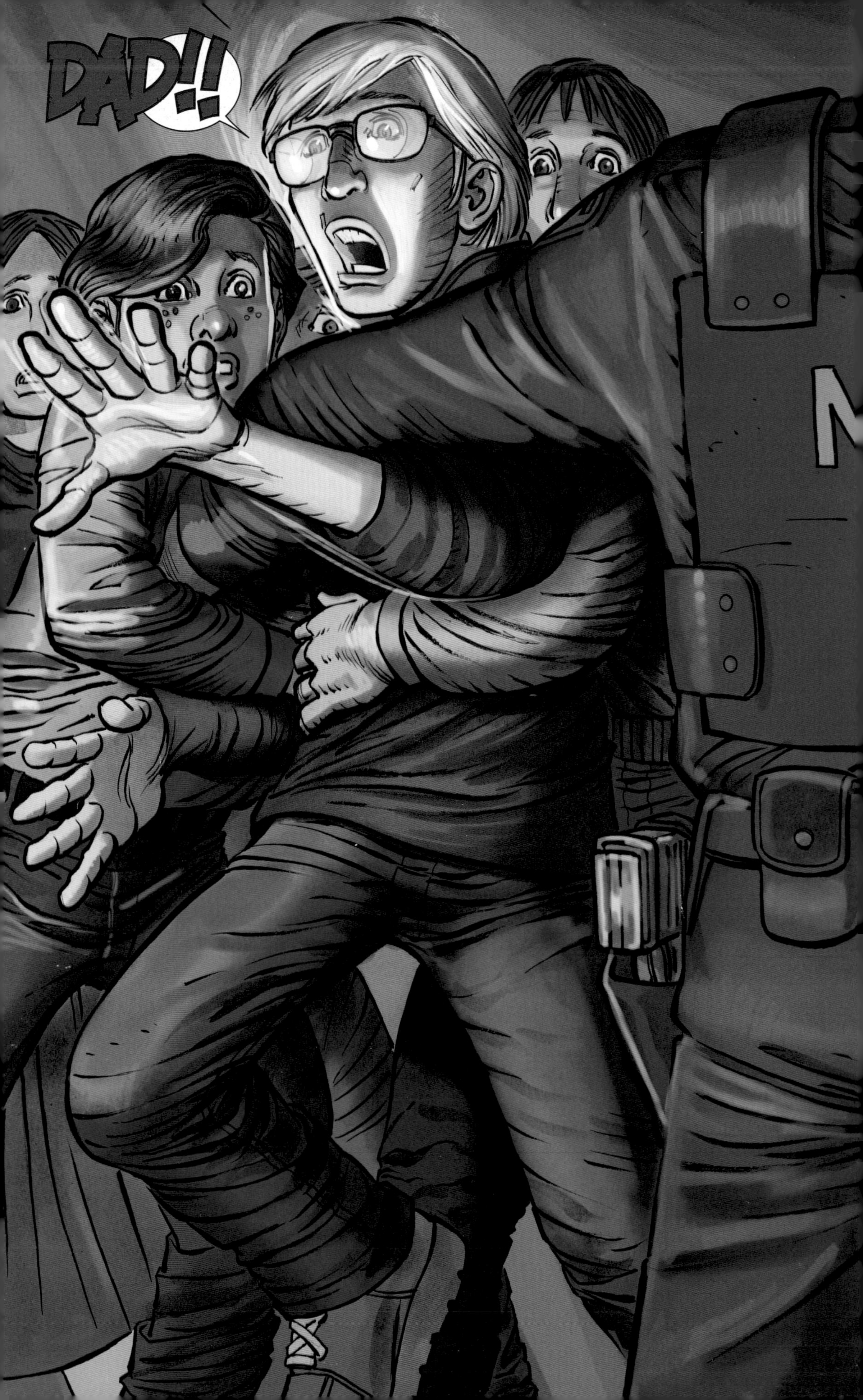
DAD!!

FIVE

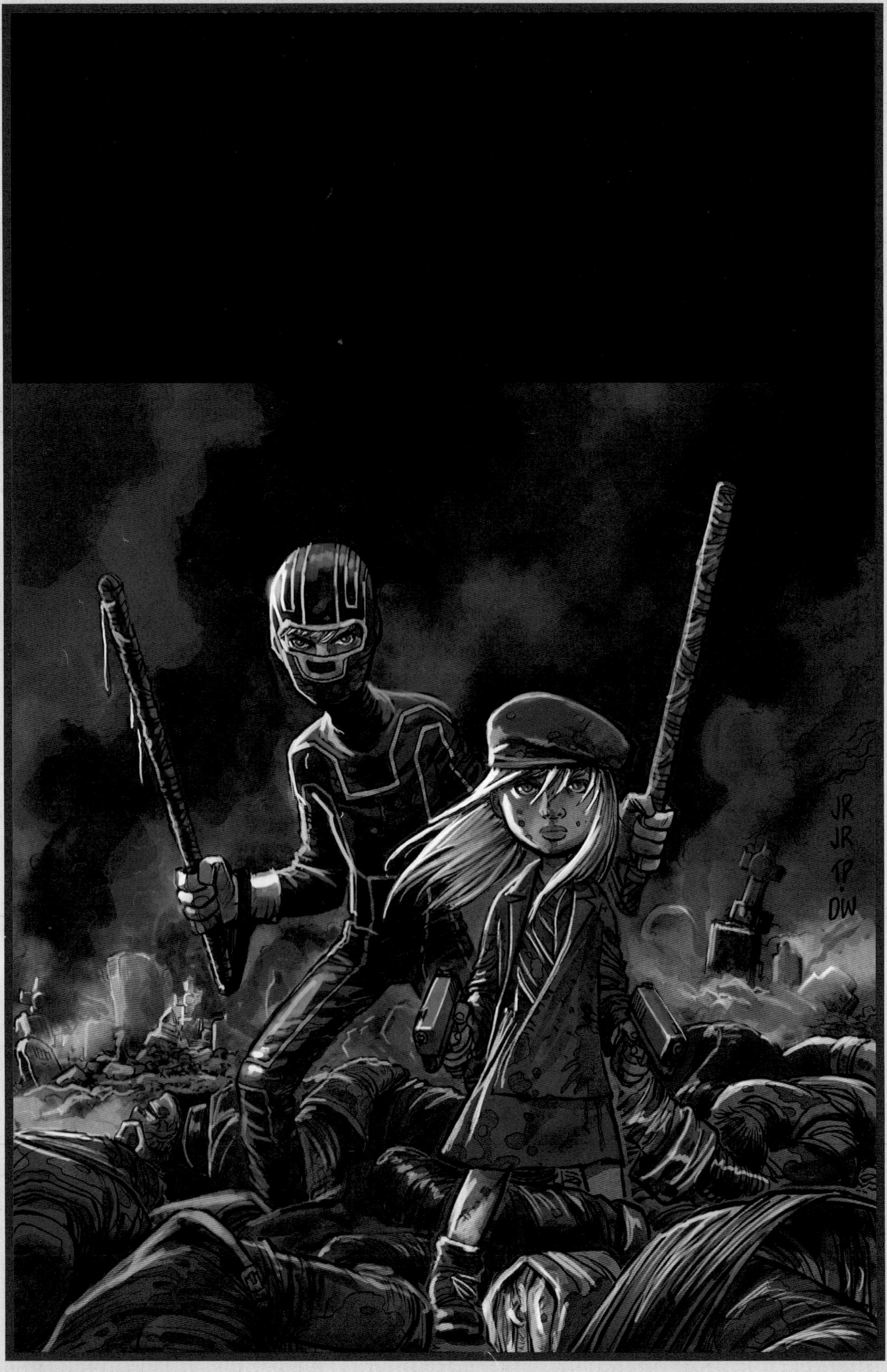
JR
JR
TP
DW

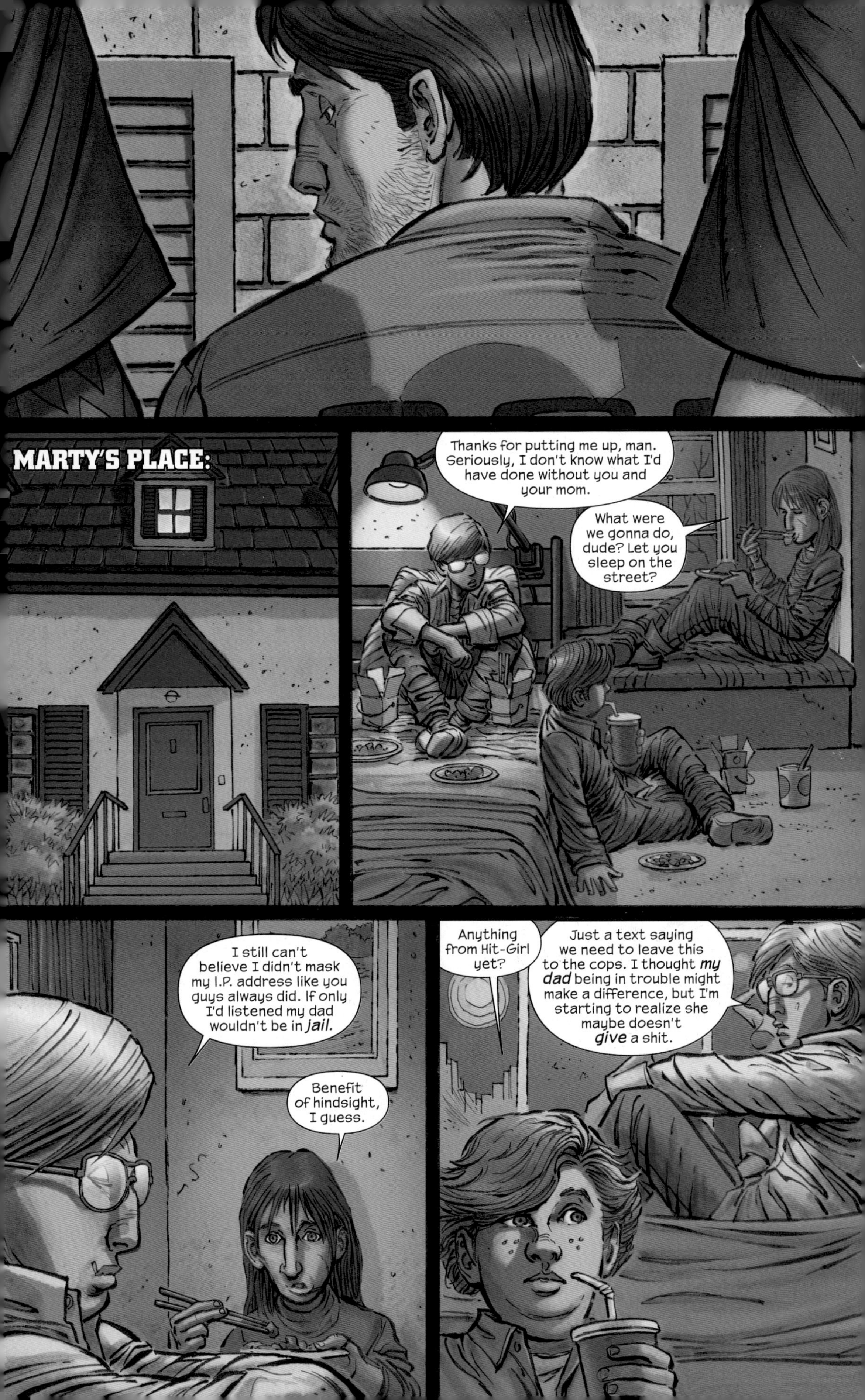
MARTY'S PLACE:
Thanks for putting me up, man. Seriously, I don't know what I'd have done without you and your mom.
What were we gonna do, dude? Let you sleep on the street?
I still can't believe I didn't mask my I.P. address like you guys always did. If only I'd listened my dad wouldn't be in jail.
Benefit of hindsight, I guess.
Anything from Hit-Girl yet?
Just a text saying we need to leave this to the cops. I thought my dad being in trouble might make a difference, but I'm starting to realize she maybe doesn't give a shit.

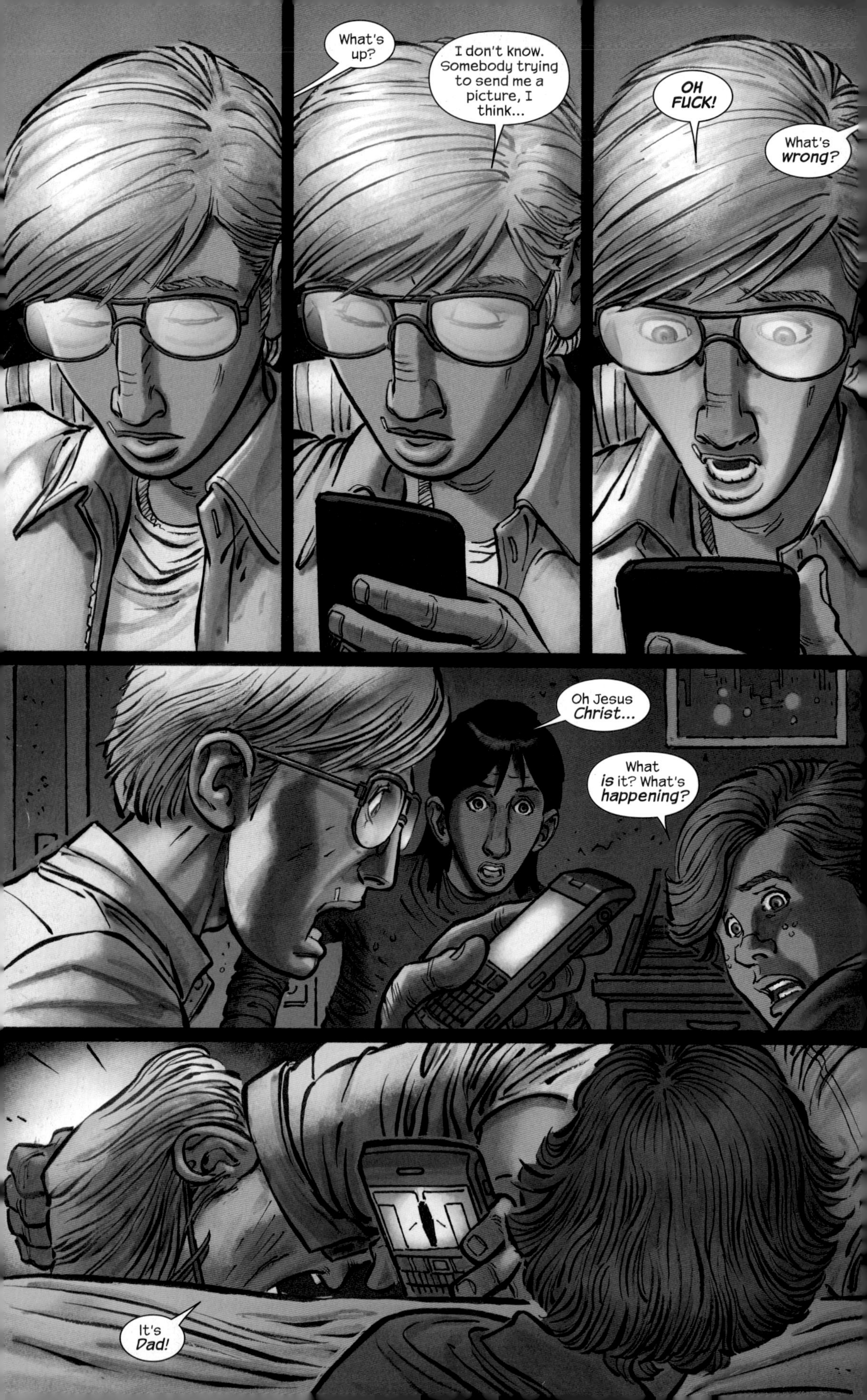

What's up?
I don't know. Somebody trying to send me a picture, I think...
OH FUCK!
What's wrong?
Oh Jesus Christ...
What is it? What's happening?
It's Dad!

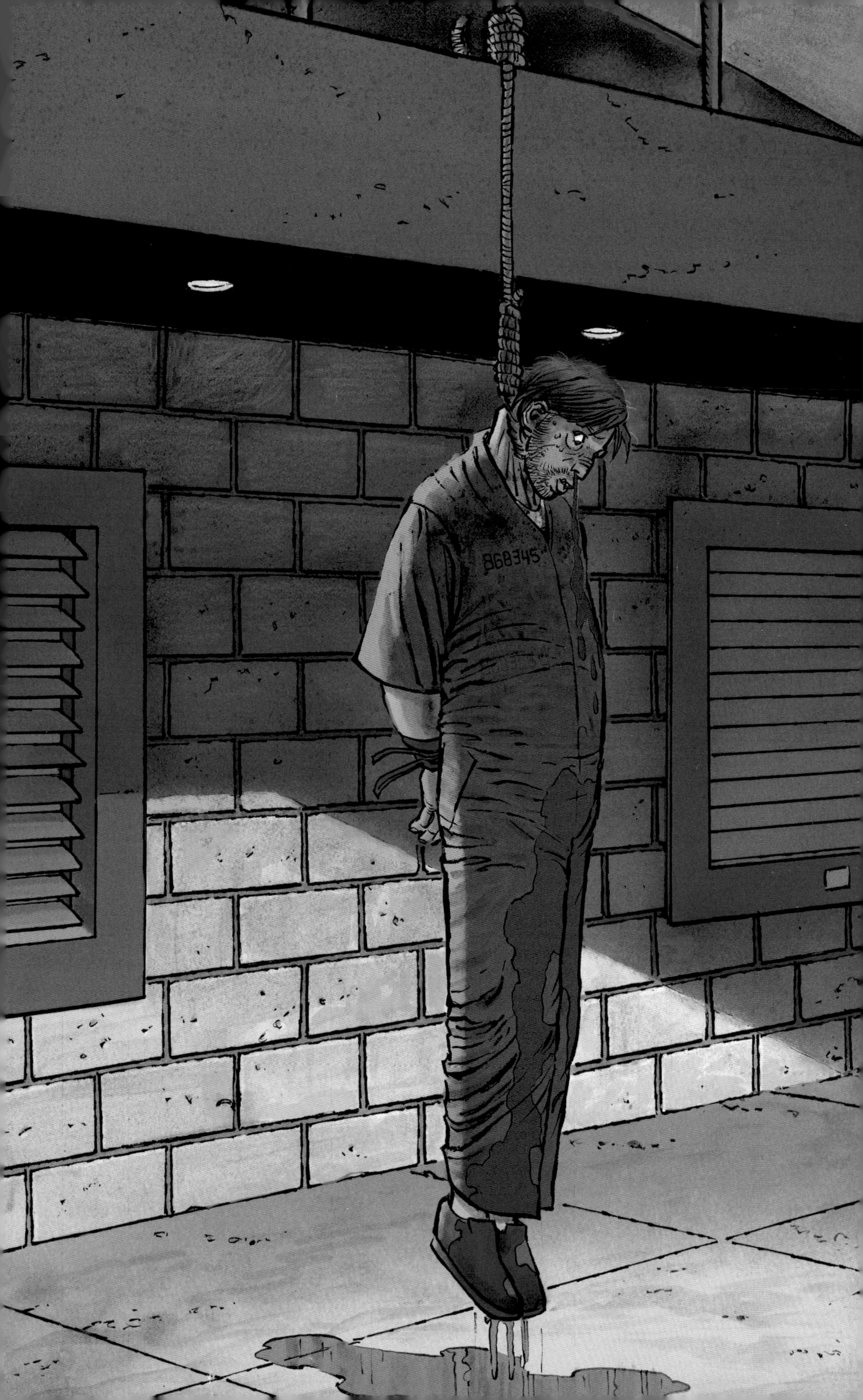
868345

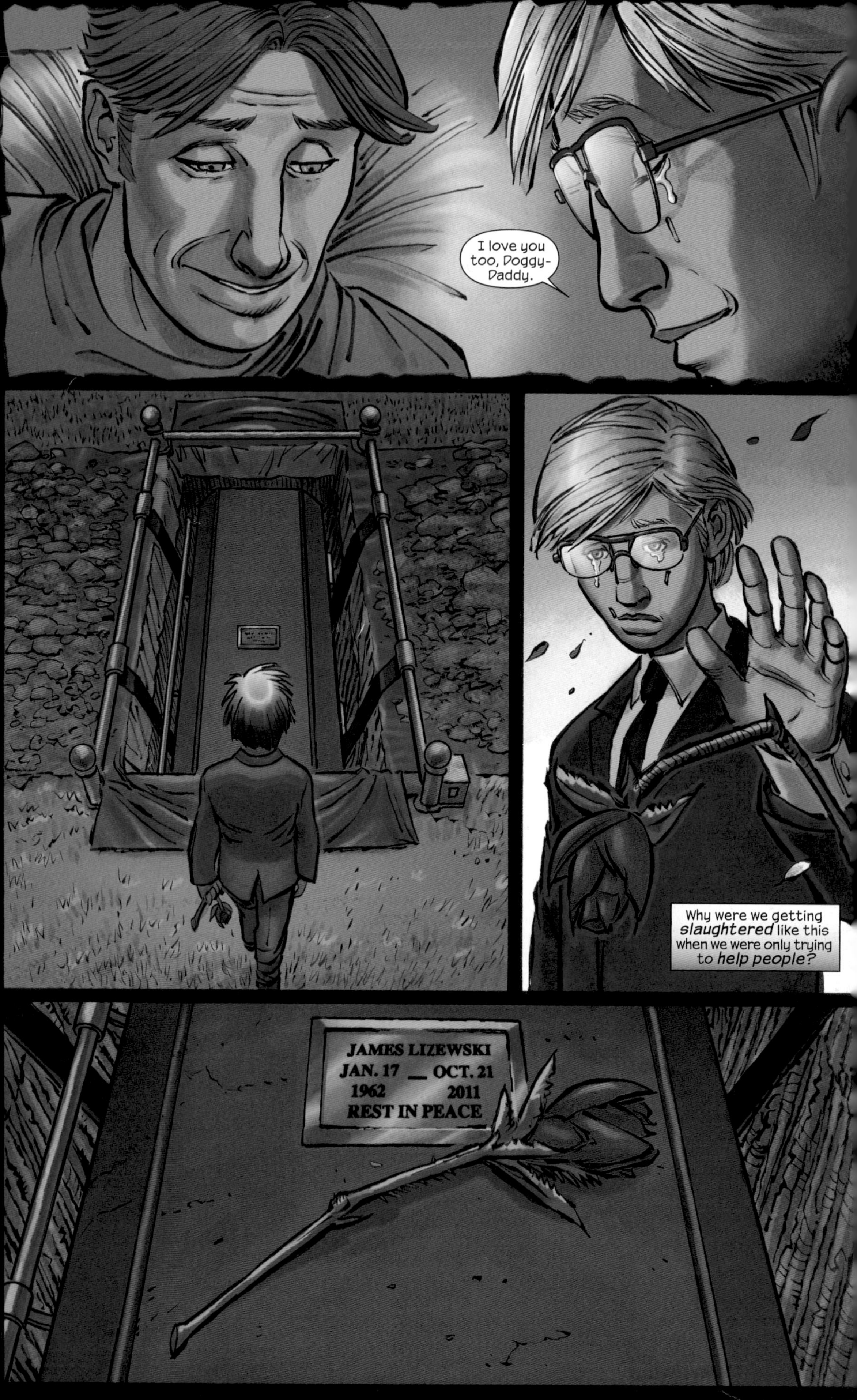
I love you too, Doggy-Daddy.
Why were we getting *slaughtered* like this when we were only trying to *help people?*
JAMES LIZEWSKI
JAN. 17 — OCT. 21
1962 2011
REST IN PEACE

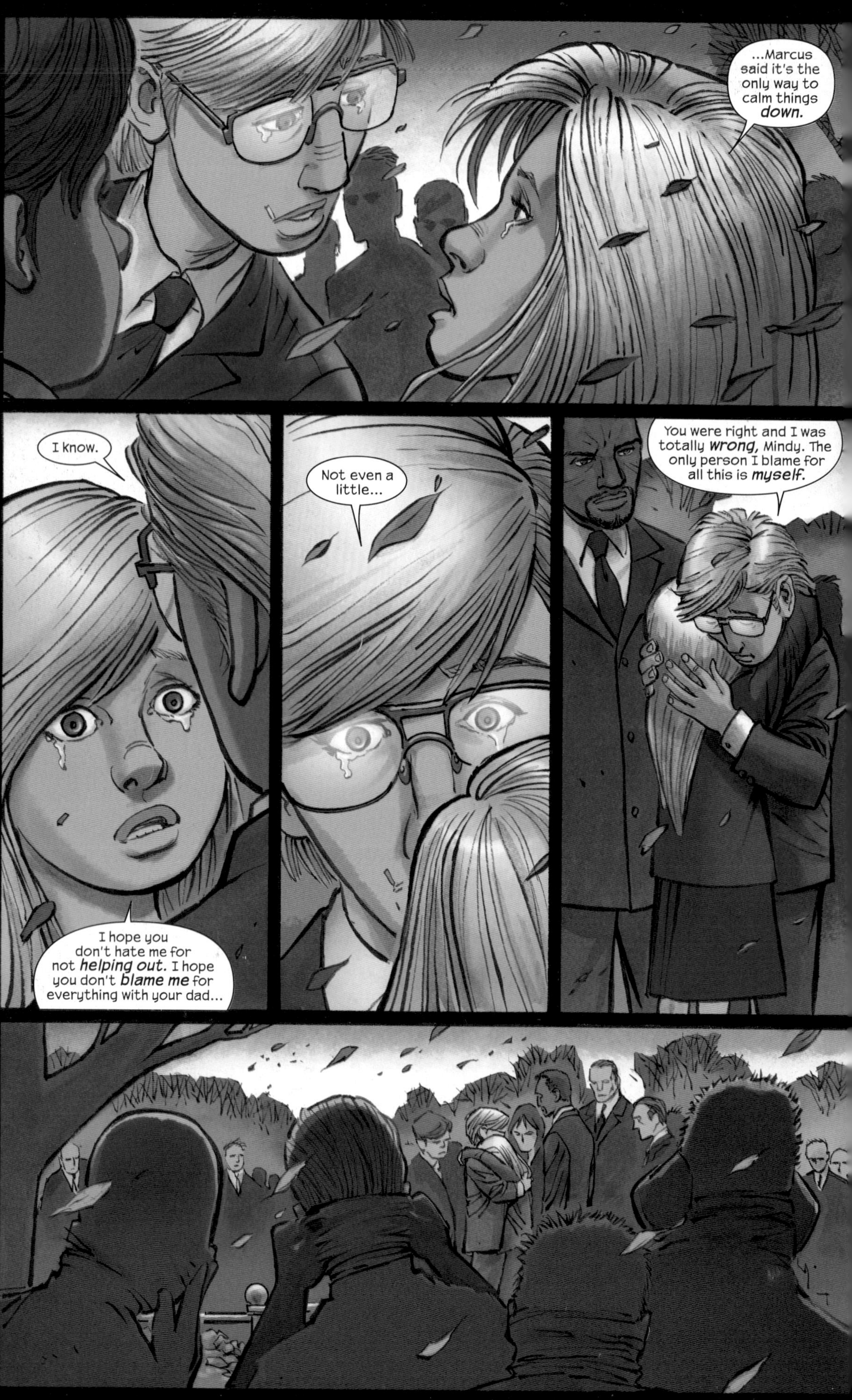
...Marcus said it's the only way to calm things down.
I know.
I hope you don't hate me for not helping out. I hope you don't blame me for everything with your dad...
Not even a little...
You were right and I was totally wrong, Mindy. The only person I blame for all this is myself.

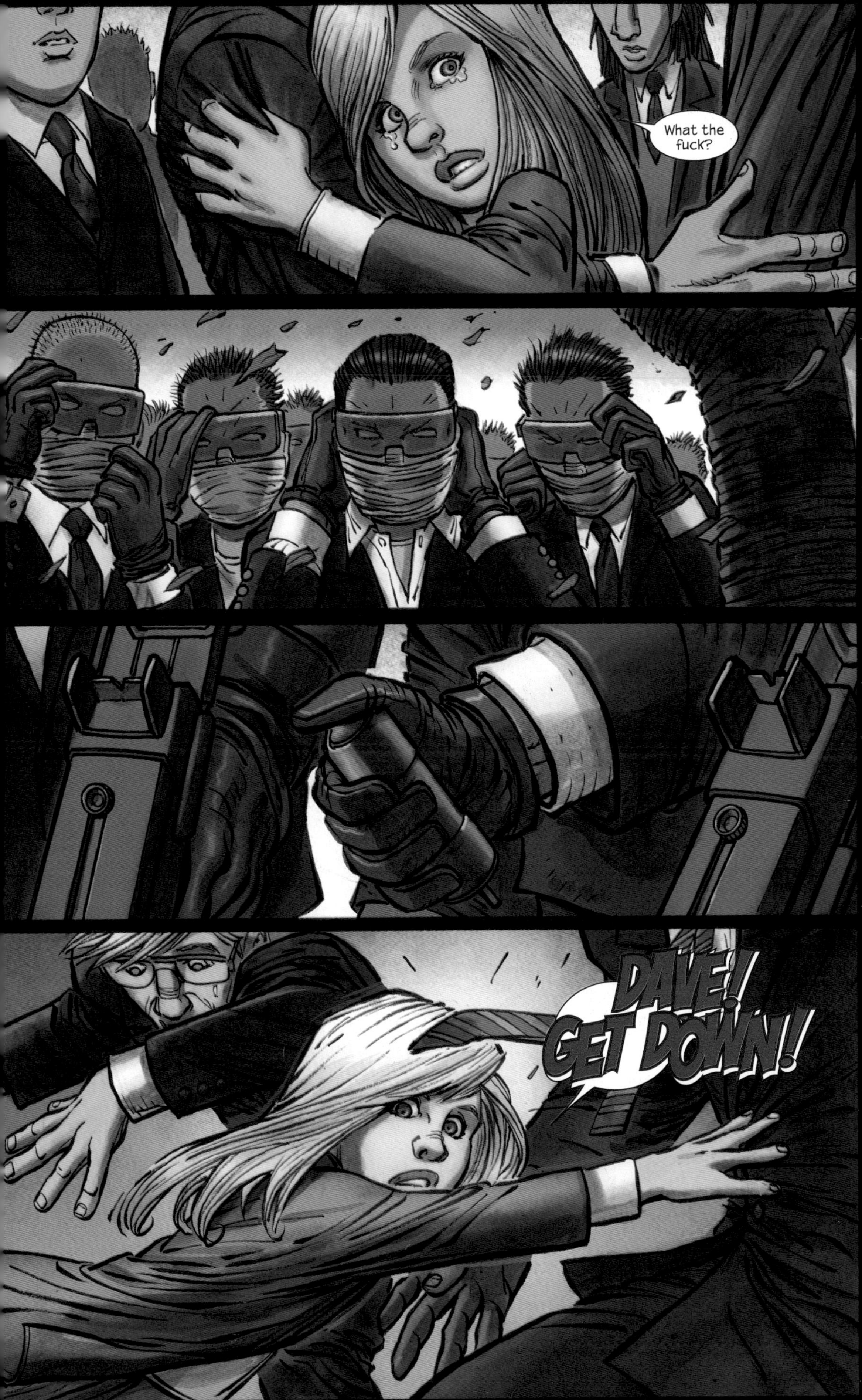
What the fuck?
DAVE! GET DOWN!

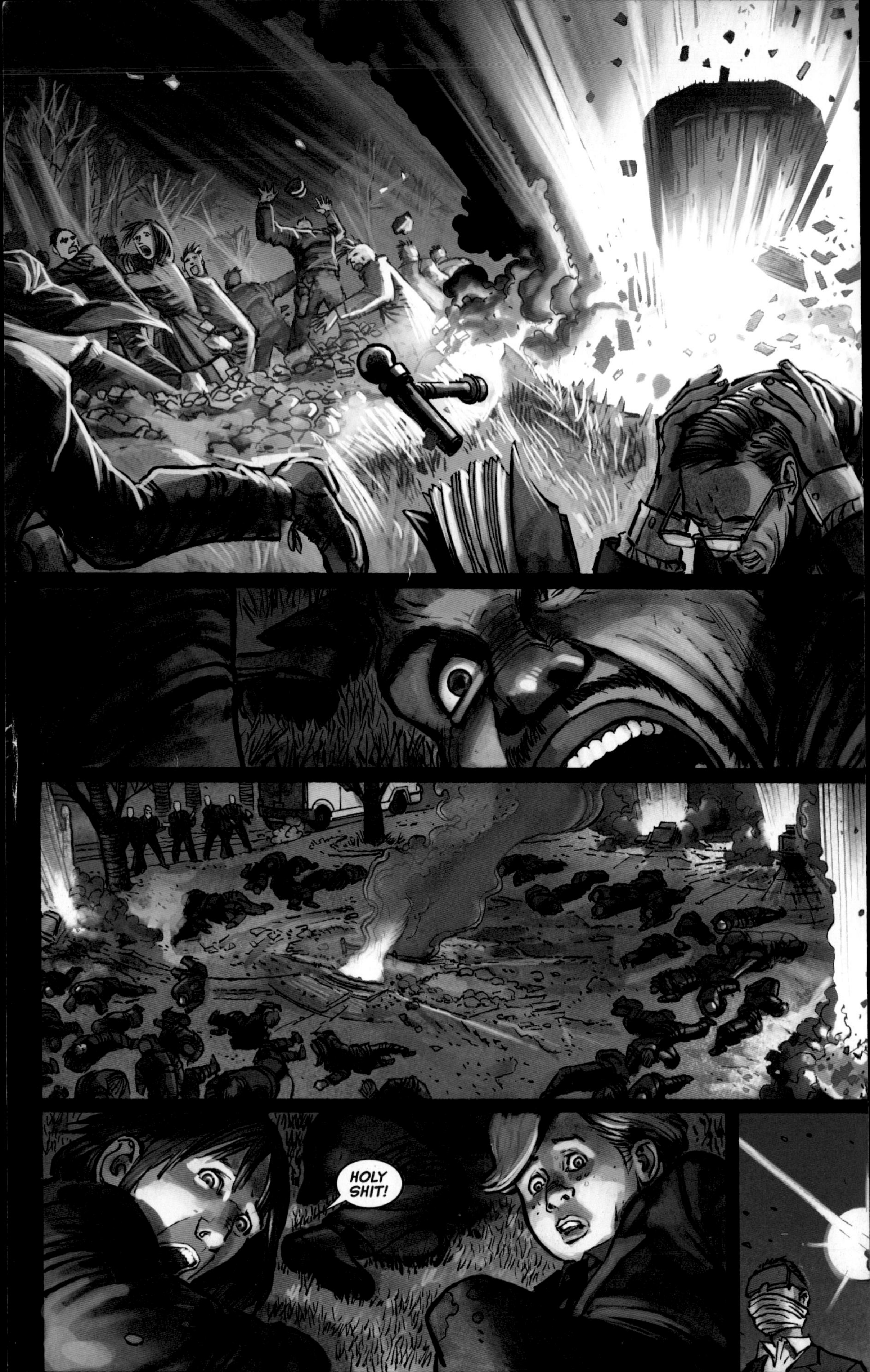
HOLY SHIT!

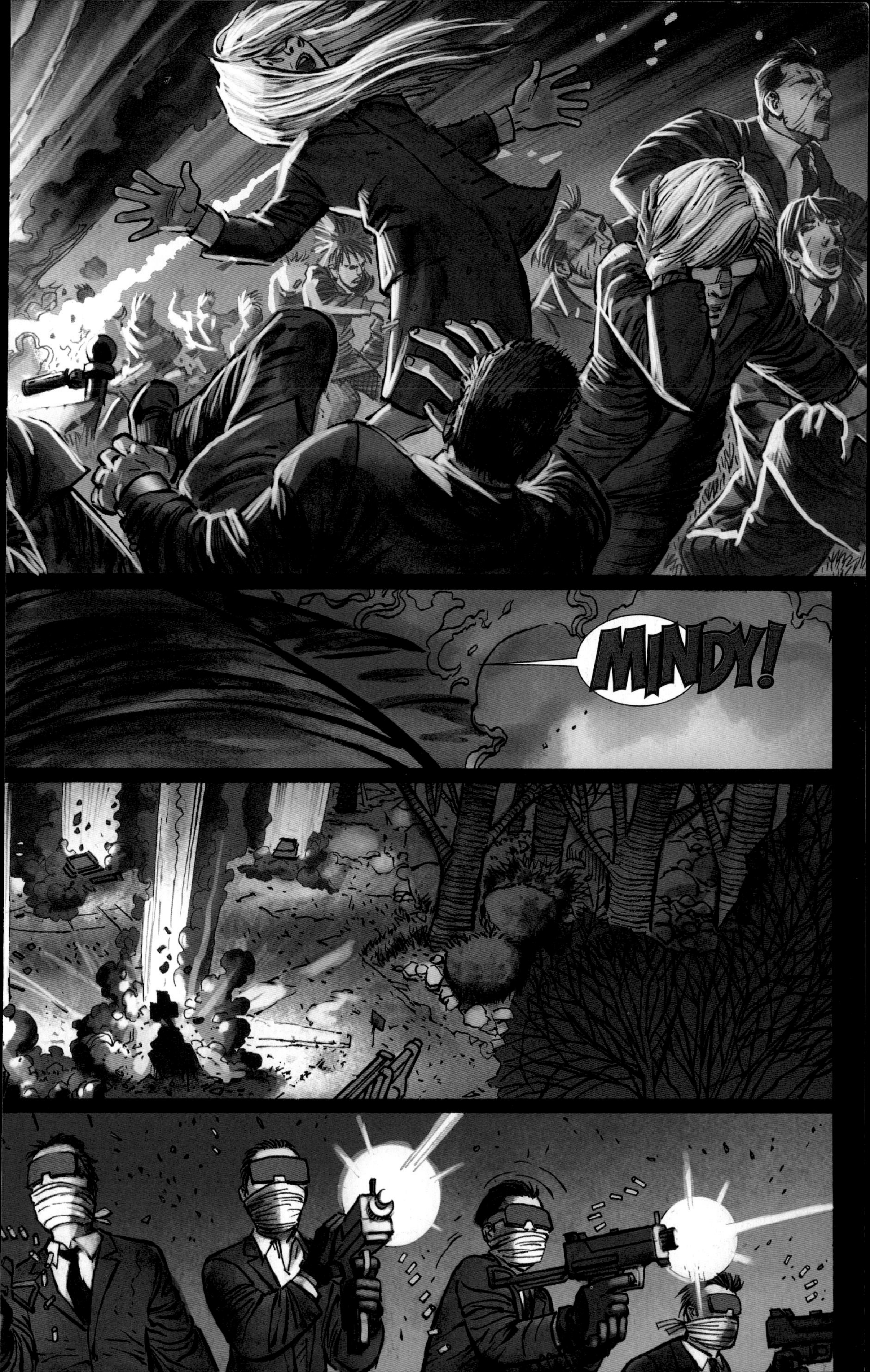
MINDY!

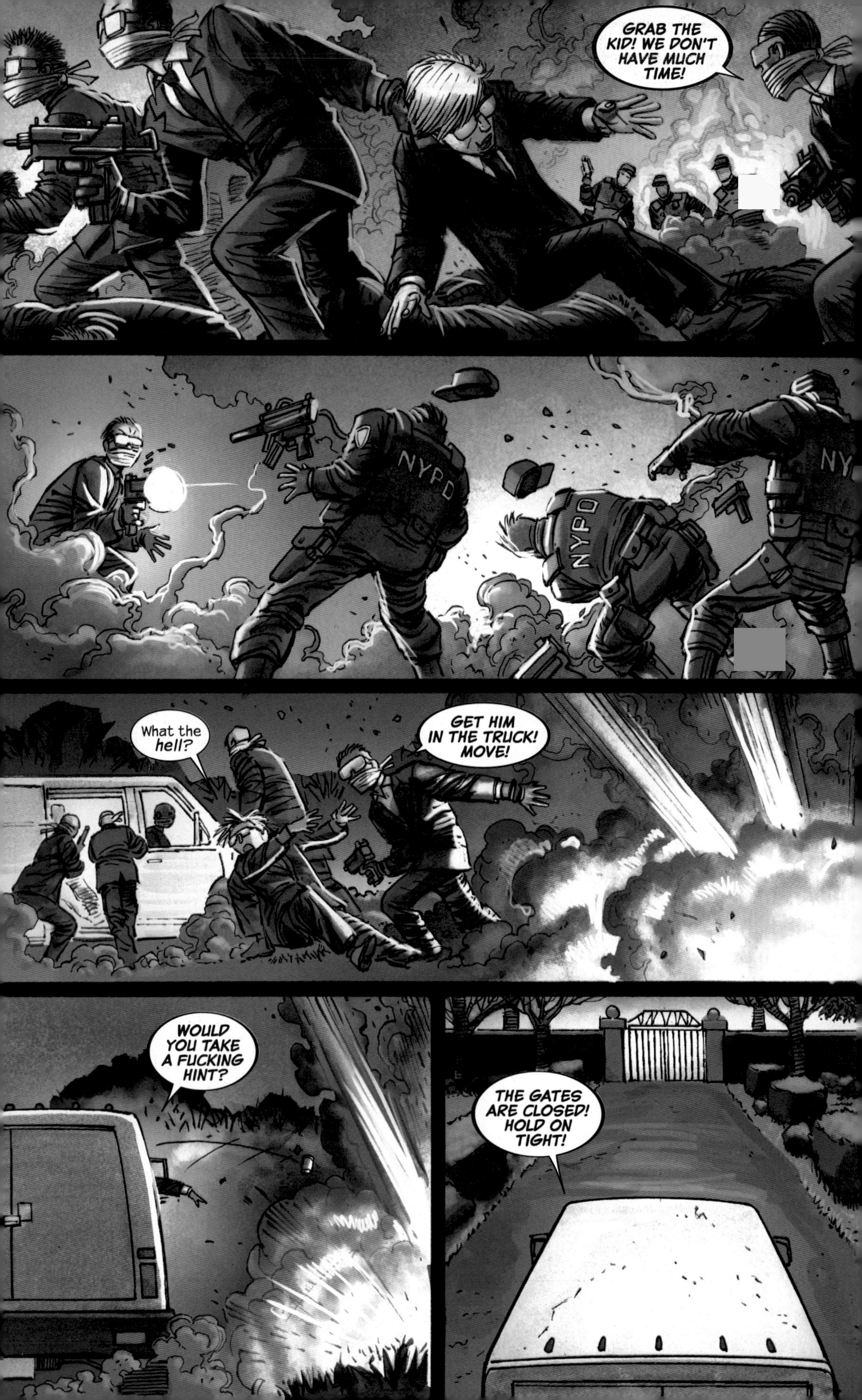
GRAB THE KID! WE DON'T HAVE MUCH TIME!
What the hell?
GET HIM IN THE TRUCK! MOVE!
WOULD YOU TAKE A FUCKING HINT?
THE GATES ARE CLOSED! HOLD ON TIGHT!

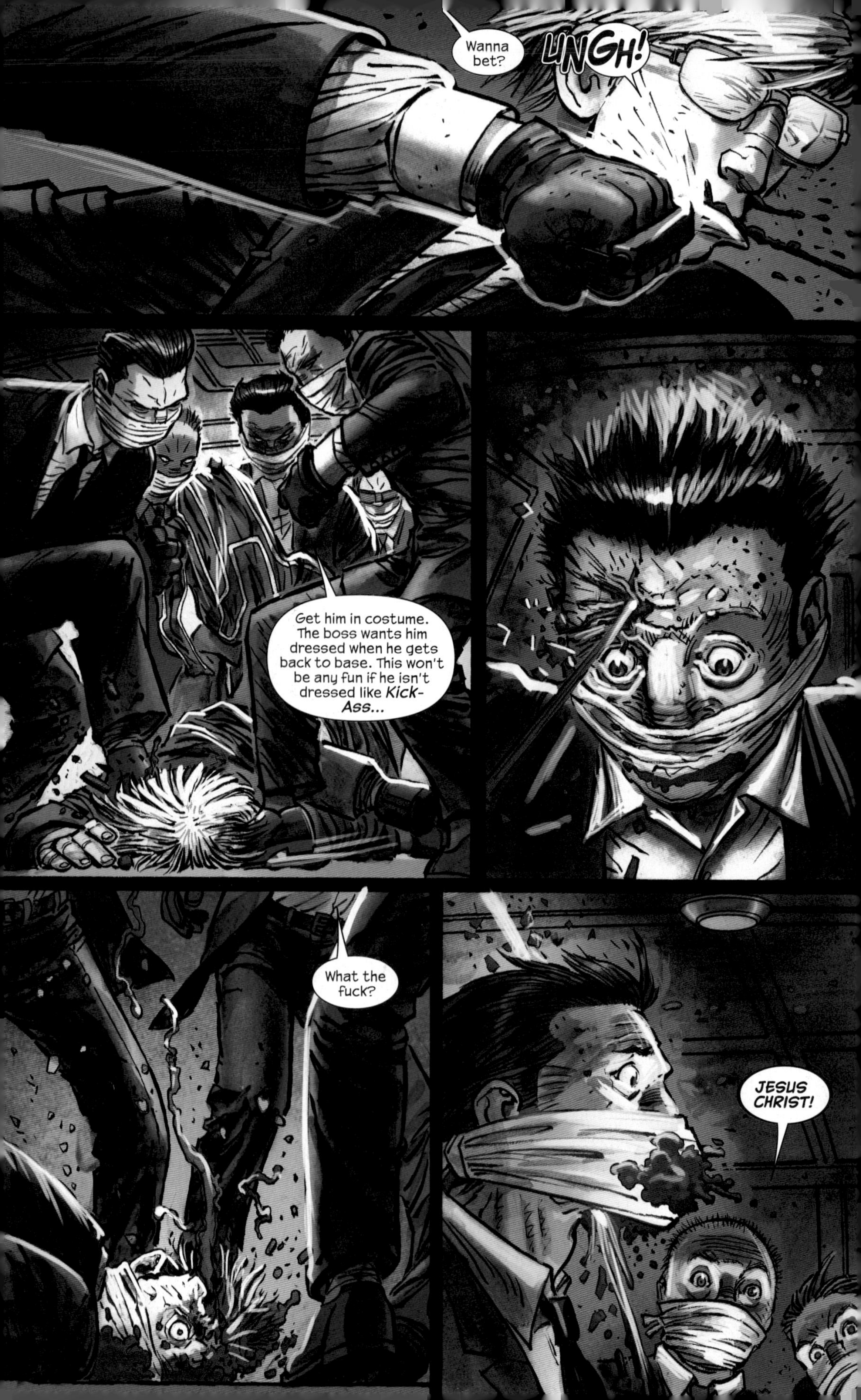
Wanna bet?
UNGH!
Get him in costume. The boss wants him dressed when he gets back to base. This won't be any fun if he isn't dressed like *Kick-Ass...*
What the fuck?
JESUS CHRIST!

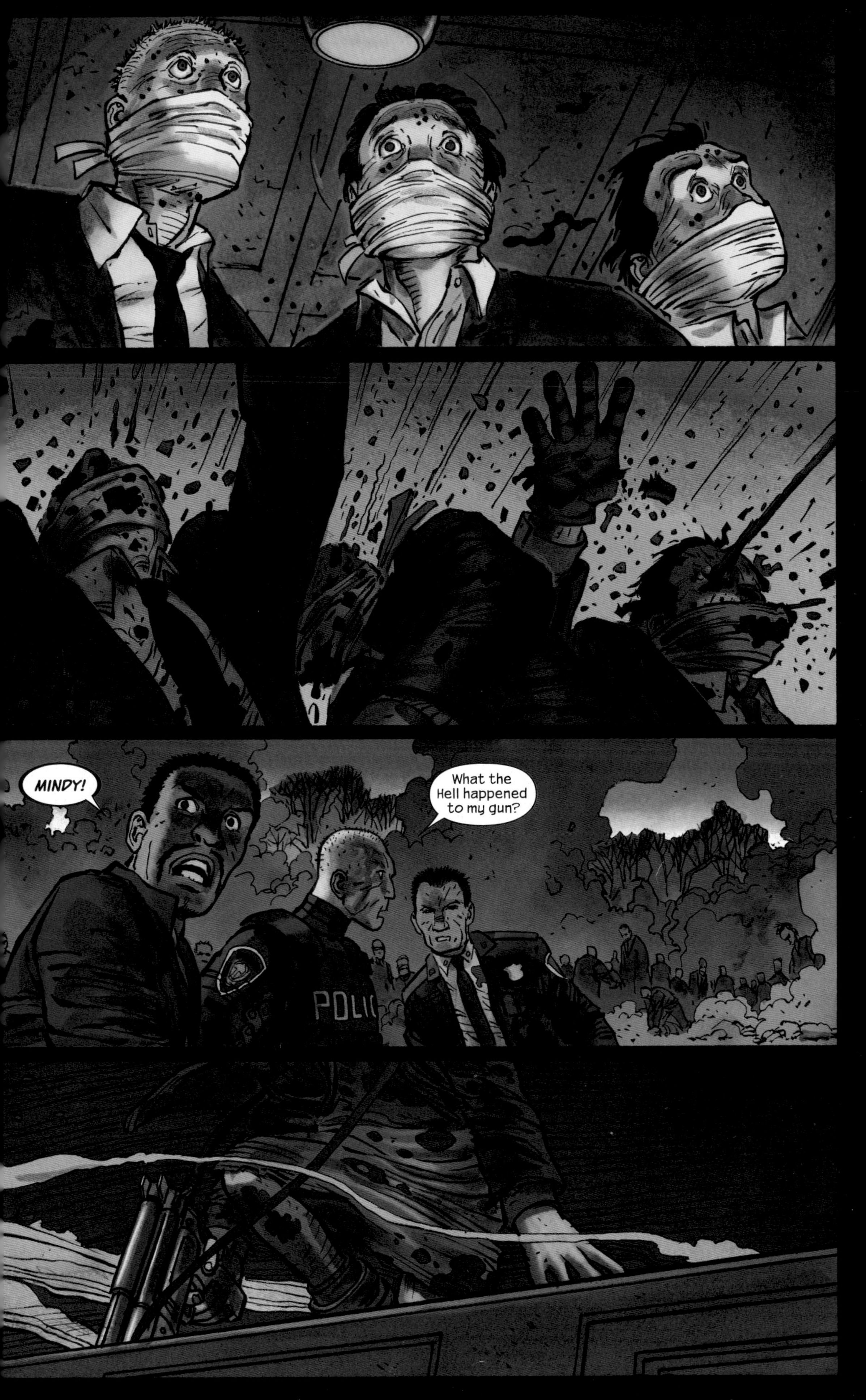
MINDY!
What the Hell happened to my gun?
POLIC

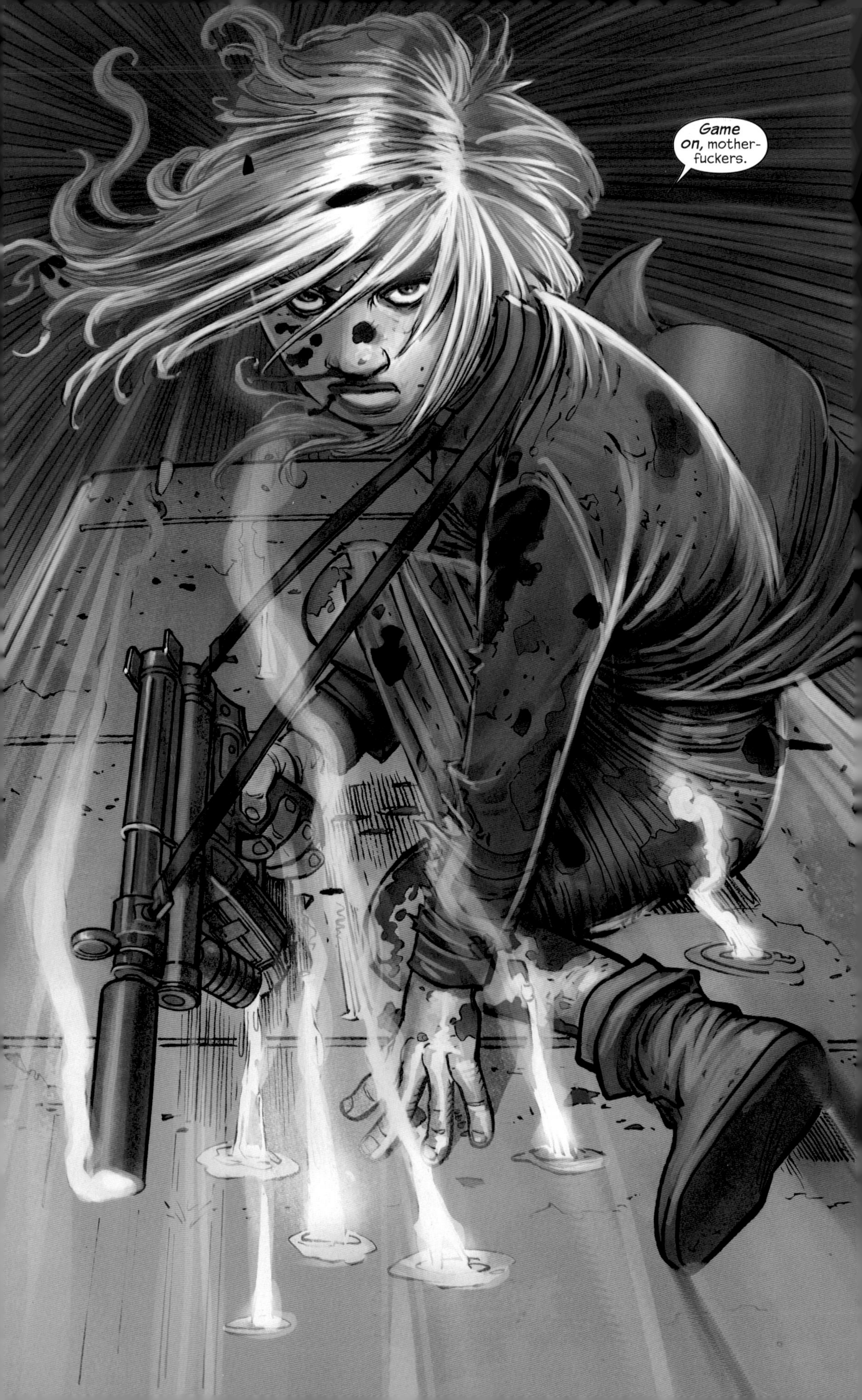
Game on, mother-fuckers.

SIX

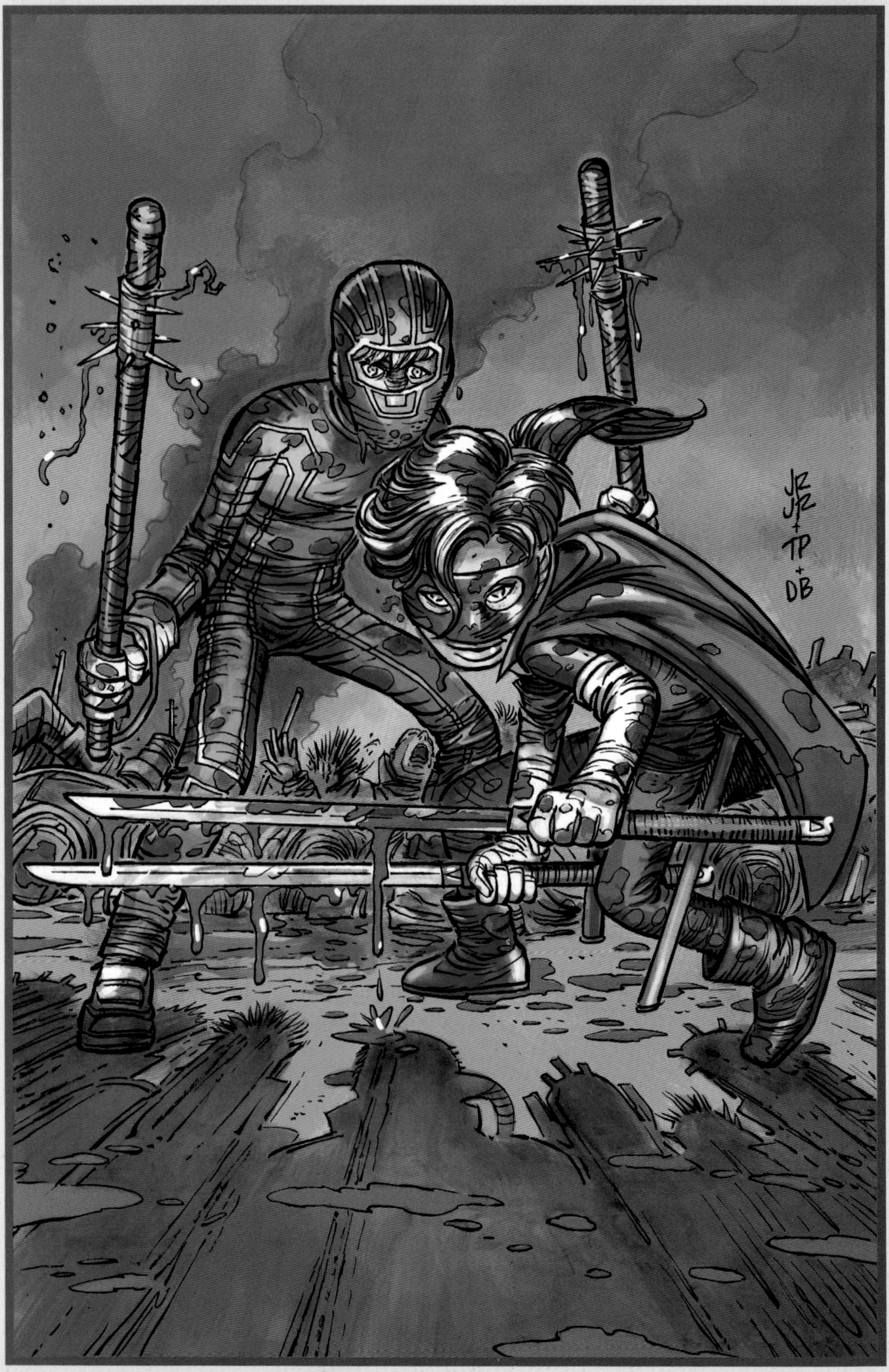
JR JR + TP + DB

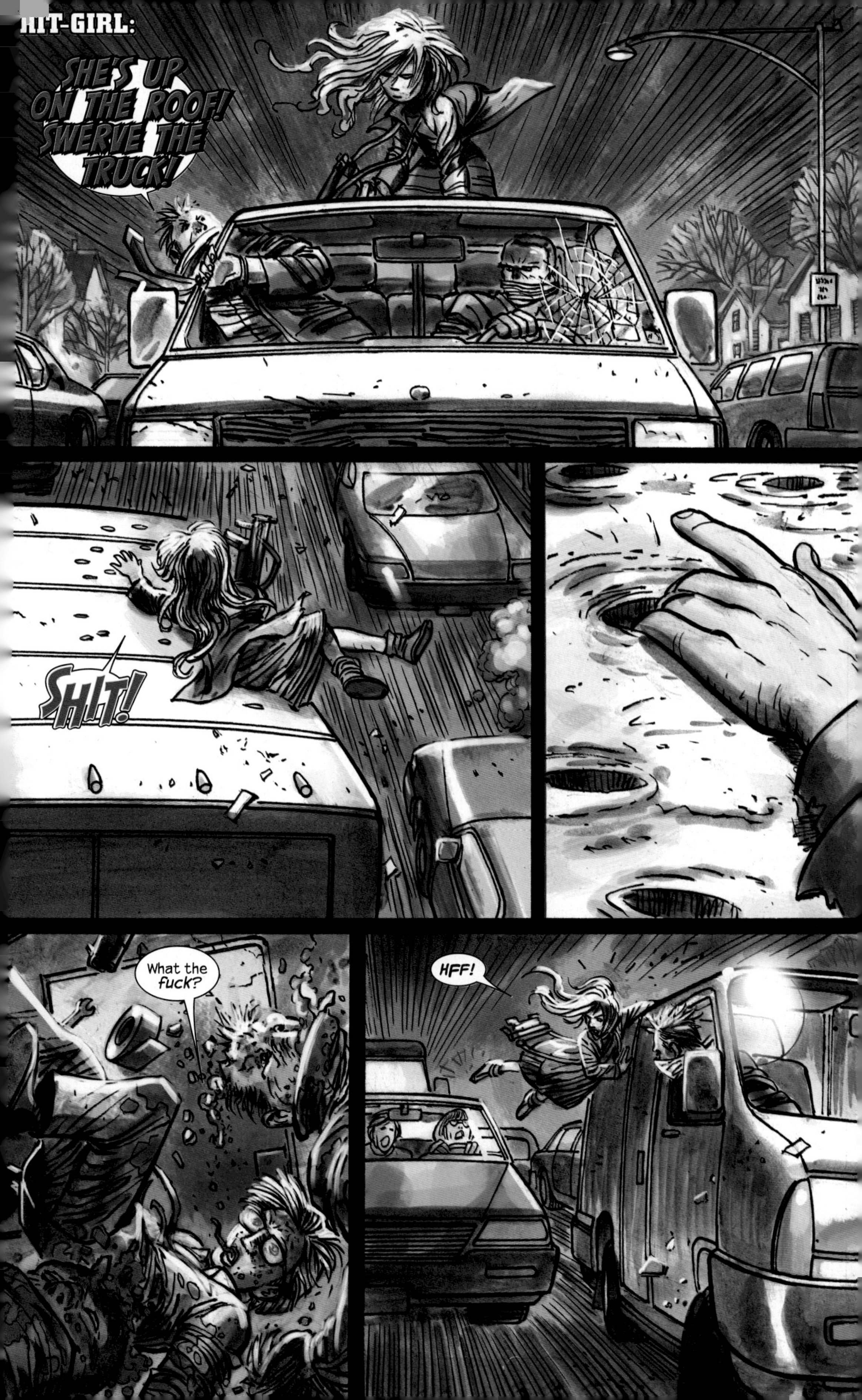
HIT-GIRL:
SHE'S UP ON THE ROOF! SWERVE THE TRUCK!
SHIT!
What the fuck?
HFF!

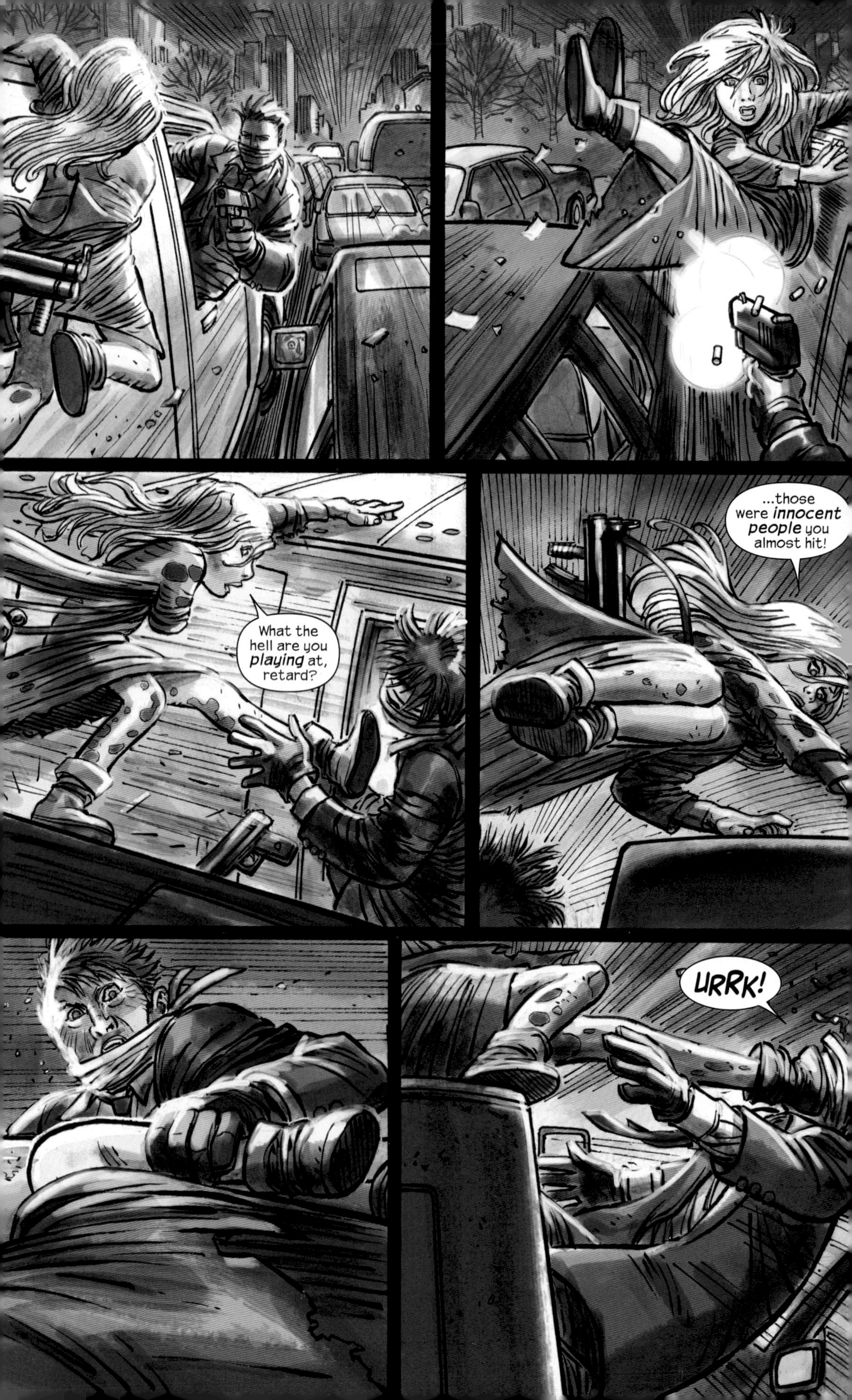
What the hell are you playing at, retard?
...those were innocent people you almost hit!
URRK!

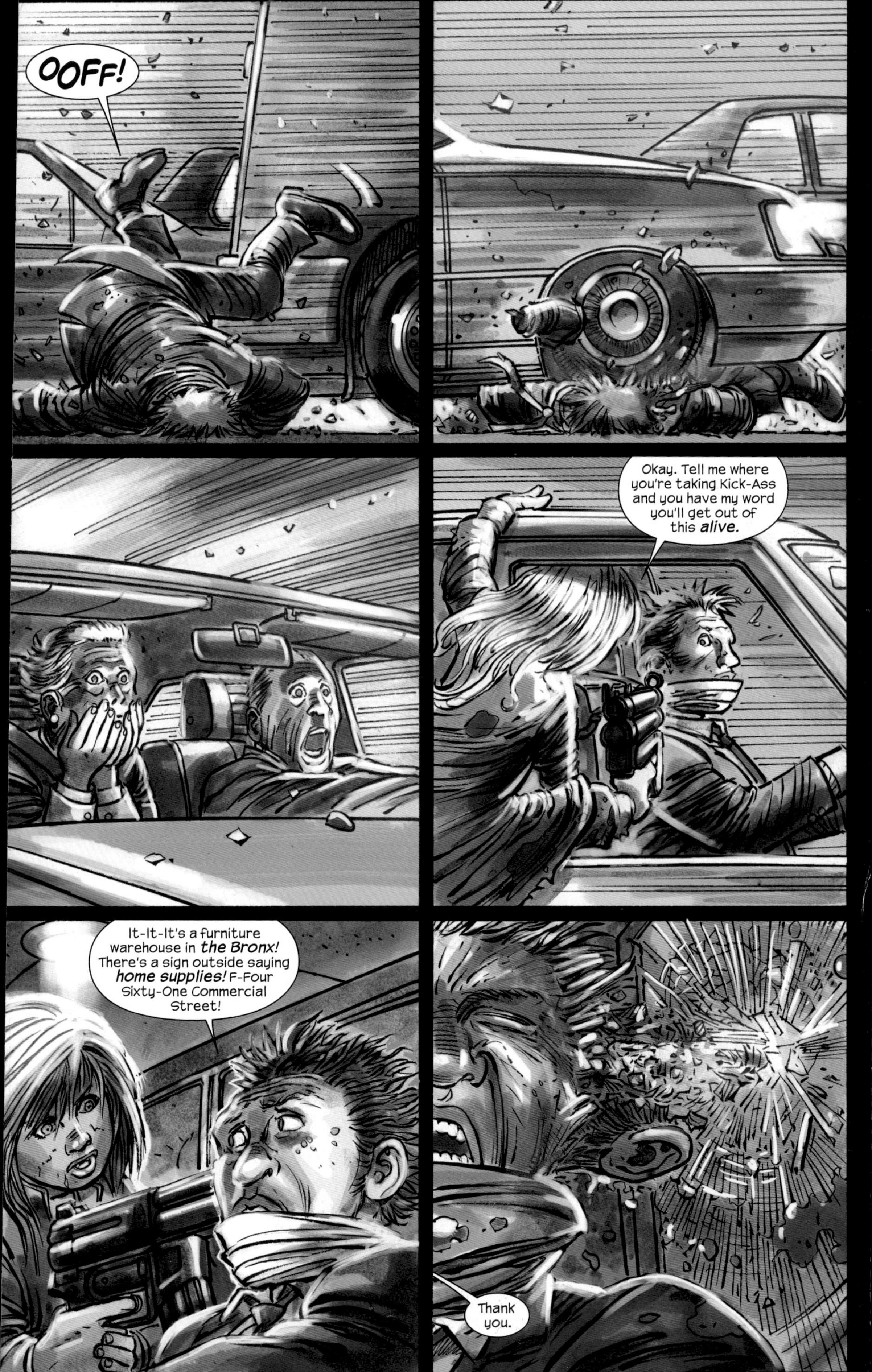
OOFF!
Okay. Tell me where you're taking Kick-Ass and you have my word you'll get out of this *alive.*
It-It-It's a furniture warehouse in *the Bronx!* There's a sign outside saying *home supplies!* F-Four Sixty-One Commercial Street!
Thank you.

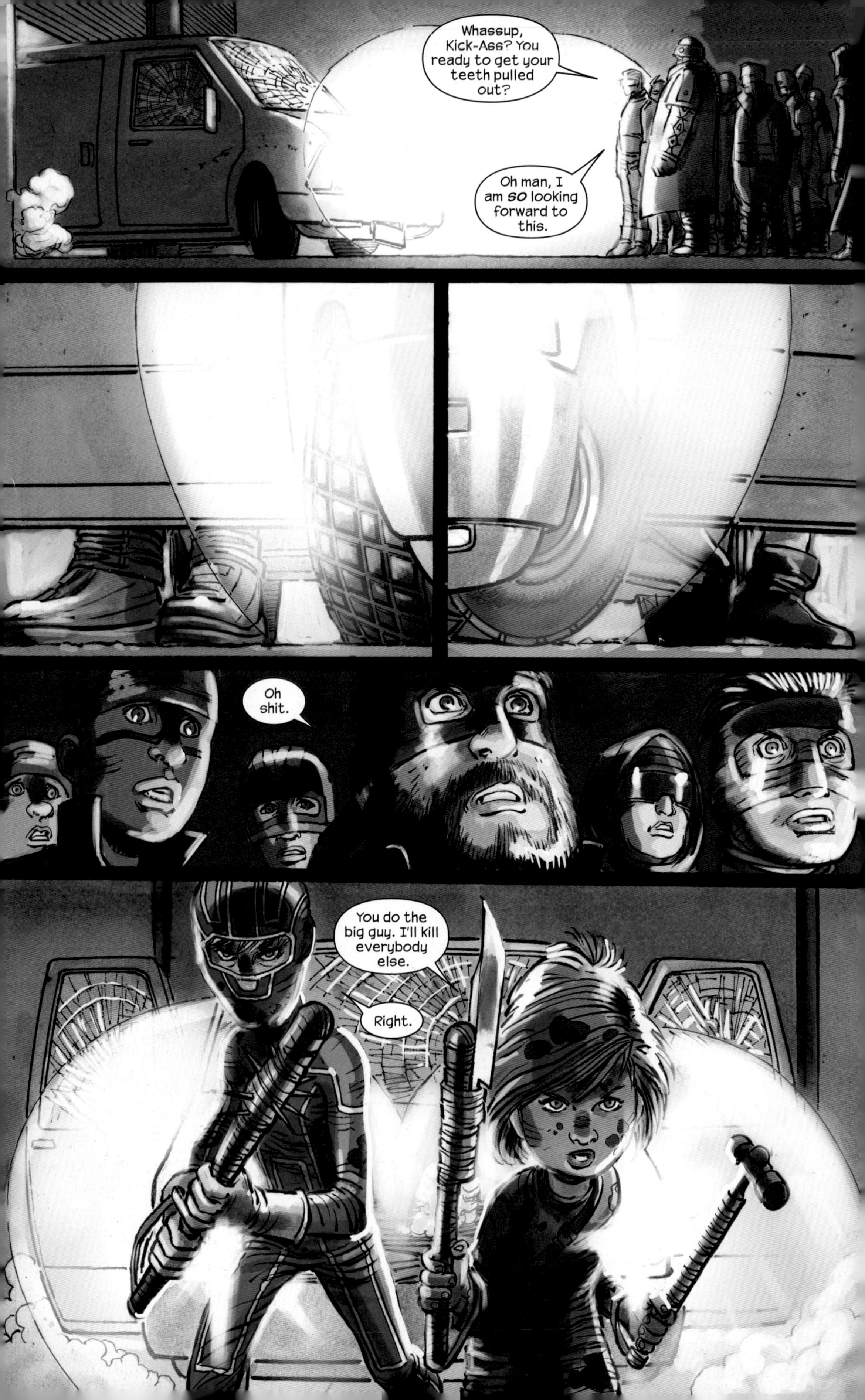
Whassup, Kick-Ass? You ready to get your teeth pulled out?
Oh man, I am SO looking forward to this.
Oh shit.
You do the big guy. I'll kill everybody else.
Right.

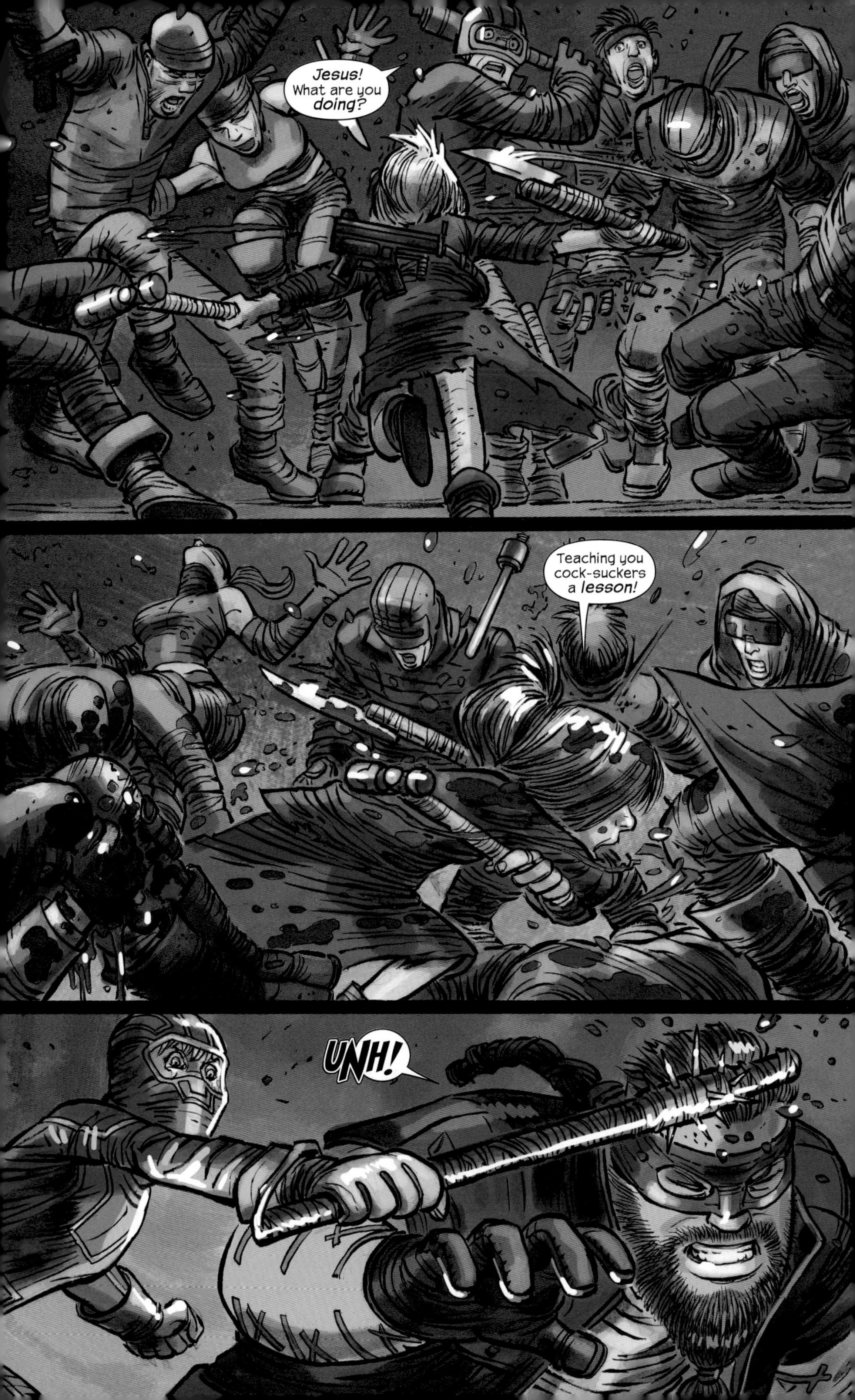
Jesus! What are you doing?
Teaching you cock-suckers a lesson!
UNH!

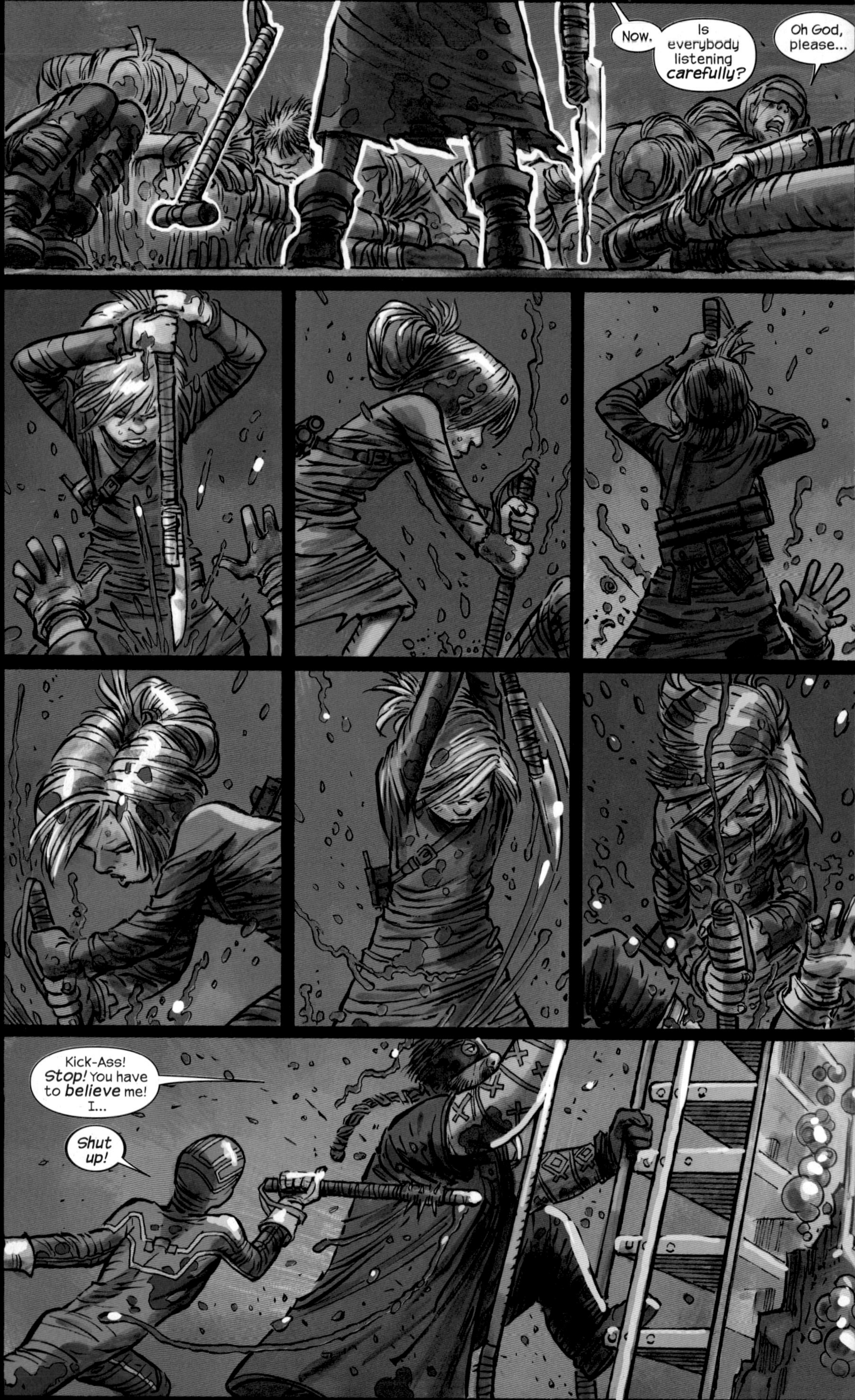
Now.
Is everybody listening carefully?
Oh God, please...
Kick-Ass! Stop! You have to believe me! I...
Shut up!

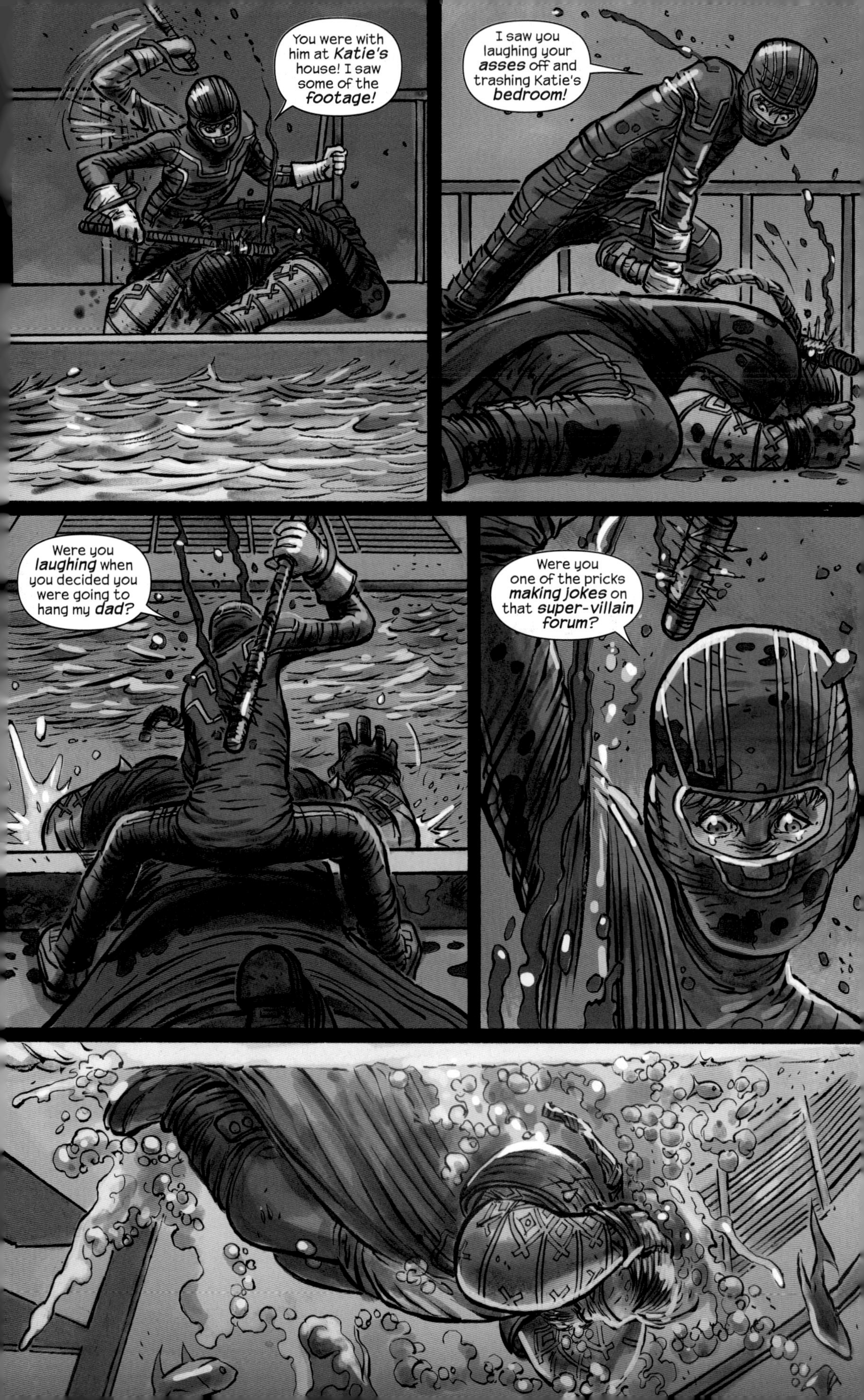
You were with him at *Katie's* house! I saw some of the *footage!*
I saw you laughing your *asses* off and trashing Katie's *bedroom!*
Were you *laughing* when you decided you were going to hang my *dad?*
Were you one of the pricks *making jokes* on that *super-villain forum?*

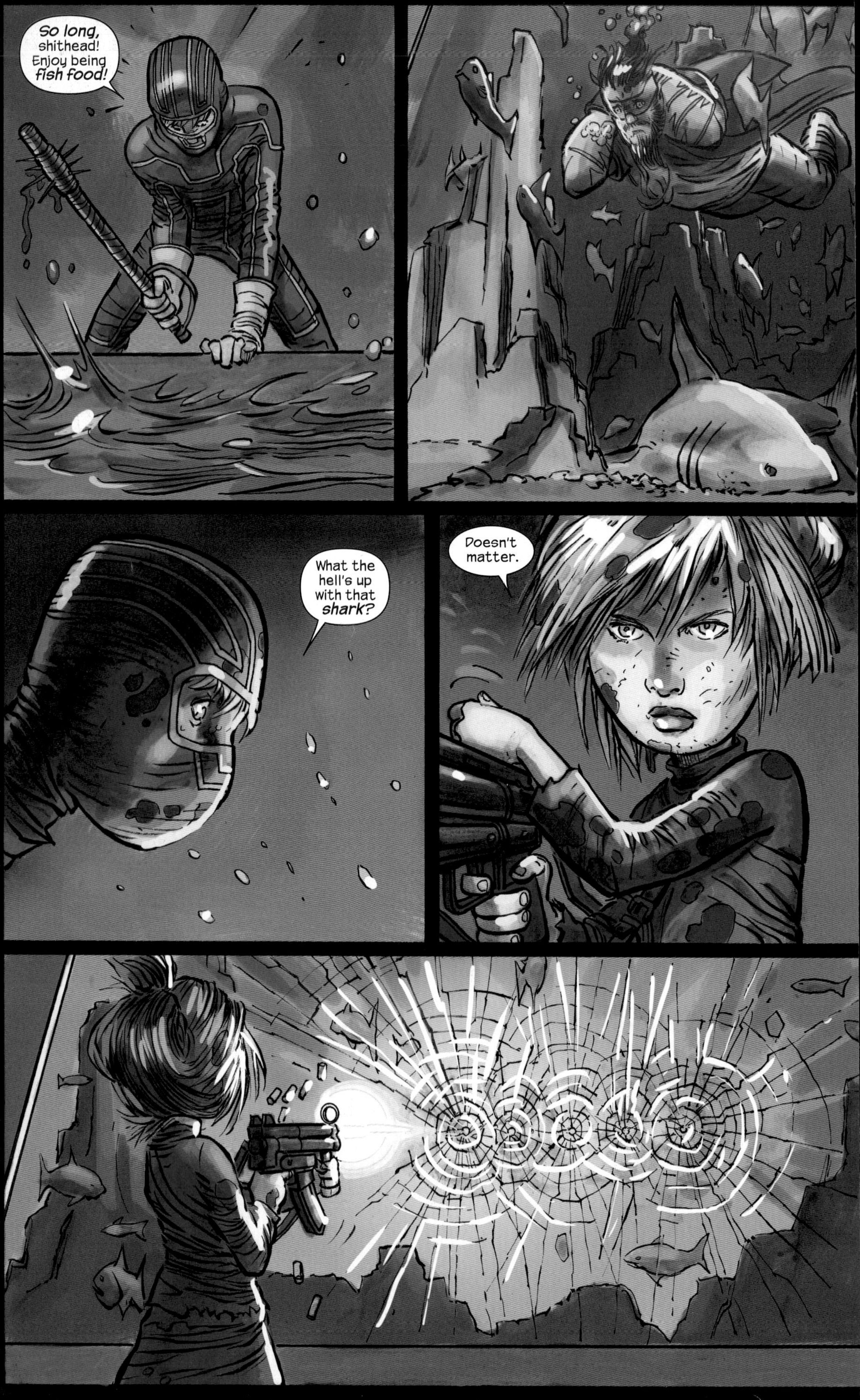
So long, shithead! Enjoy being fish food!
What the hell's up with that shark?
Doesn't matter.

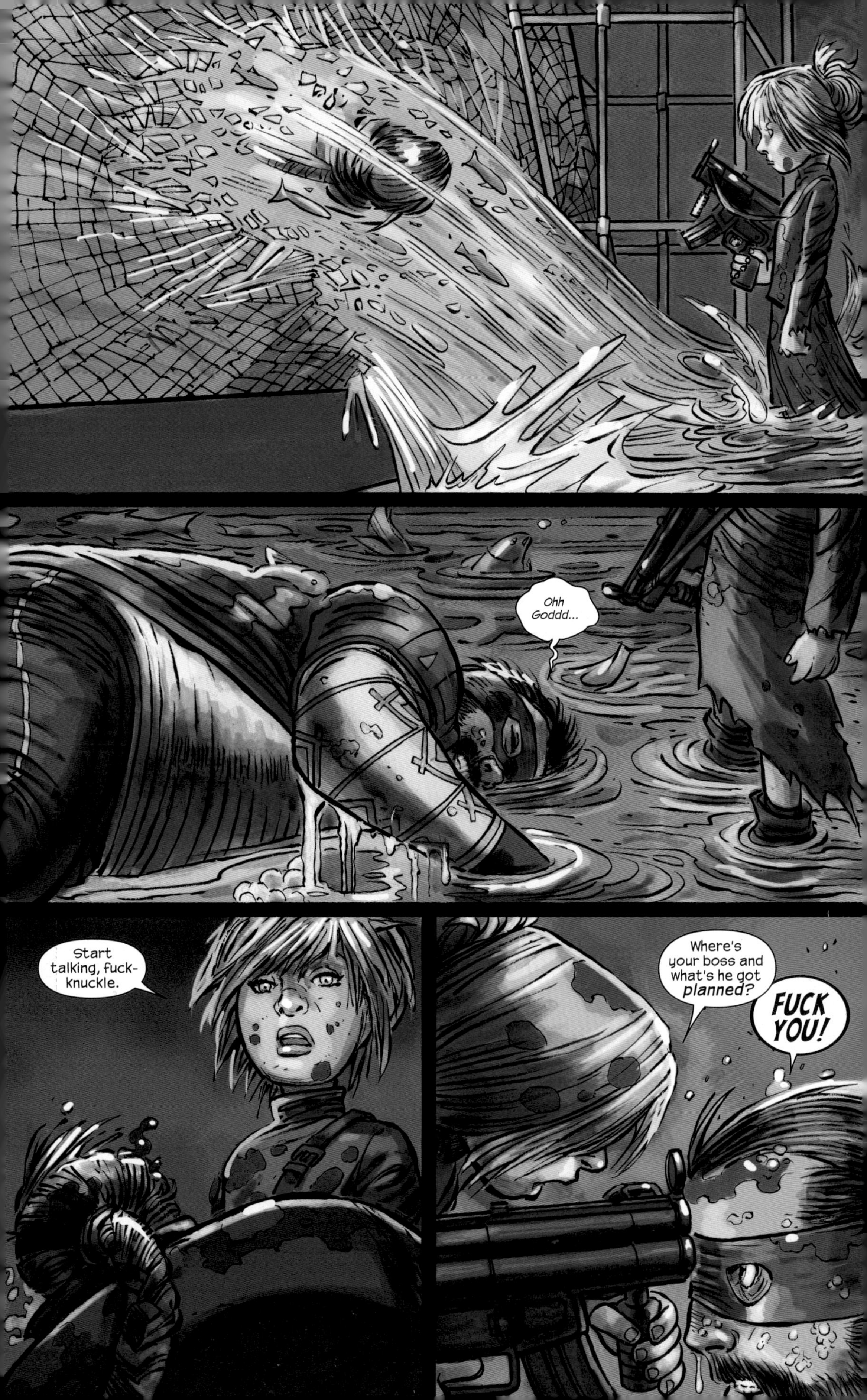
Ohh Goddd...
Start talking, fuck-knuckle.
Where's your boss and what's he got planned?
FUCK YOU!

SAFE-HOUSE #3:

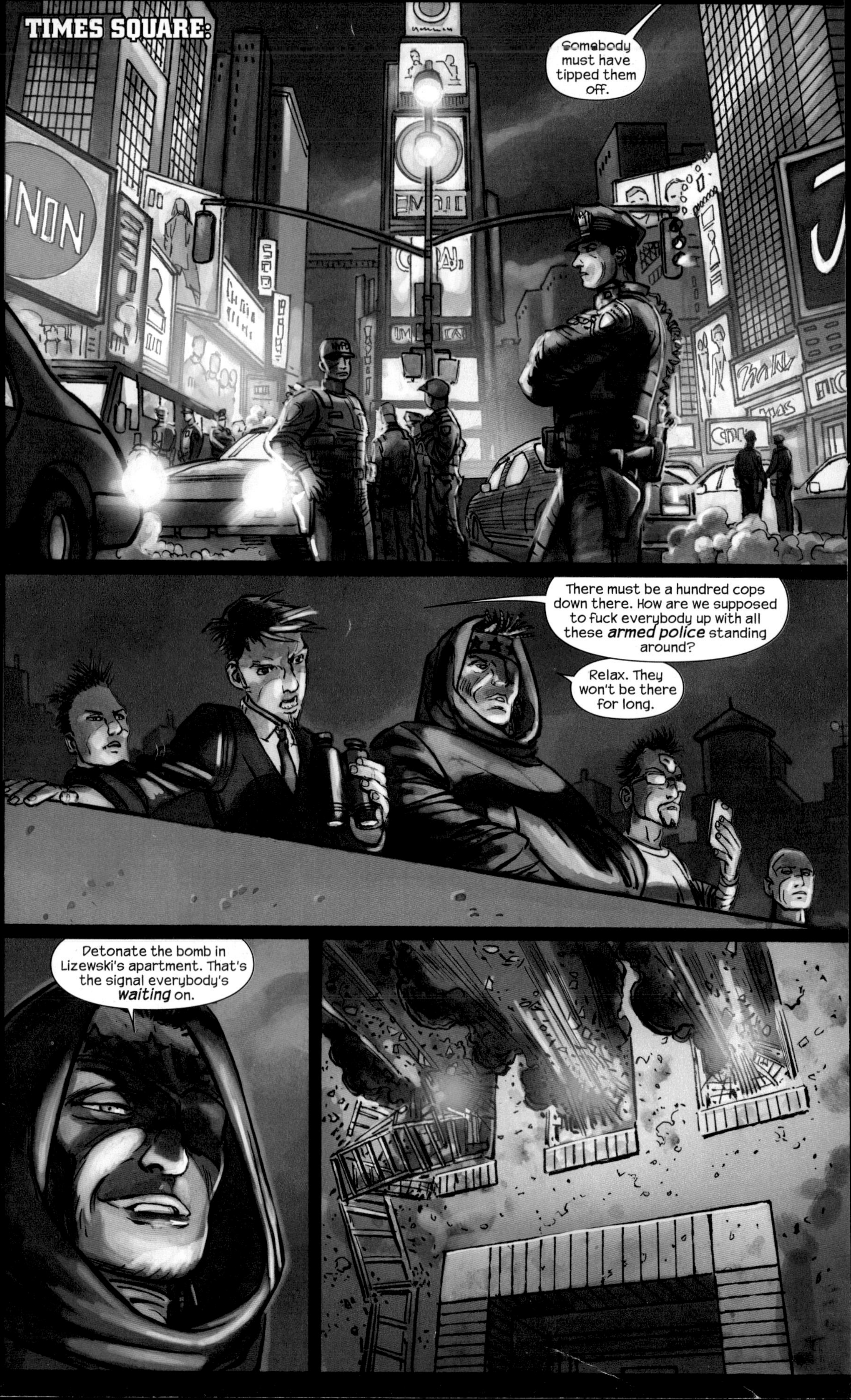
TIMES SQUARE:
Somebody must have tipped them off.
There must be a hundred cops down there. How are we supposed to fuck everybody up with all these *armed police* standing around?
Relax. They won't be there for long.
Detonate the bomb in Lizewski's apartment. That's the signal everybody's *waiting* on.

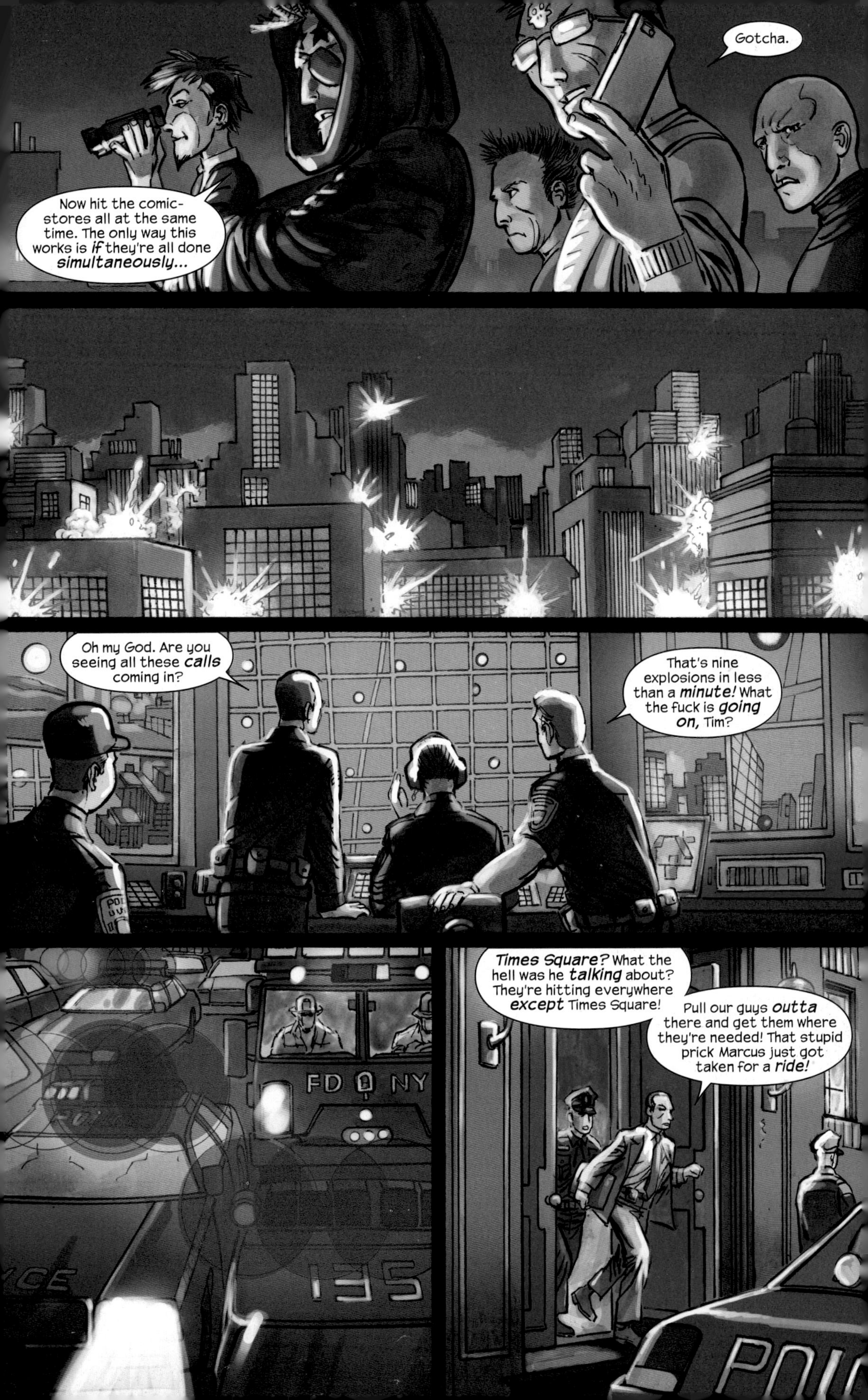
Gotcha.
Now hit the comic-stores all at the same time. The only way this works is *if* they're all done *simultaneously*...
Oh my God. Are you seeing all these *calls* coming in?
That's nine explosions in less than a *minute!* What the fuck is *going on,* Tim?
FD NY
135
Times Square? What the hell was he *talking* about? They're hitting everywhere *except* Times Square!
Pull our guys *outta* there and get them where they're needed! That stupid prick Marcus just got taken for a *ride!*

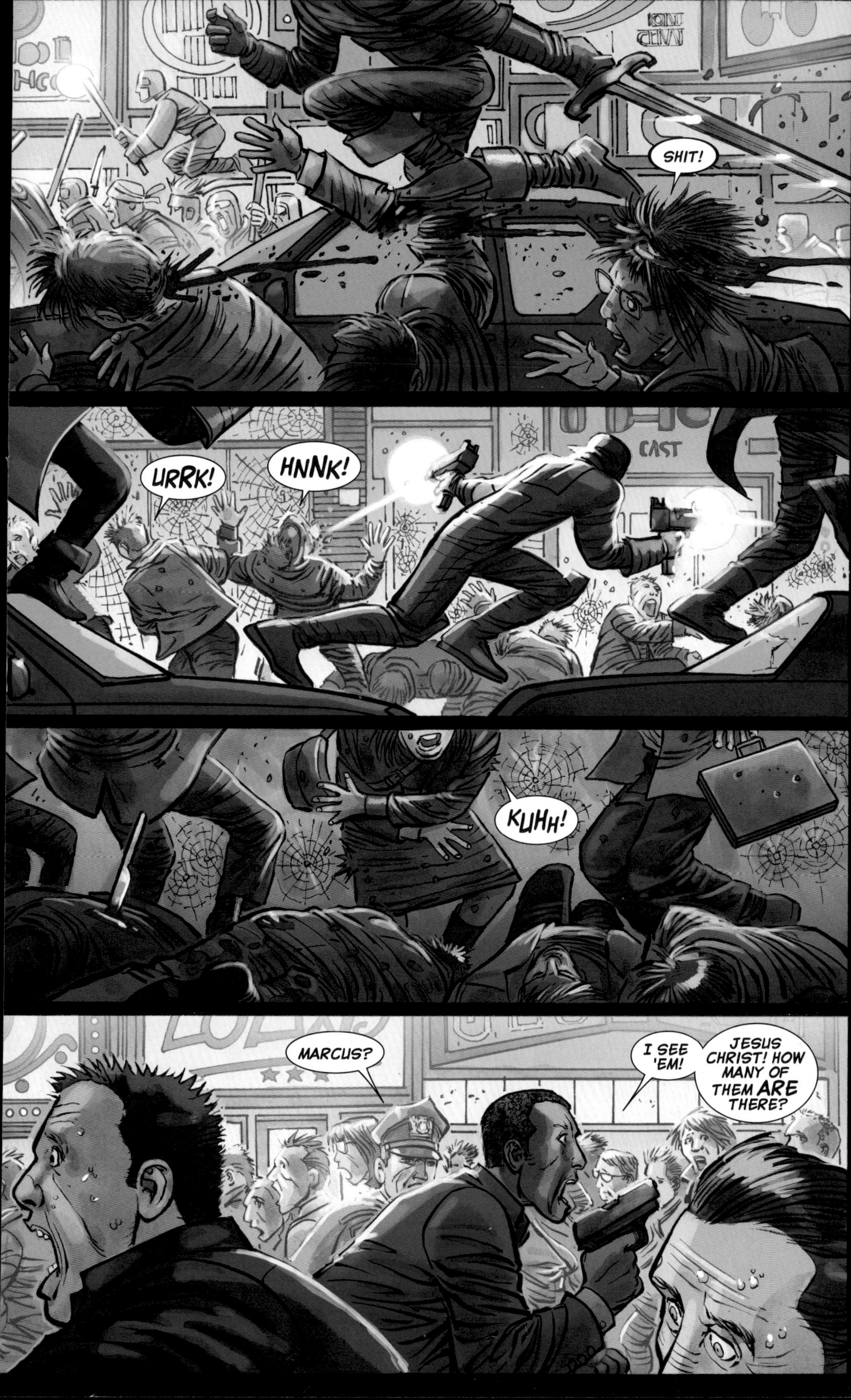
SHIT!
URRK!
HNNK!
KUHH!
MARCUS?
I SEE 'EM!
JESUS CHRIST! HOW MANY OF THEM ARE THERE?

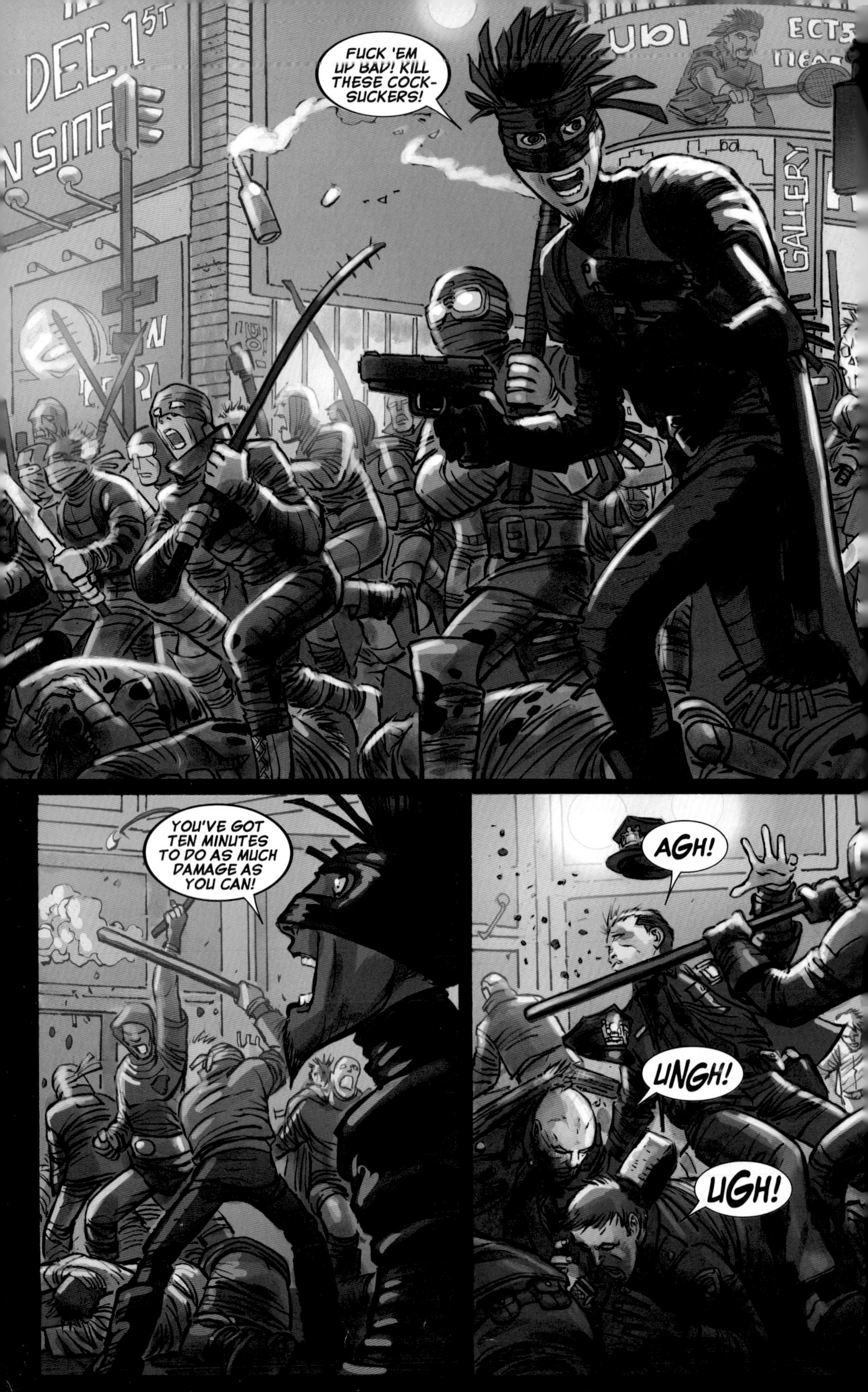
DEC 1ST
GALLERY
FUCK 'EM UP BAD! KILL THESE COCK-SUCKERS!
YOU'VE GOT TEN MINUTES TO DO AS MUCH DAMAGE AS YOU CAN!
AGH!
UNGH!
UGH!

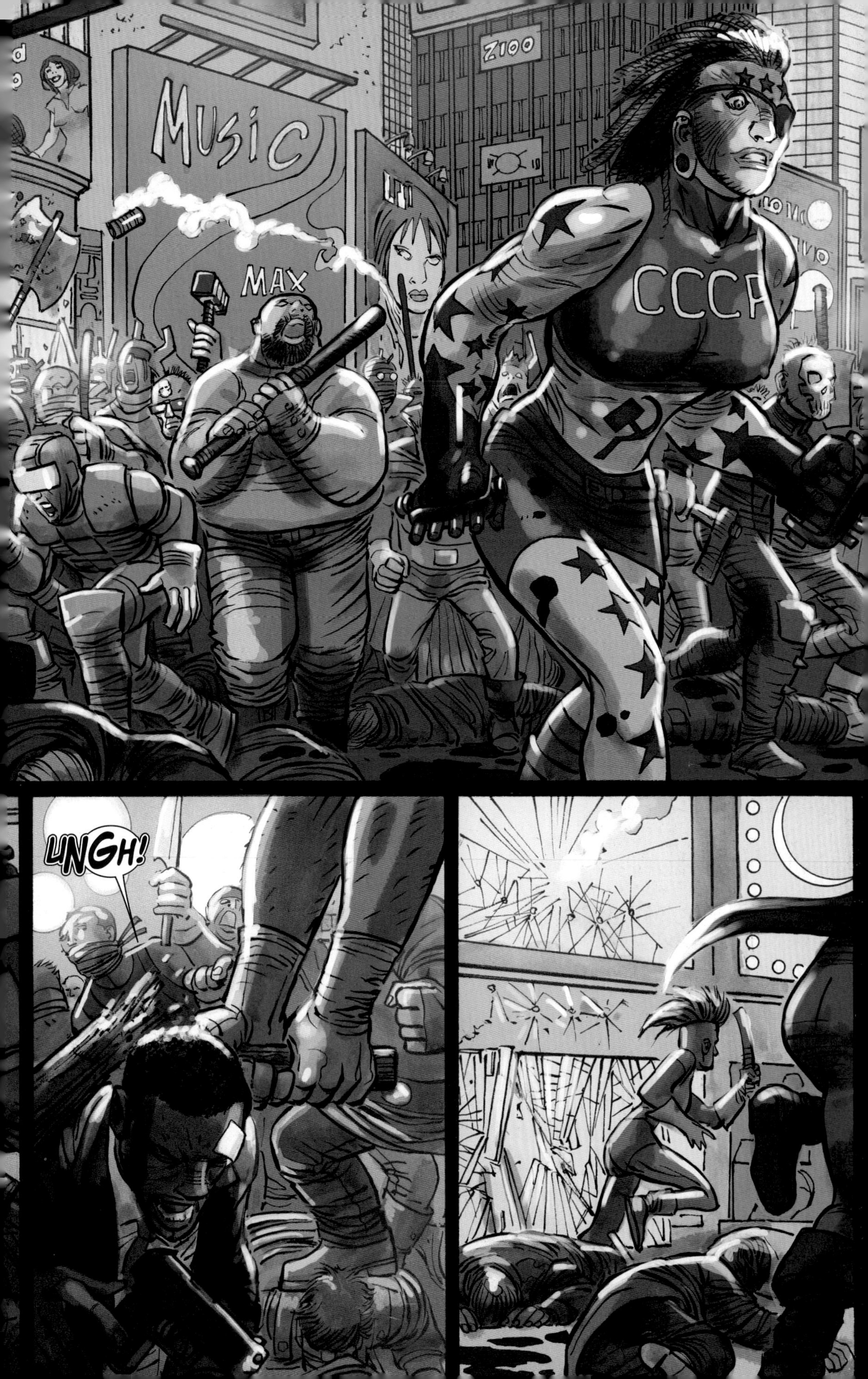
ZIOO
MUSIC
MAX
CCCP
UNGH!

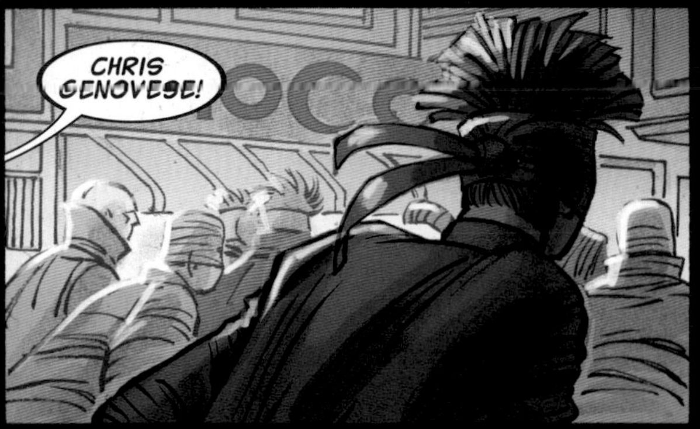
CHRIS GENOVESE!

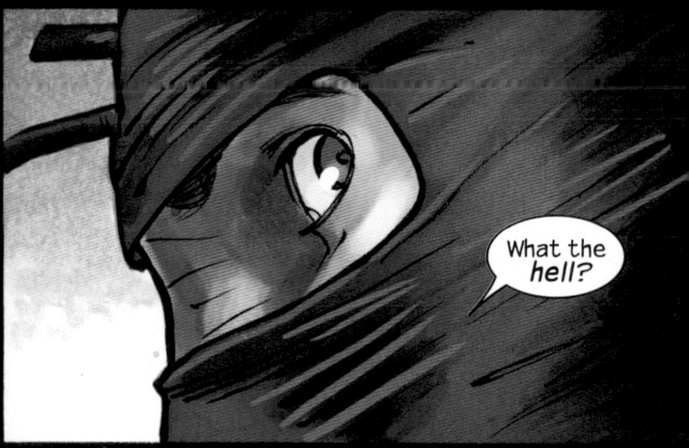
What the hell?

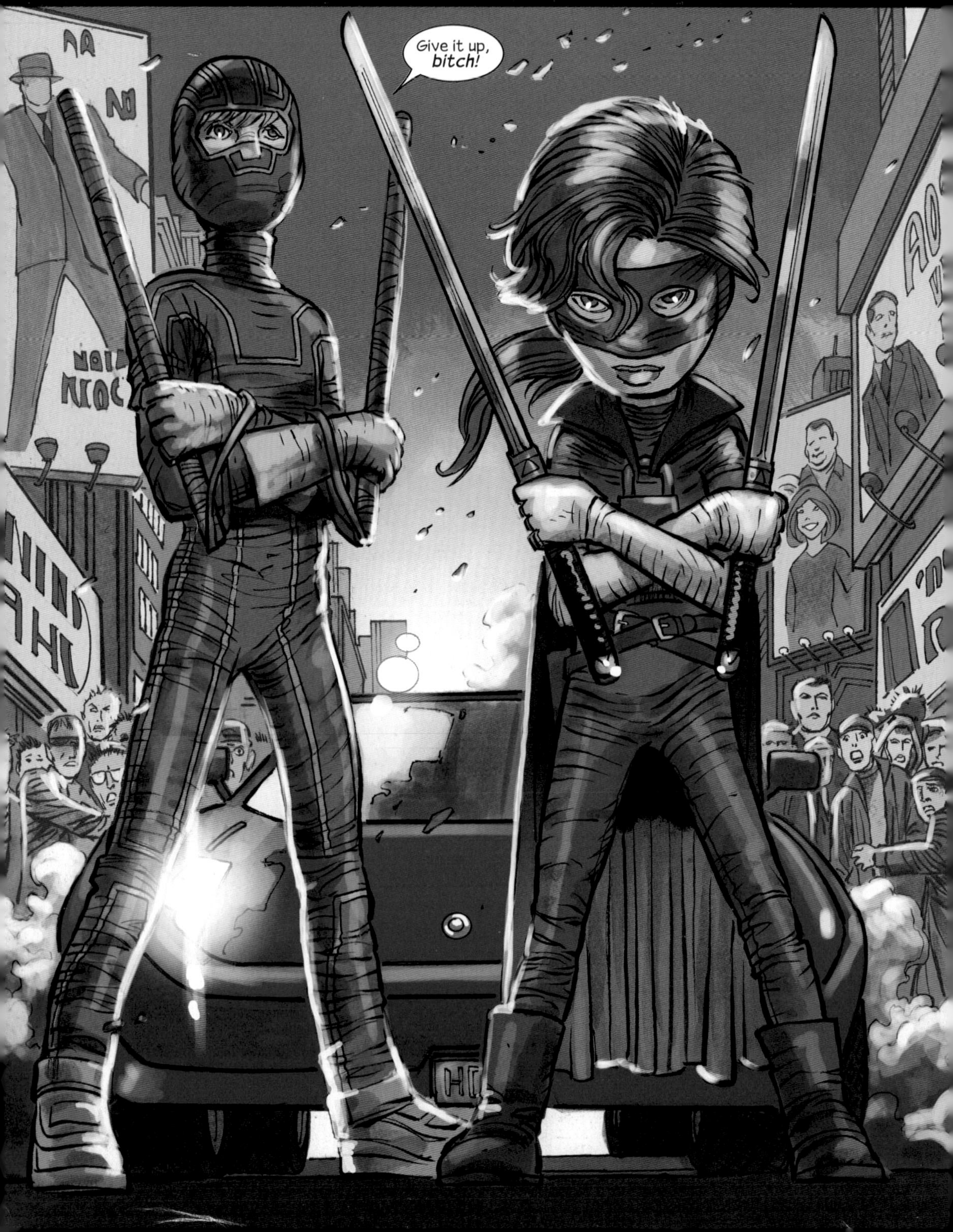
Give it up, bitch!

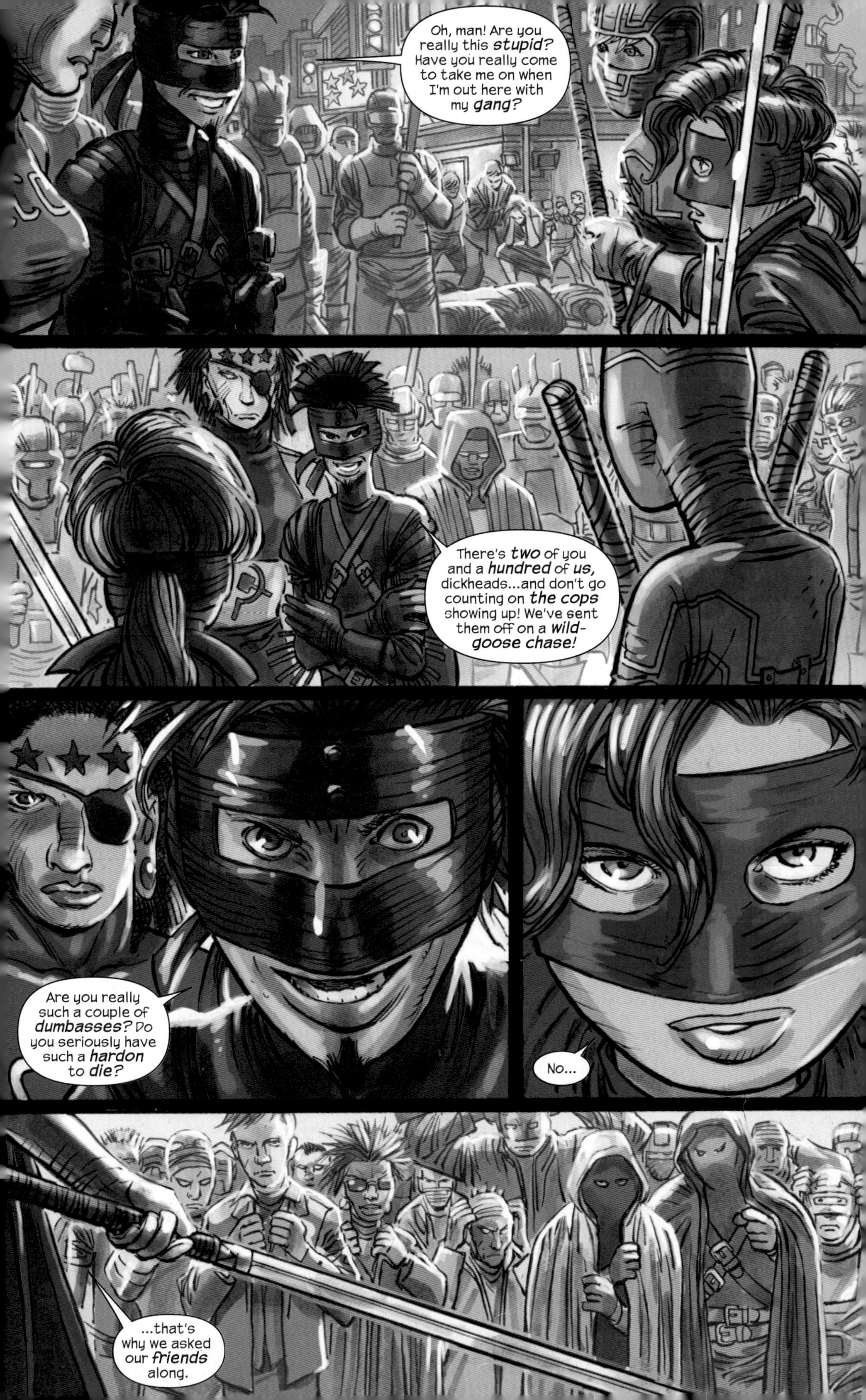
Oh, man! Are you really this *stupid?* Have you really come to take me on when I'm out here with my *gang?*
There's *two* of you and a *hundred* of *us,* dickheads...and don't go counting on *the cops* showing up! We've sent them off on a *wild-goose chase!*
Are you really such a couple of *dumbasses?* Do you seriously have such a *hardon* to *die?*
No...
...that's why we asked our *friends* along.

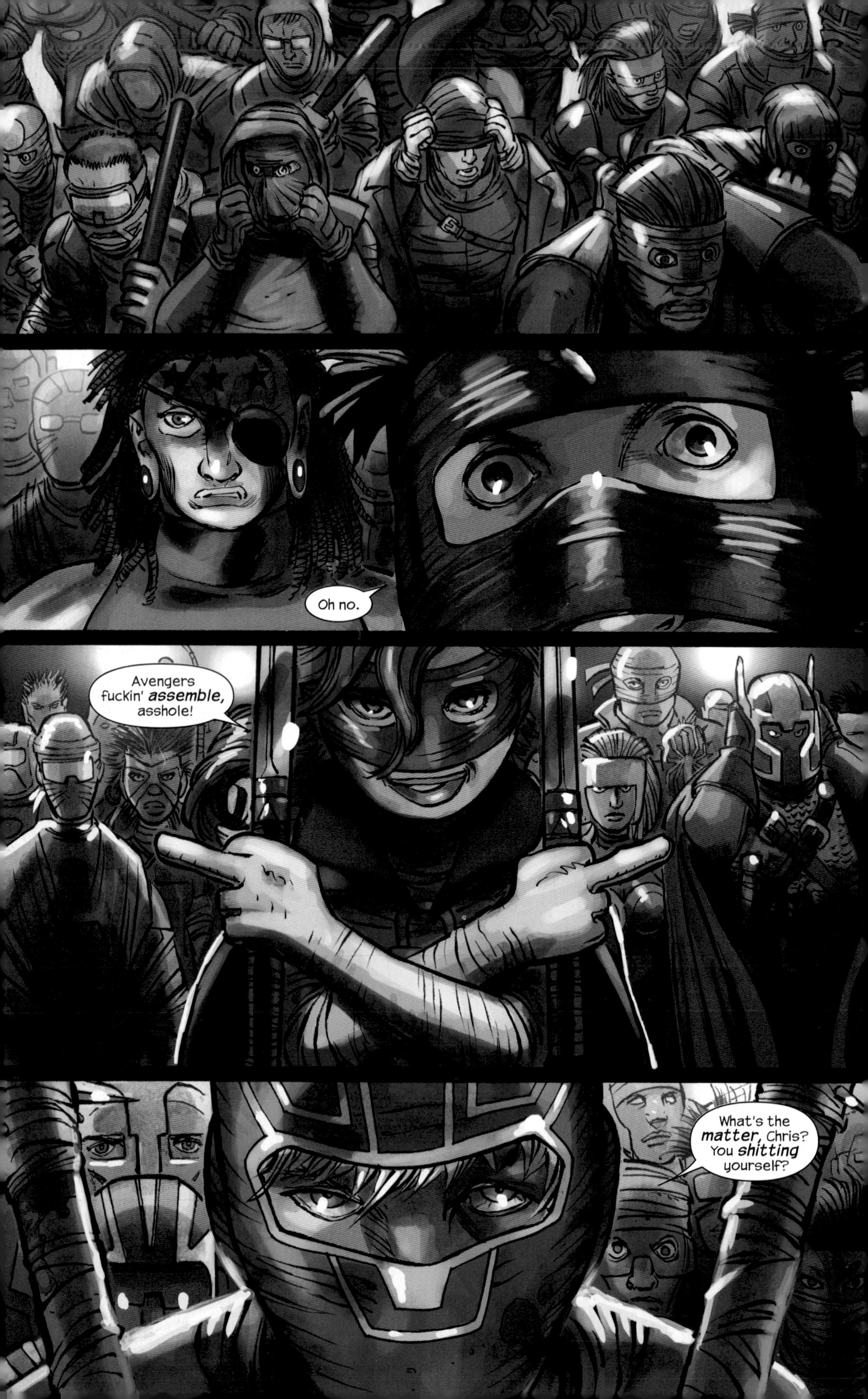
Oh no.
Avengers fuckin' *assemble,* asshole!
What's the *matter,* Chris? You *shitting* yourself?

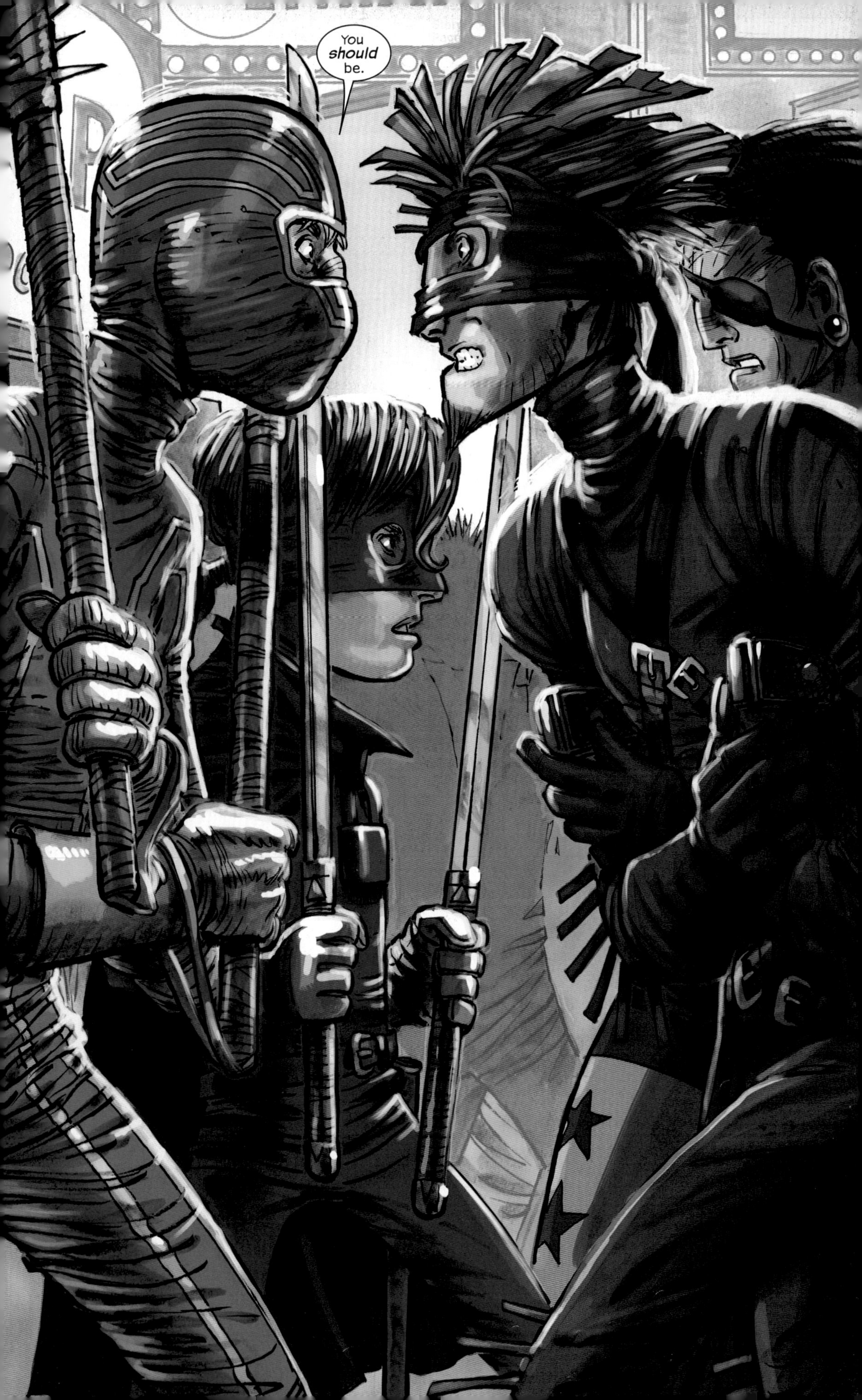
You *should* be.

SEVEN

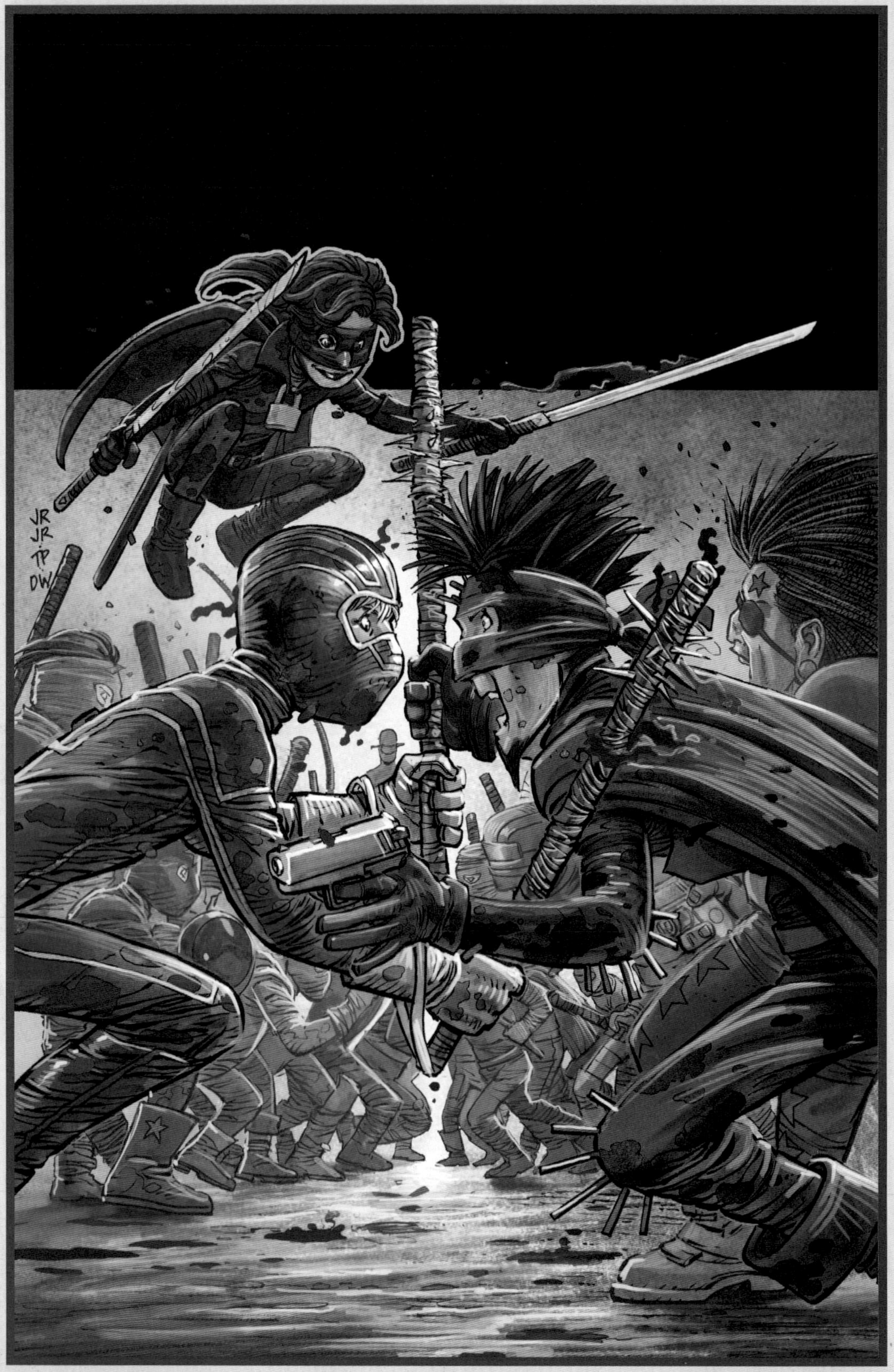
JR JR TP DW

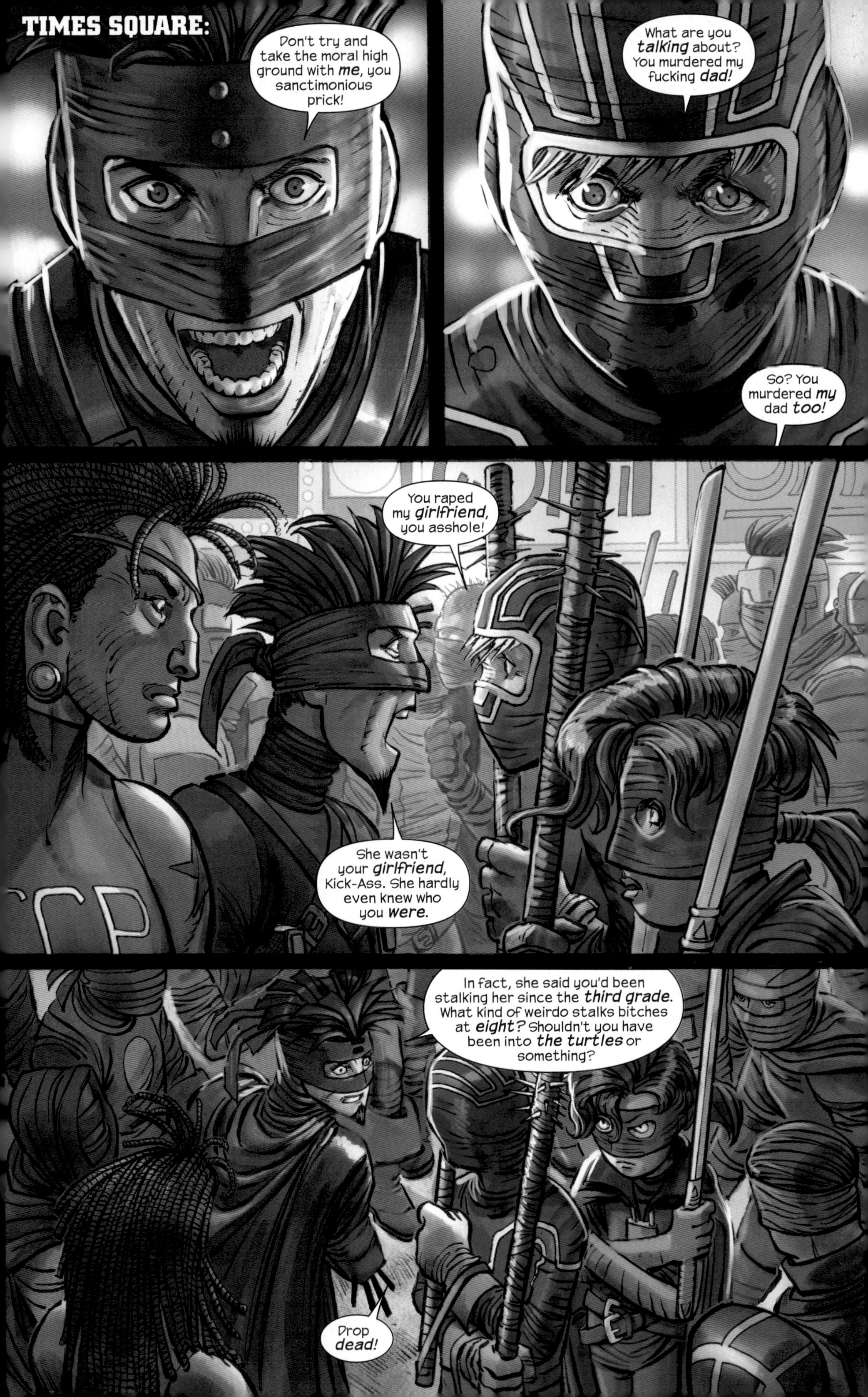
TIMES SQUARE:
Don't try and take the moral high ground with *me*, you sanctimonious prick!
What are you *talking* about? You murdered my fucking *dad!*
So? You murdered *my* dad *too!*
You raped my *girlfriend*, you asshole!
She wasn't your *girlfriend*, Kick-Ass. She hardly even knew who you *were*.
In fact, she said you'd been stalking her since the *third grade*. What kind of weirdo stalks bitches at *eight?* Shouldn't you have been into *the turtles* or something?
Drop *dead!*

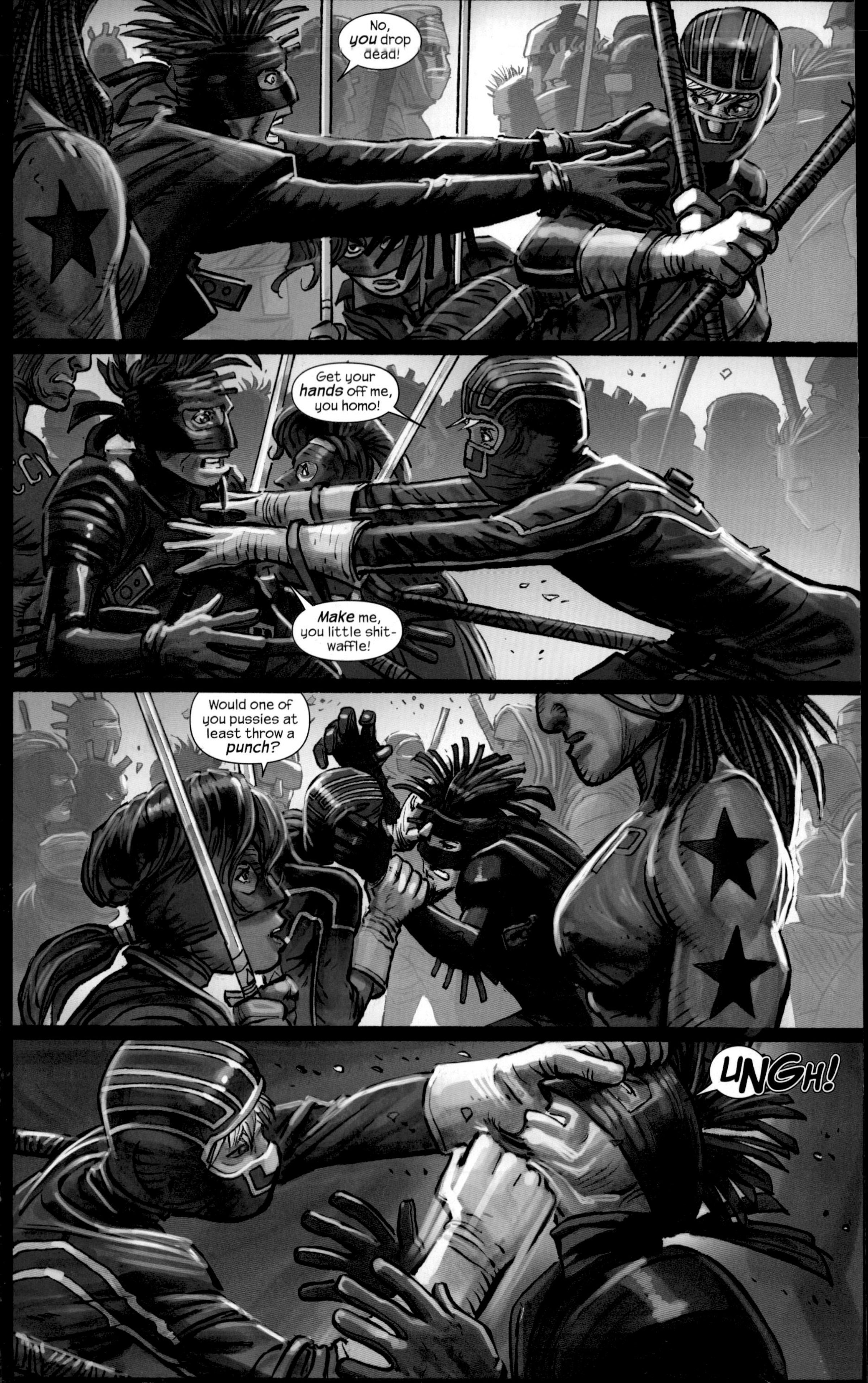
No, you drop dead!
Get your hands off me, you homo!
Make me, you little shit-waffle!
Would one of you pussies at least throw a punch?
UNGH!

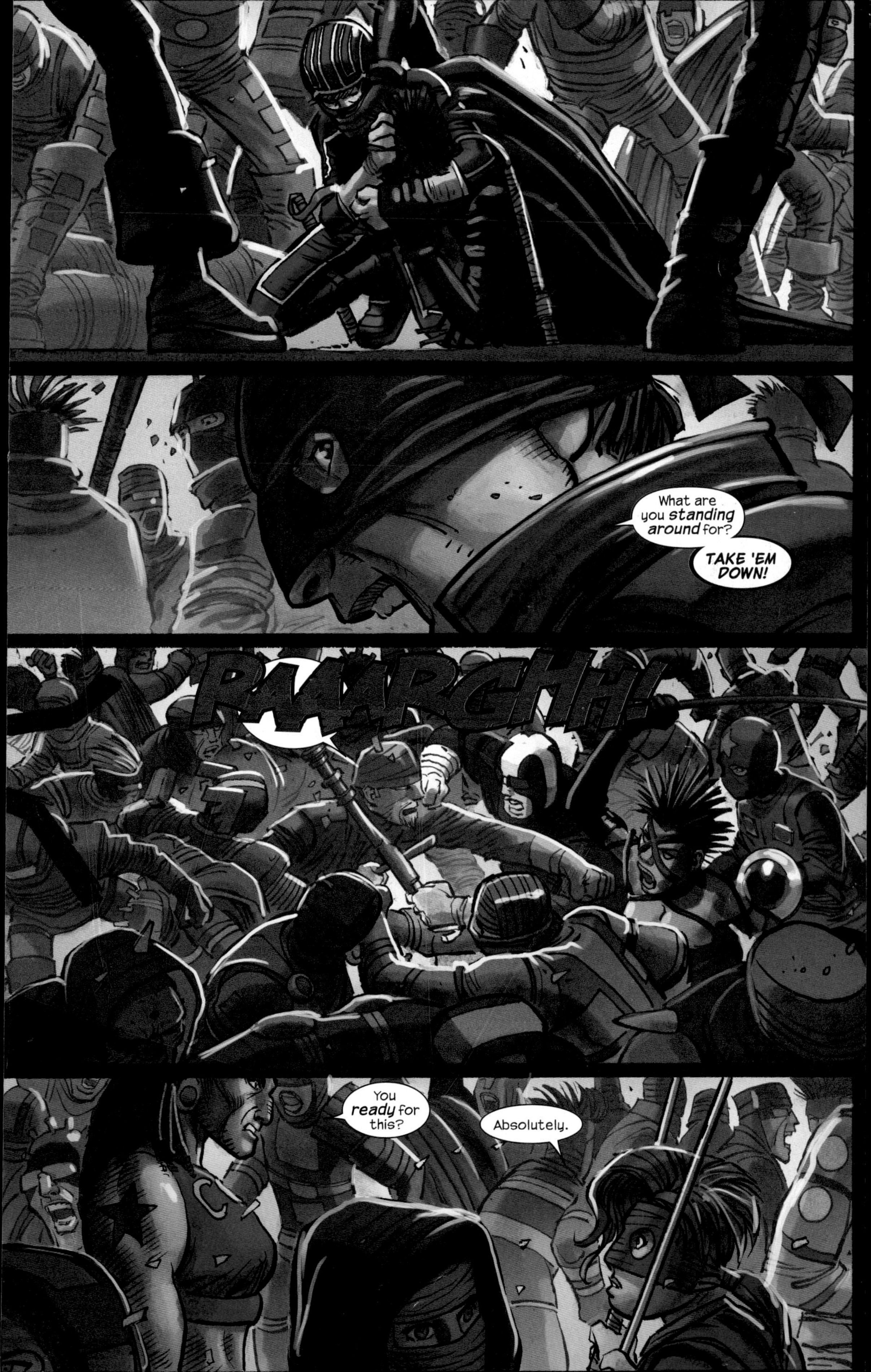
What are you *standing around* for?
TAKE 'EM DOWN!
RAAARCHHH!
You *ready* for this?
Absolutely.

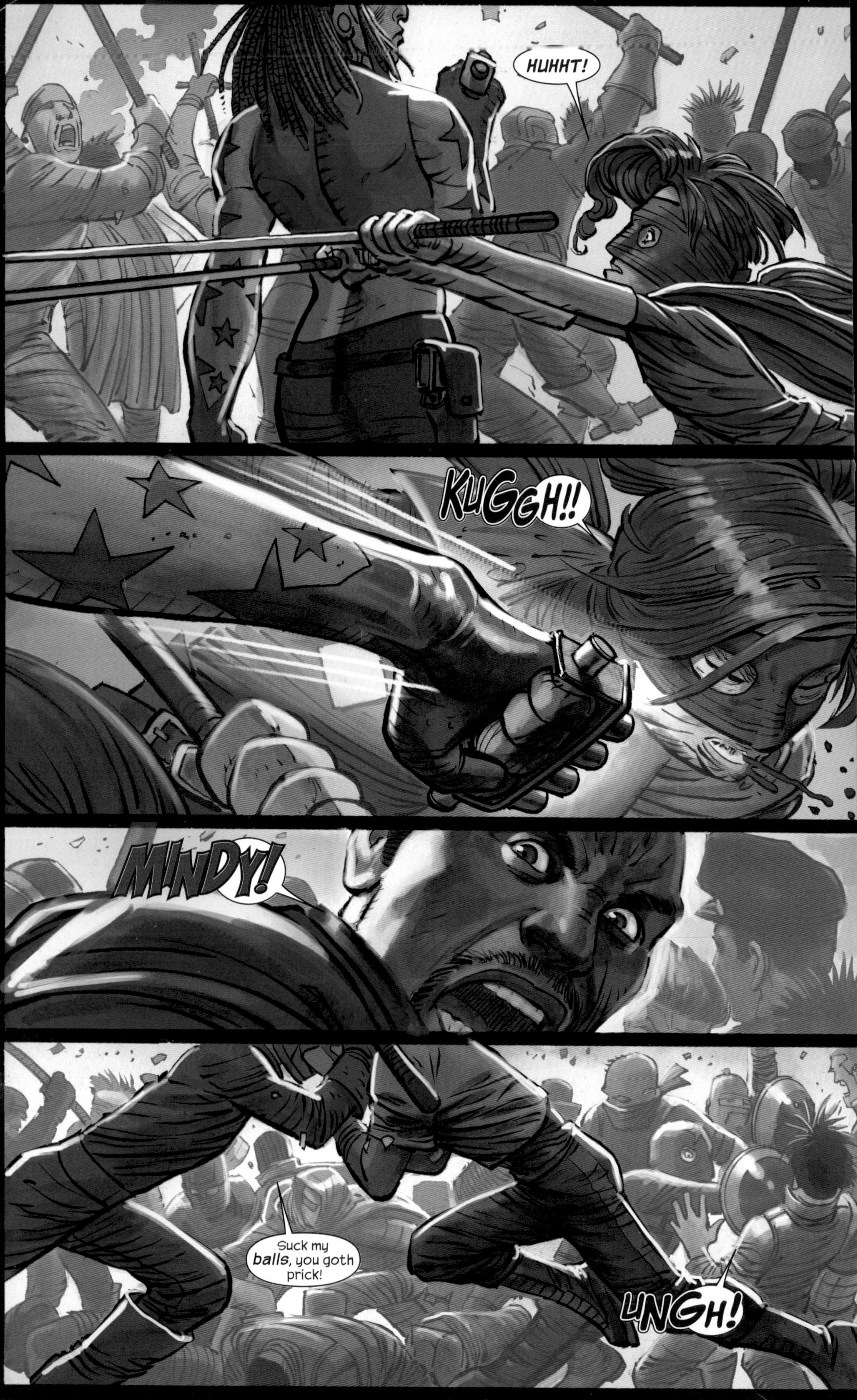
HUHHT!
KUGGH!!
MINDY!
Suck my balls, you goth prick!
UNGH!

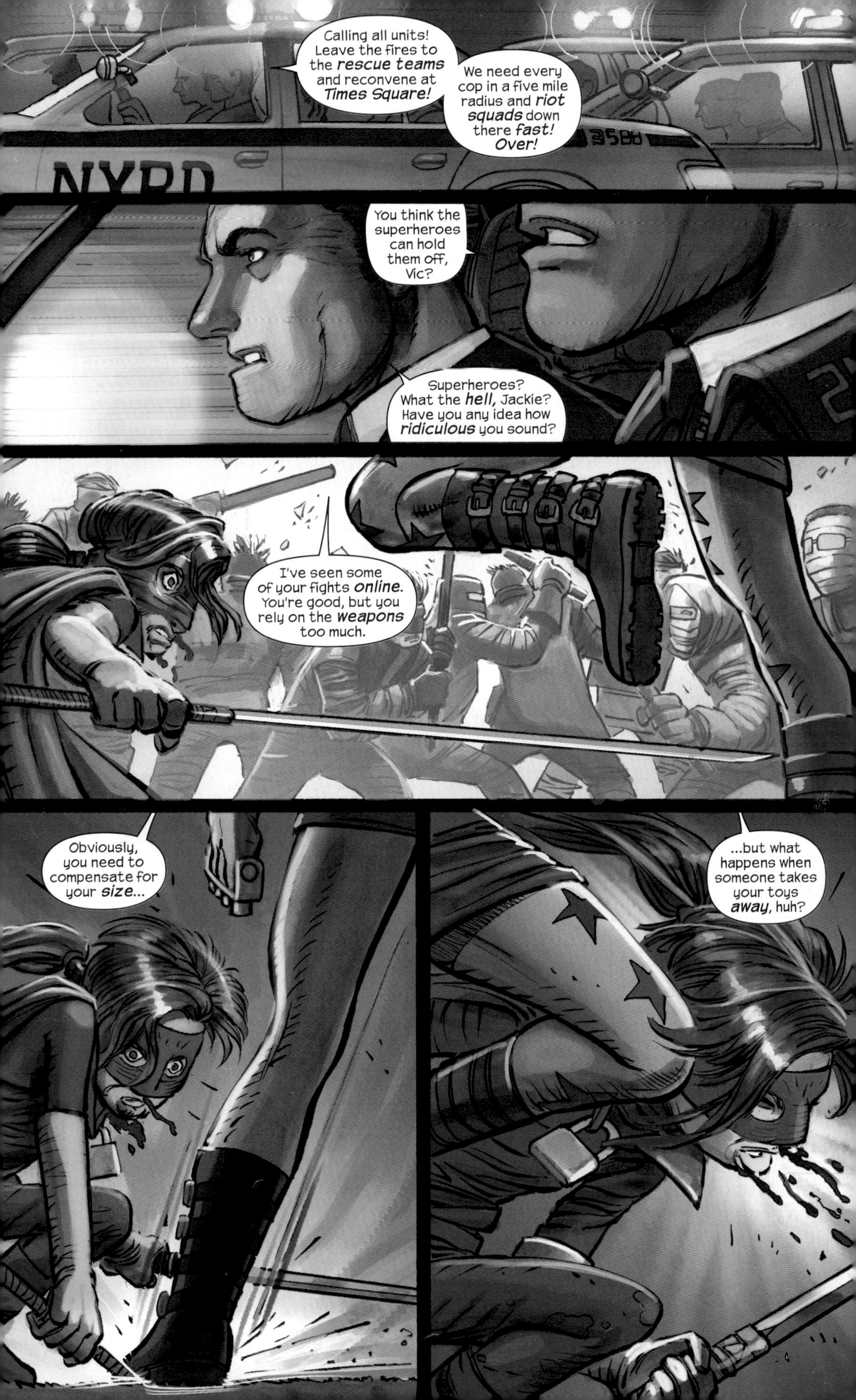
NYPD
Calling all units! Leave the fires to the *rescue teams* and reconvene at *Times Square!*
We need every cop in a five mile radius and *riot squads* down there *fast! Over!*
You think the superheroes can hold them off, Vic?
Superheroes? What the *hell,* Jackie? Have you any idea how *ridiculous* you sound?
I've seen some of your fights *online*. You're good, but you rely on the *weapons* too much.
Obviously, you need to compensate for your *size*...
...but what happens when someone takes your toys *away*, huh?

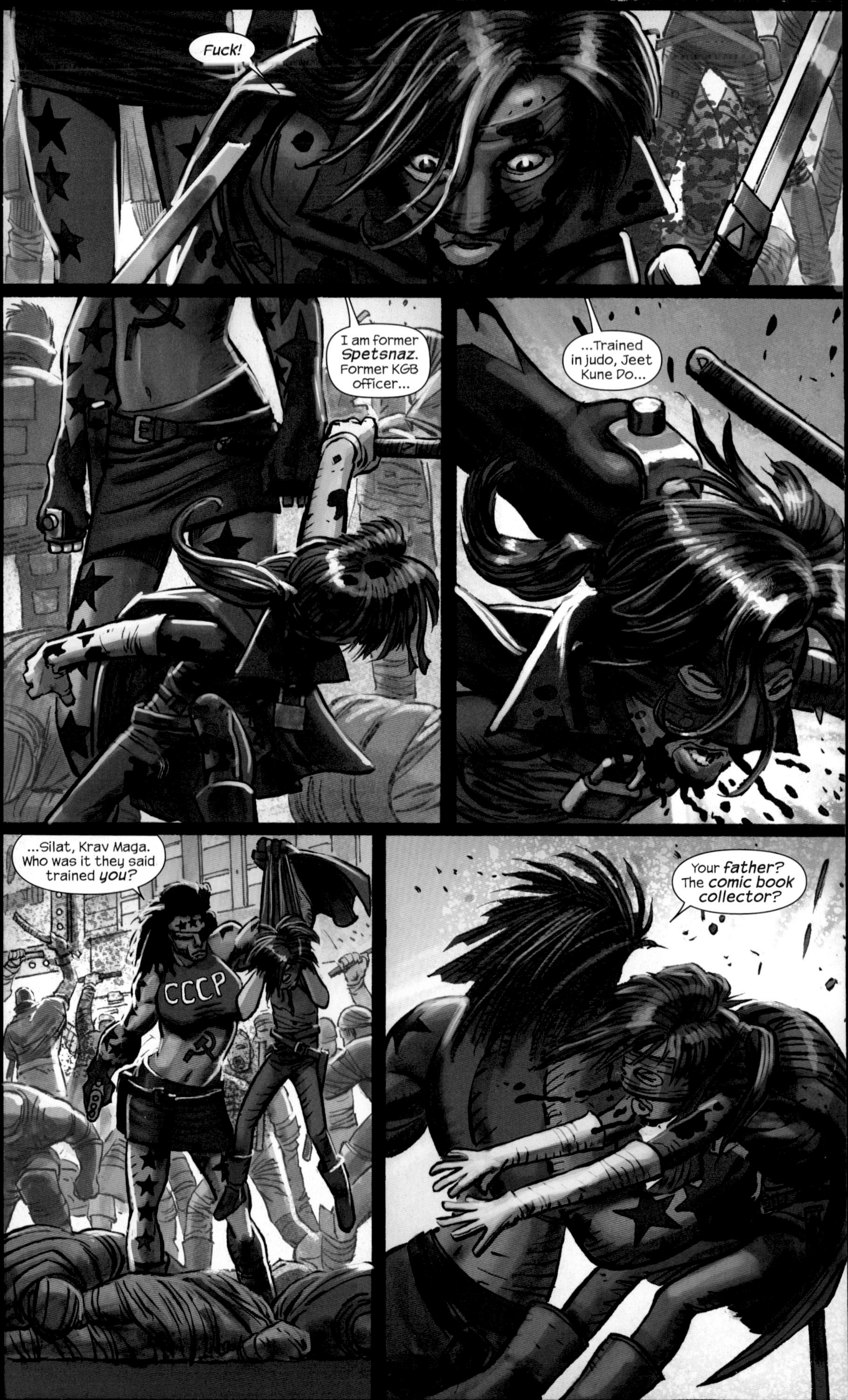
Fuck!
I am former Spetsnaz. Former KGB officer...
...Trained in judo, Jeet Kune Do...
...Silat, Krav Maga. Who was it they said trained you?
Your father? The comic book collector?
CCCP

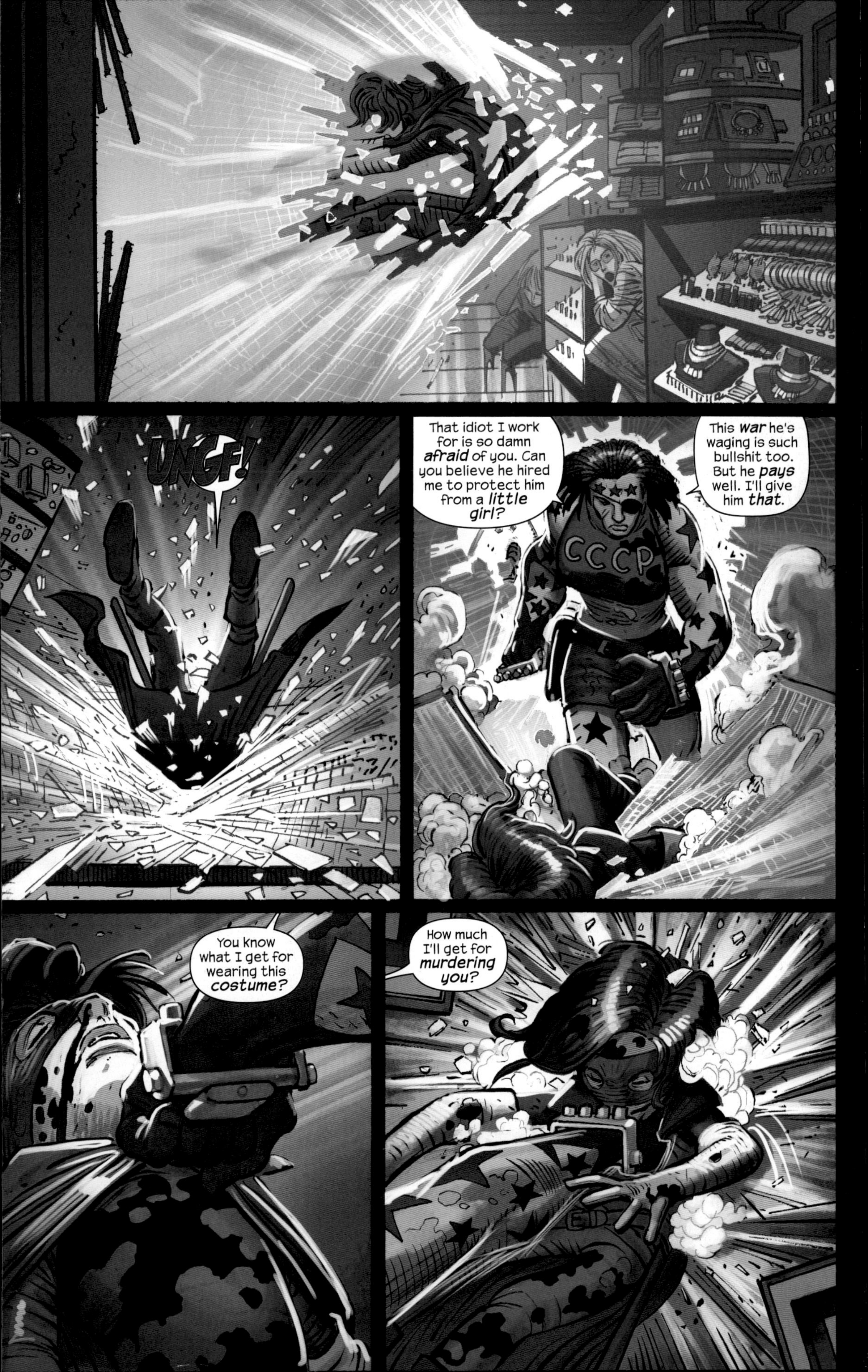
UNGF!
That idiot I work for is so damn afraid of you. Can you believe he hired me to protect him from a little girl?
This war he's waging is such bullshit too. But he pays well. I'll give him that.
You know what I get for wearing this costume?
How much I'll get for murdering you?

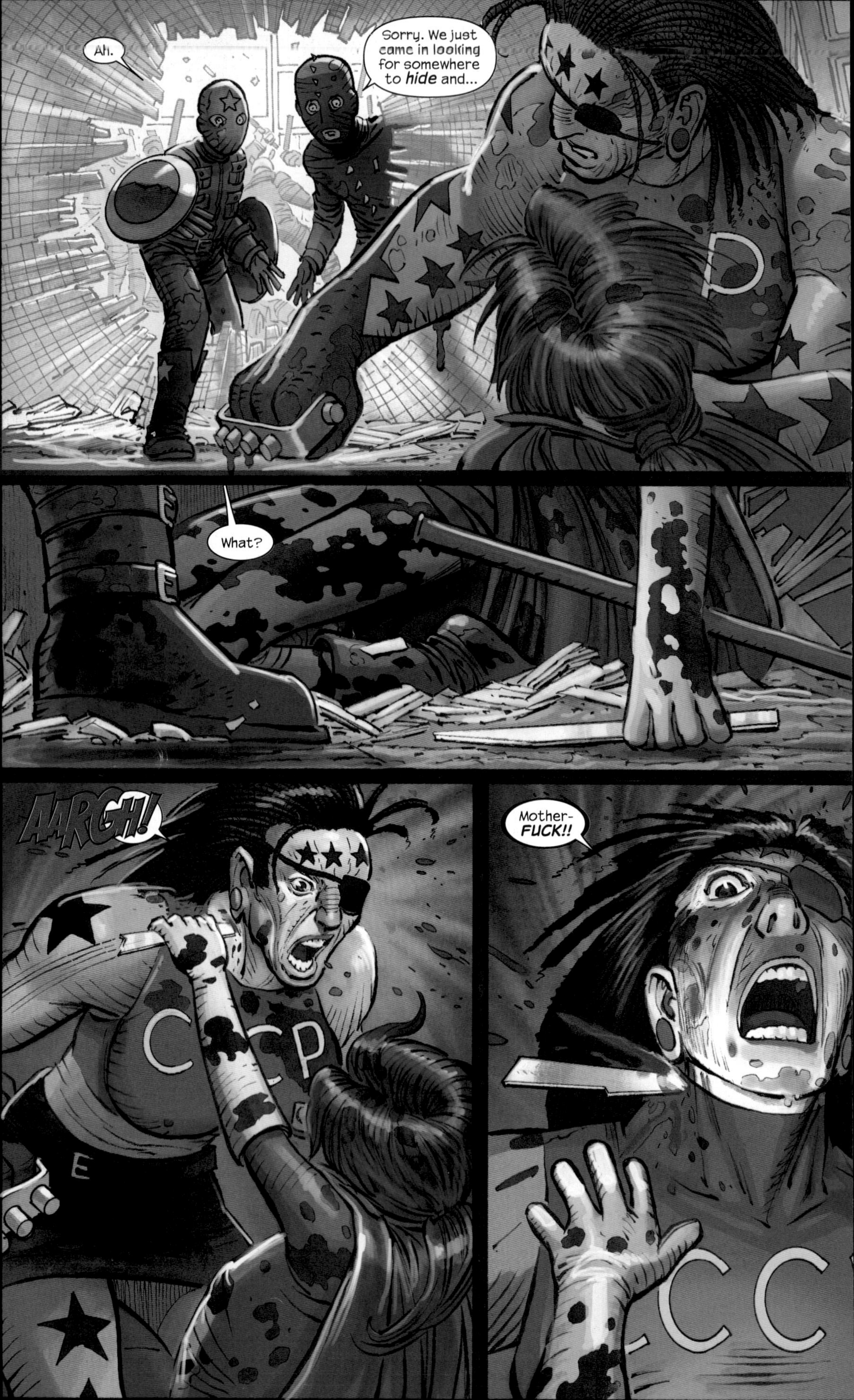
Ah.
Sorry. We just came in looking for somewhere to *hide* and...
What?
AARGH!
Mother-**FUCK!!**

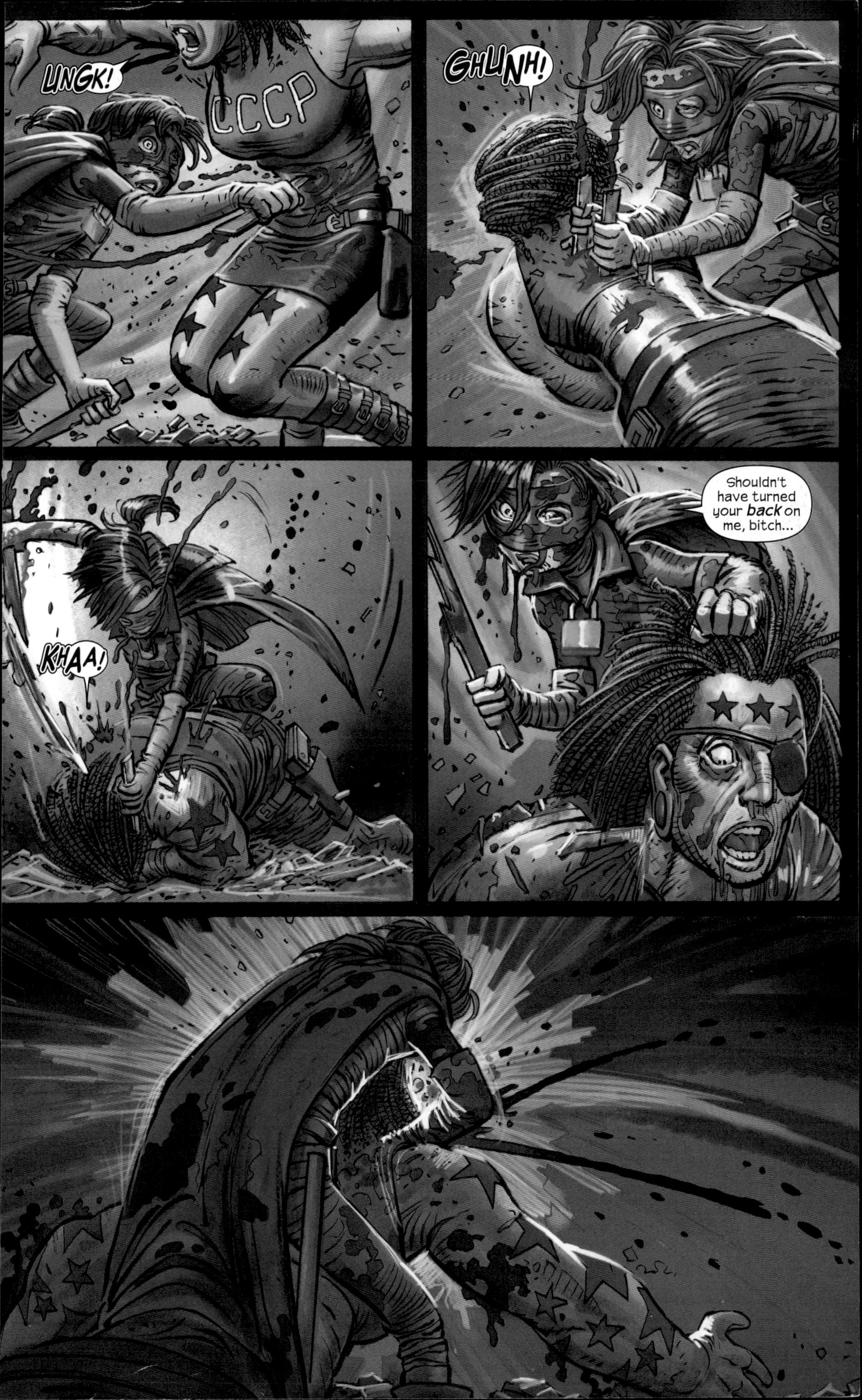
UNGK!
CCCP
GHUNH!
KHAA!
Shouldn't have turned your **back** on me, bitch...

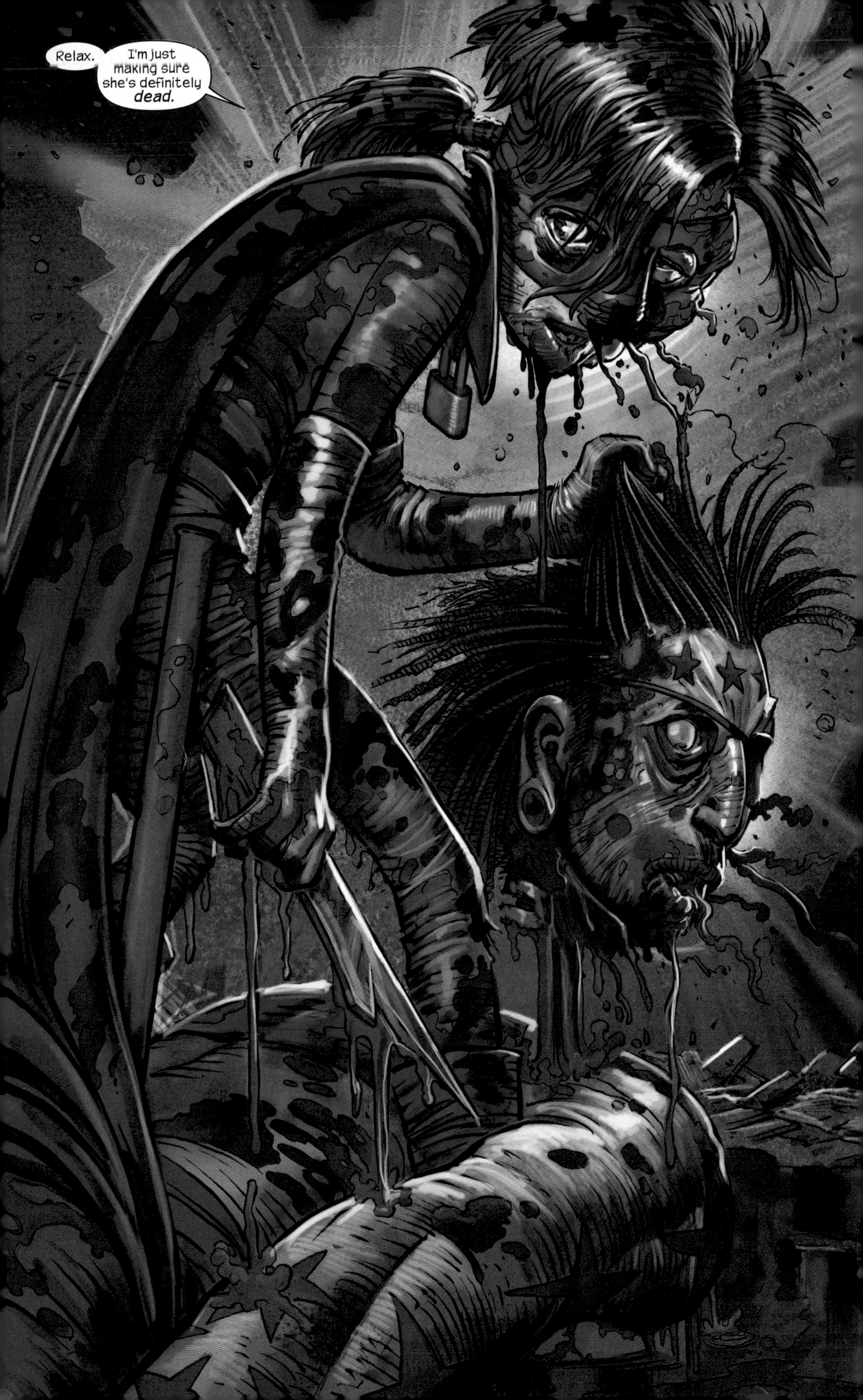
Relax.
I'm just making sure she's definitely *dead.*

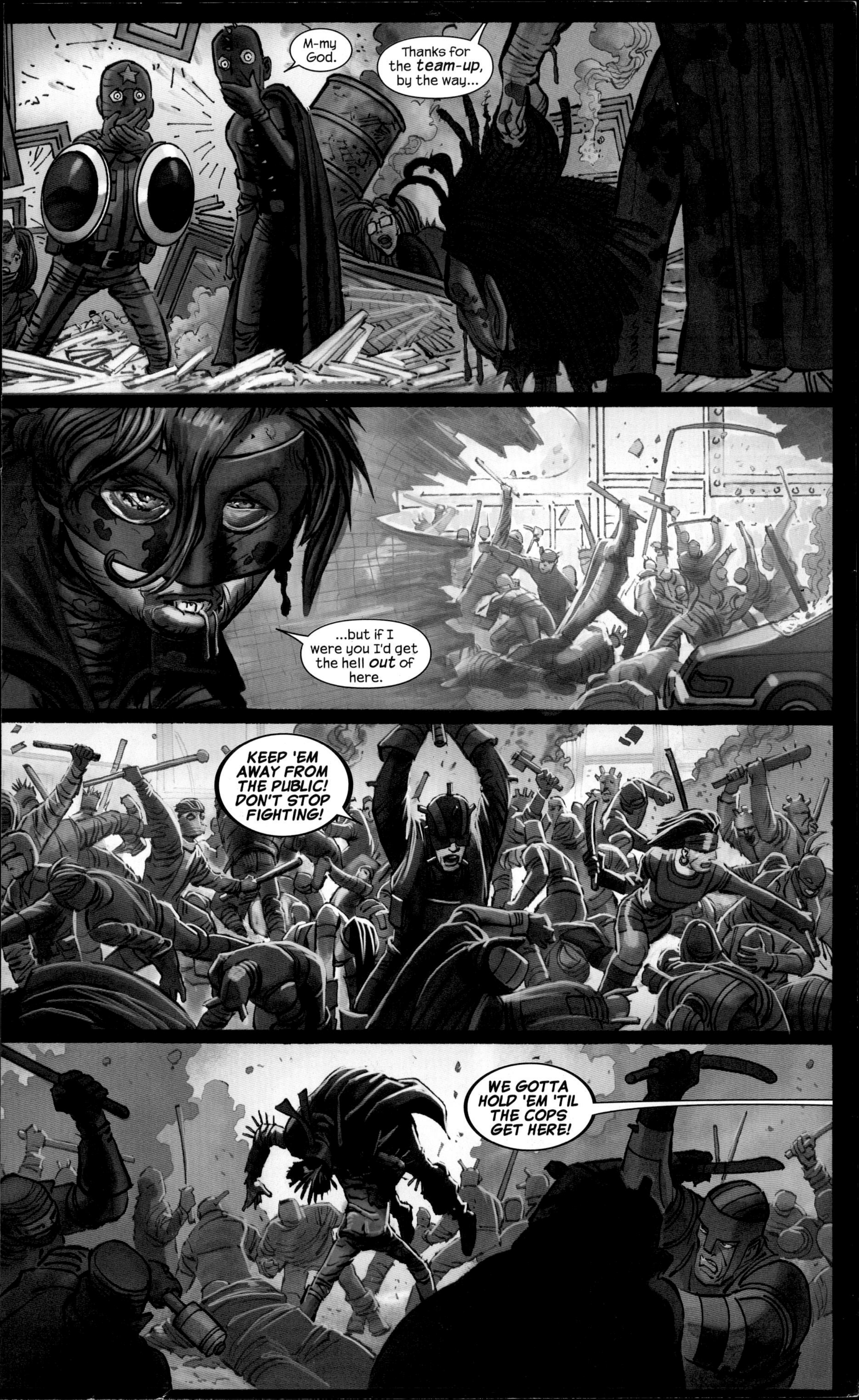
M-my God.
Thanks for the team-up, by the way...
...but if I were you I'd get the hell out of here.
KEEP 'EM AWAY FROM THE PUBLIC! DON'T STOP FIGHTING!
WE GOTTA HOLD 'EM 'TIL THE COPS GET HERE!

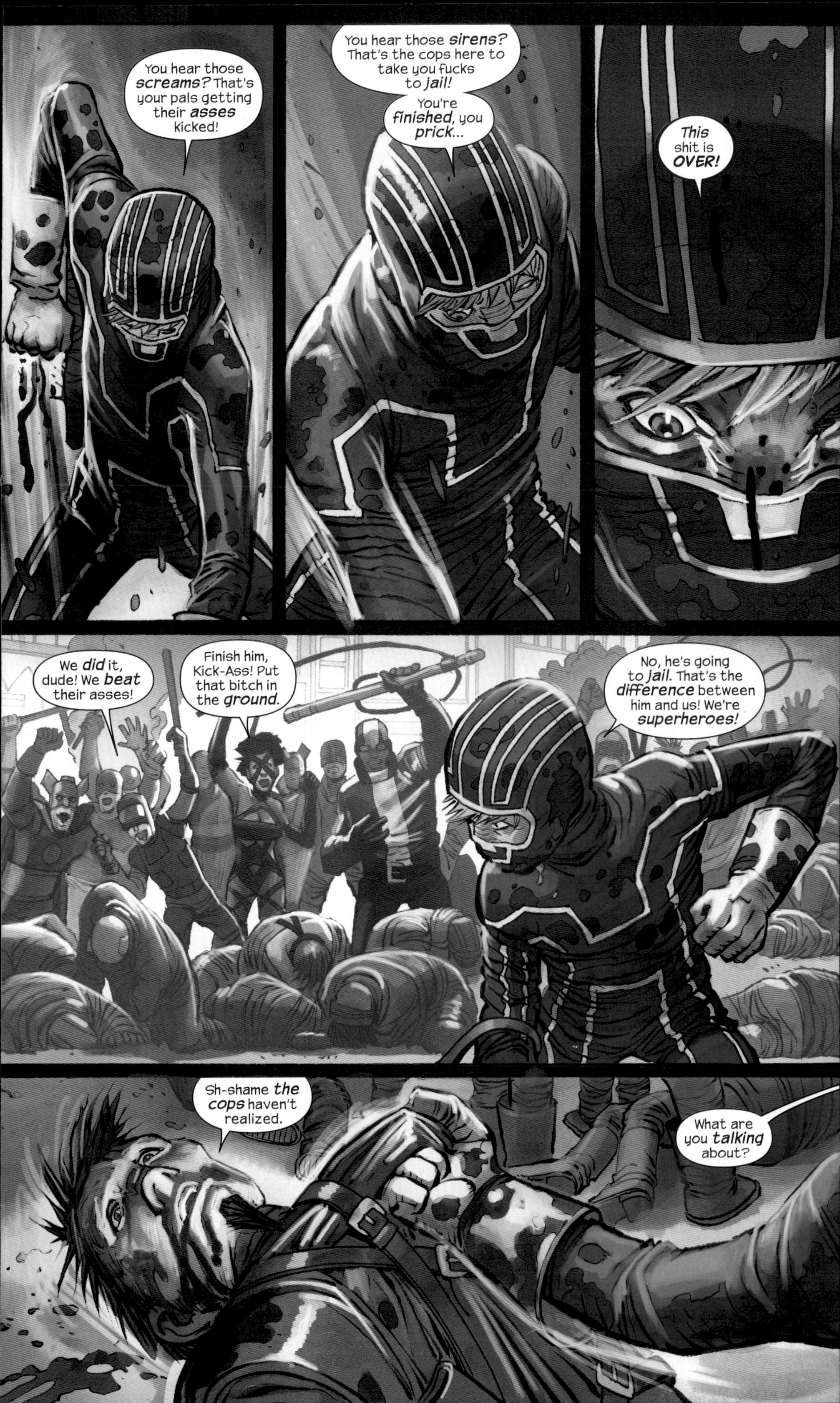
You hear those screams? That's your pals getting their asses kicked!
You hear those sirens? That's the cops here to take you fucks to jail!
You're finished, you prick...
This shit is OVER!
We did it, dude! We beat their asses!
Finish him, Kick-Ass! Put that bitch in the ground.
No, he's going to jail. That's the difference between him and us! We're superheroes!
Sh-shame the cops haven't realized.
What are you talking about?

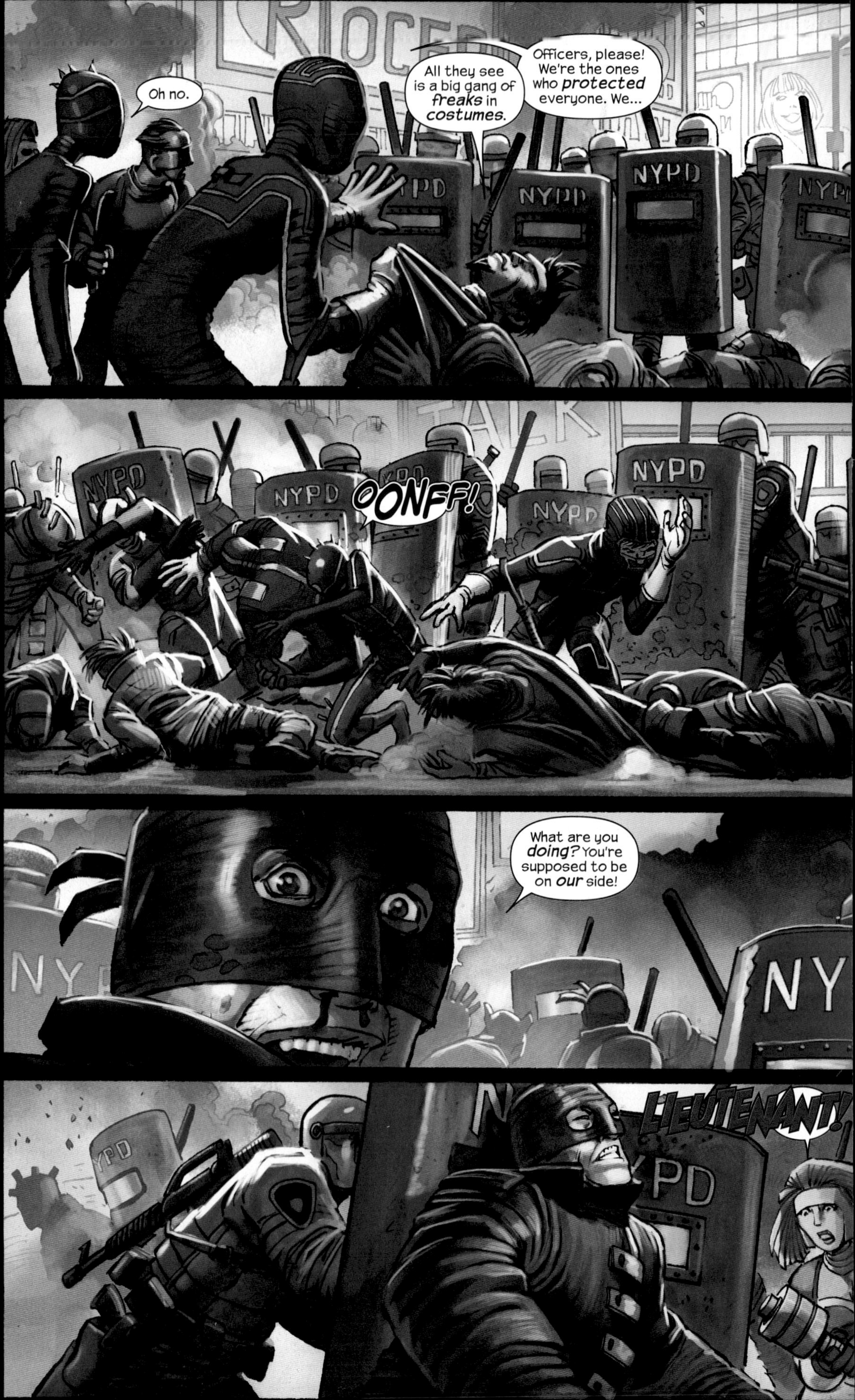

Oh no.
All they see is a big gang of *freaks* in *costumes*.
Officers, please! We're the ones who *protected* everyone. We...
OONFF!
What are you *doing?* You're supposed to be on *our* side!
LIEUTENANT!

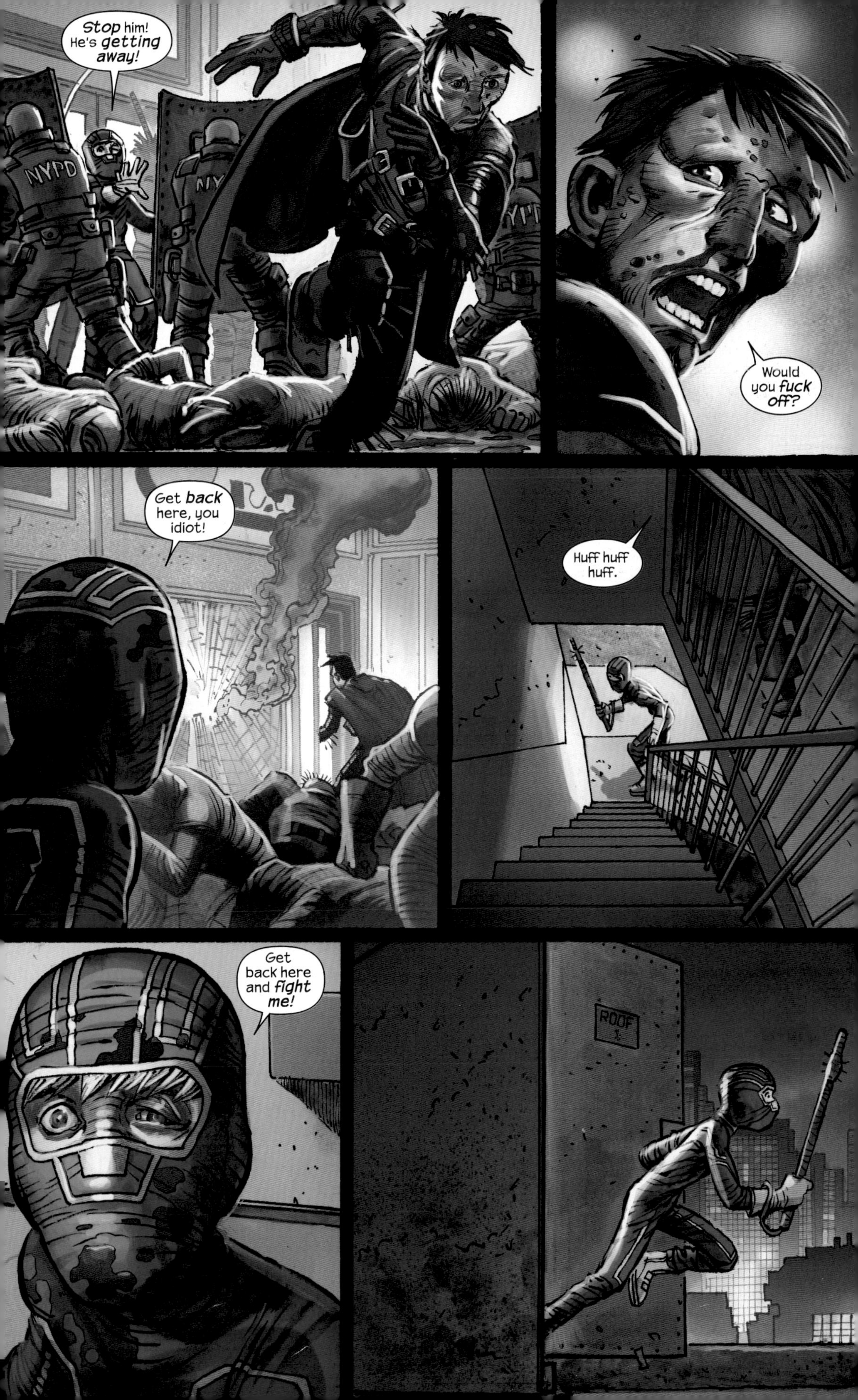
Stop him! He's getting away!
NYPD
Would you fuck off?
Get back here, you idiot!
Huff huff huff.
Get back here and fight me!
ROOF

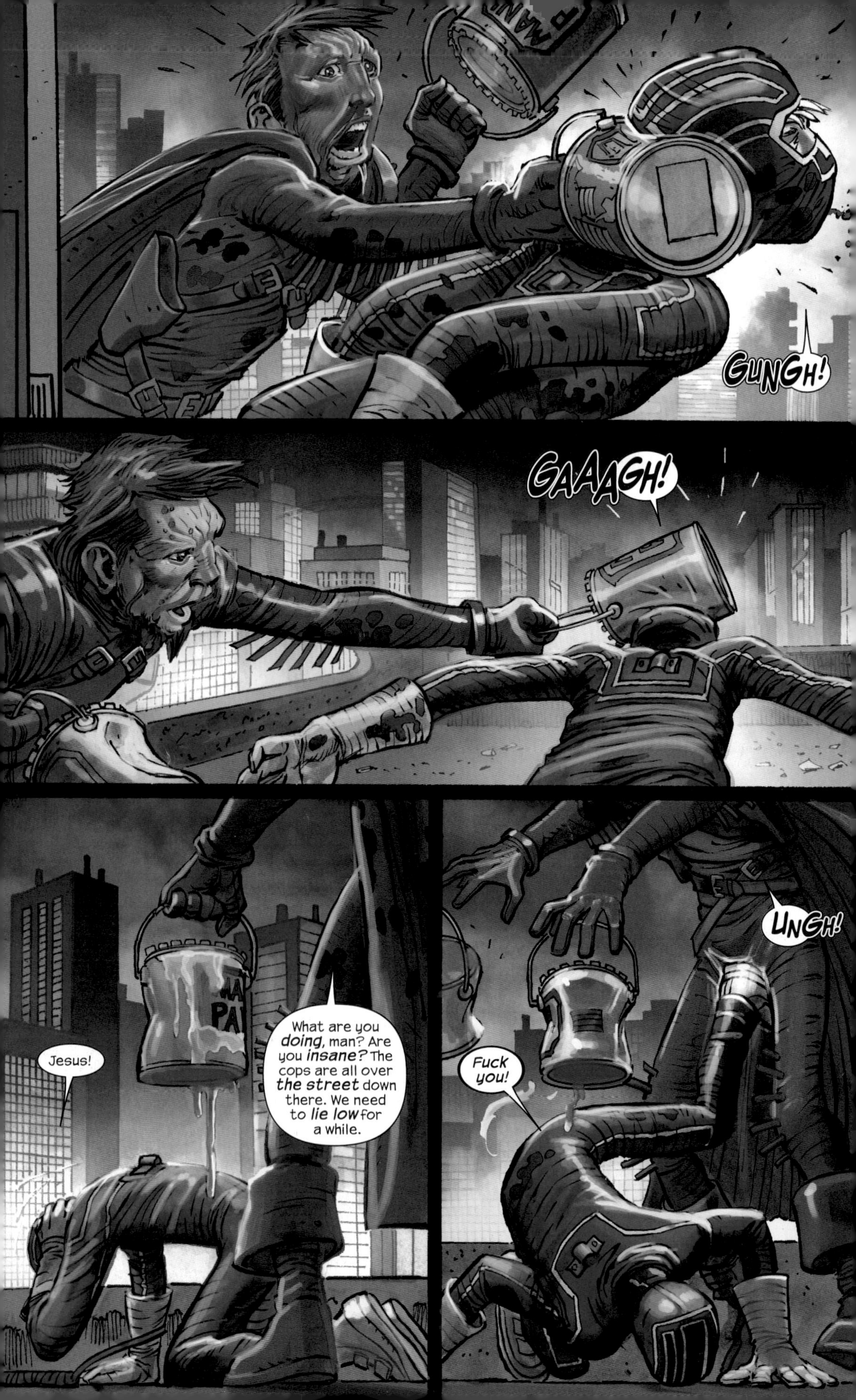
GUNGH!
GAAAGH!
Jesus!
What are you doing, man? Are you insane? The cops are all over the street down there. We need to lie low for a while.
UNGH!
Fuck you!

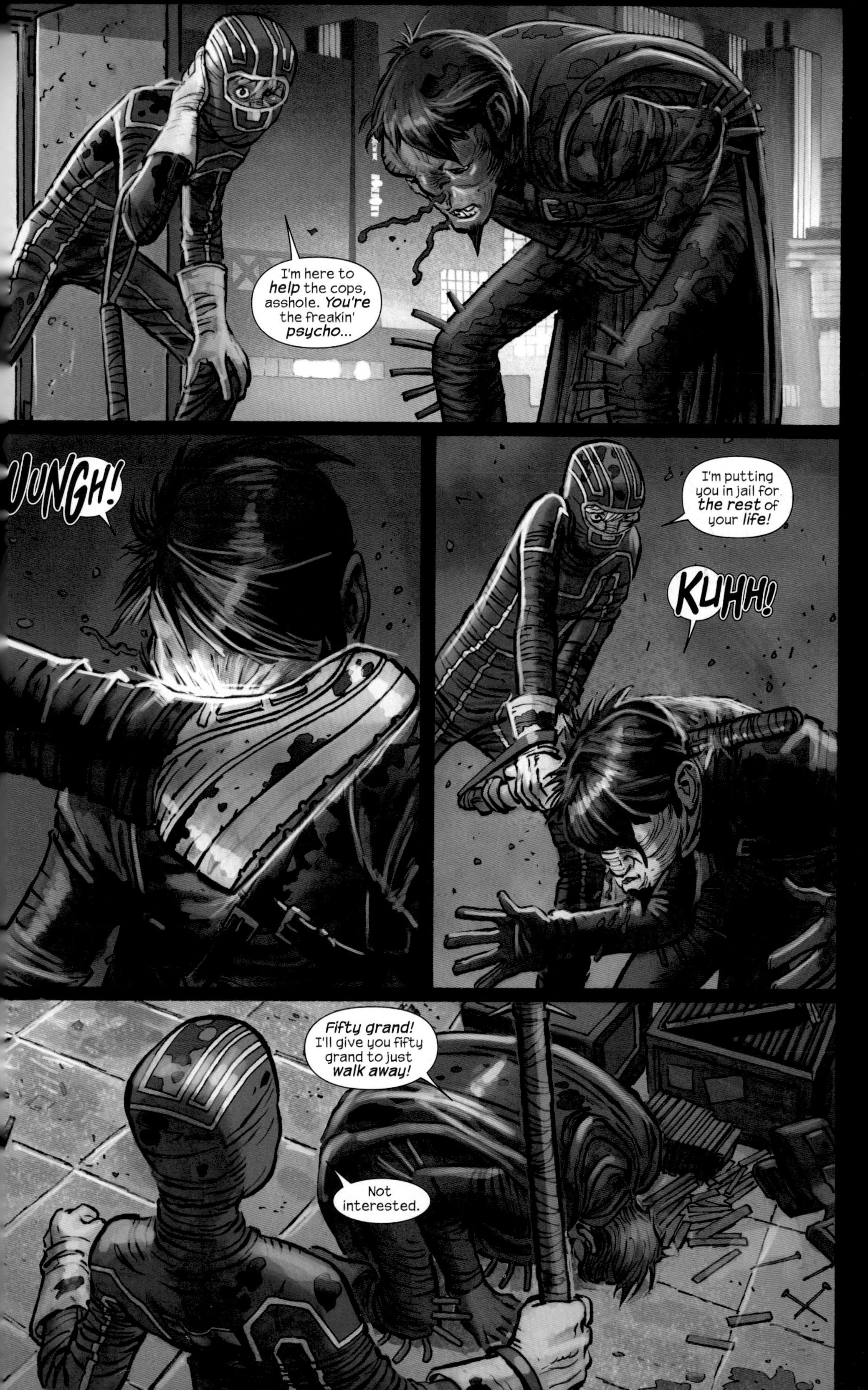
I'm here to *help* the cops, asshole. *You're* the freakin' *psycho*...
UUNGH!
I'm putting you in jail for *the rest* of your *life!*
KUHH!
Fifty grand! I'll give you fifty grand to just *walk away!*
Not interested.

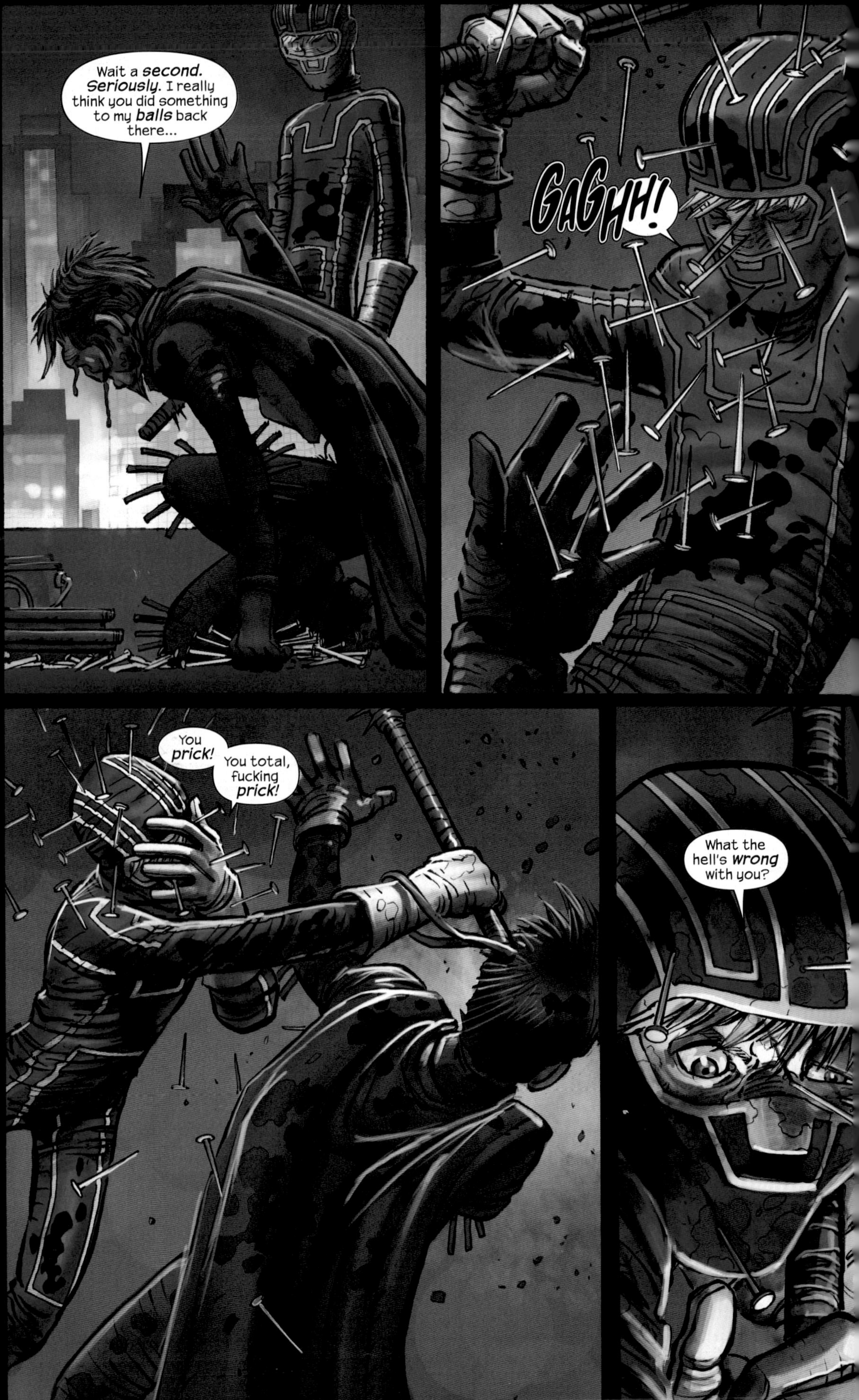
Wait a *second.* *Seriously.* I really think you did something to my *balls* back there...
GAGHH!
You *prick!*
You total, fucking *prick!*
What the hell's *wrong* with you?

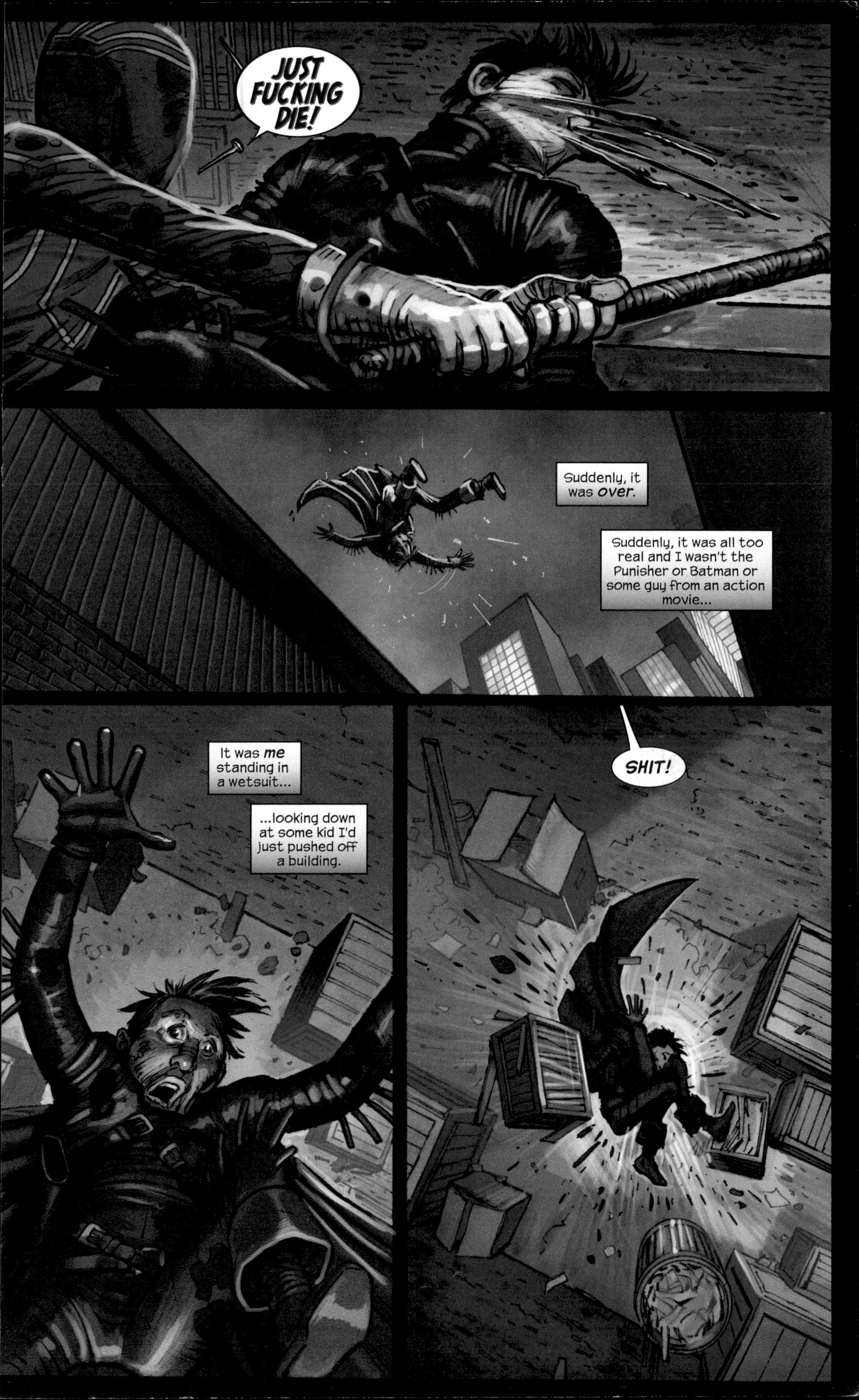
JUST FUCKING DIE!
Suddenly, it was *over*.
Suddenly, it was all too real and I wasn't the Punisher or Batman or some guy from an action movie...
It was *me* standing in a wetsuit...
...looking down at some kid I'd just pushed off a building.
SHIT!

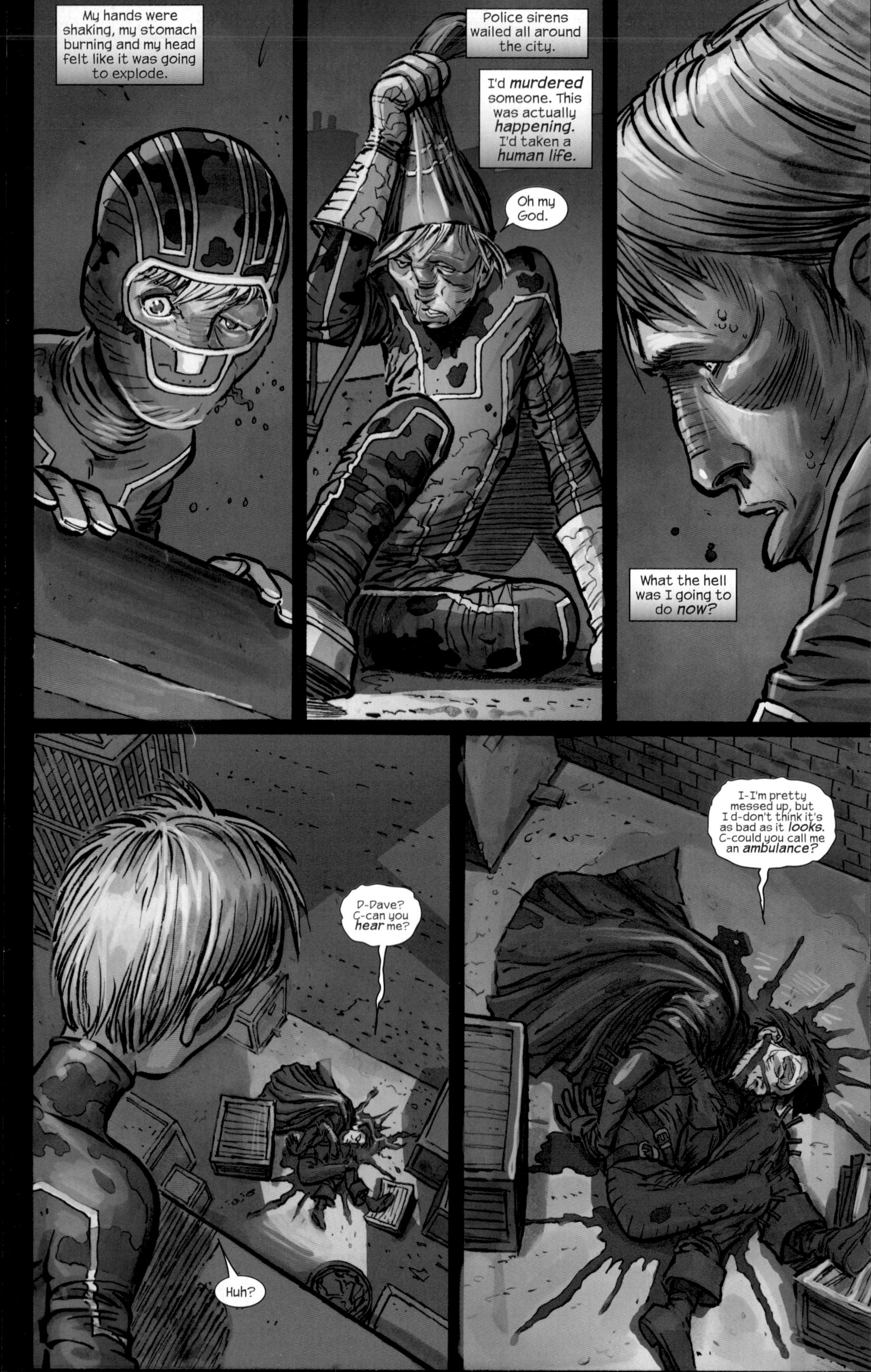

My hands were shaking, my stomach burning and my head felt like it was going to explode.
Police sirens wailed all around the city.
I'd *murdered* someone. This was actually *happening*. I'd taken a *human life.*
Oh my God.
What the hell was I going to do *now?*
D-Dave? C-can you *hear* me?
Huh?
I-I'm pretty messed up, but I d-don't think it's as bad as it *looks.* C-could you call me an *ambulance?*

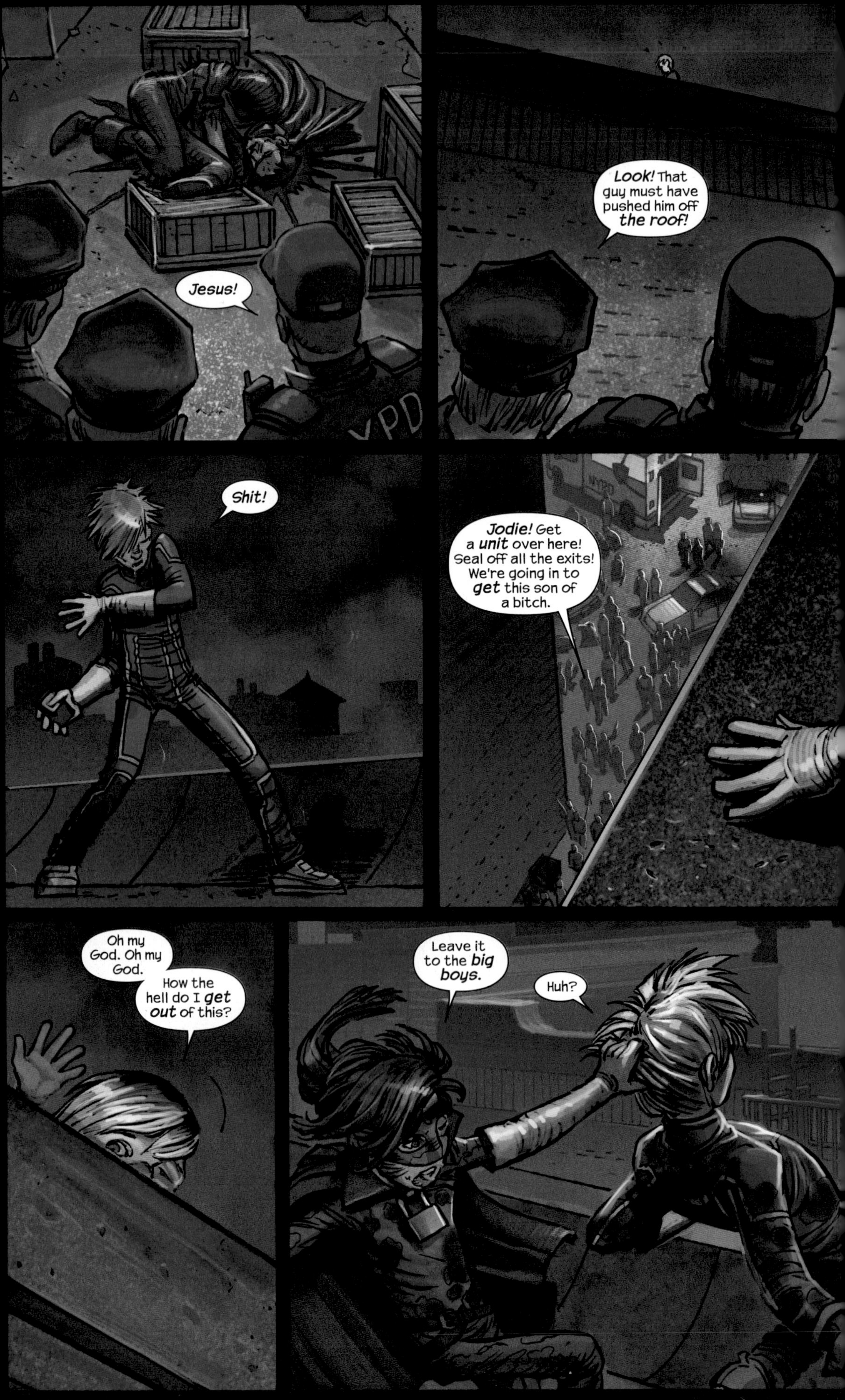
Jesus!
Look! That guy must have pushed him off the roof!
Shit!
Jodie! Get a unit over here! Seal off all the exits! We're going in to get this son of a bitch.
Oh my God. Oh my God.
How the hell do I get out of this?
Leave it to the big boys.
Huh?

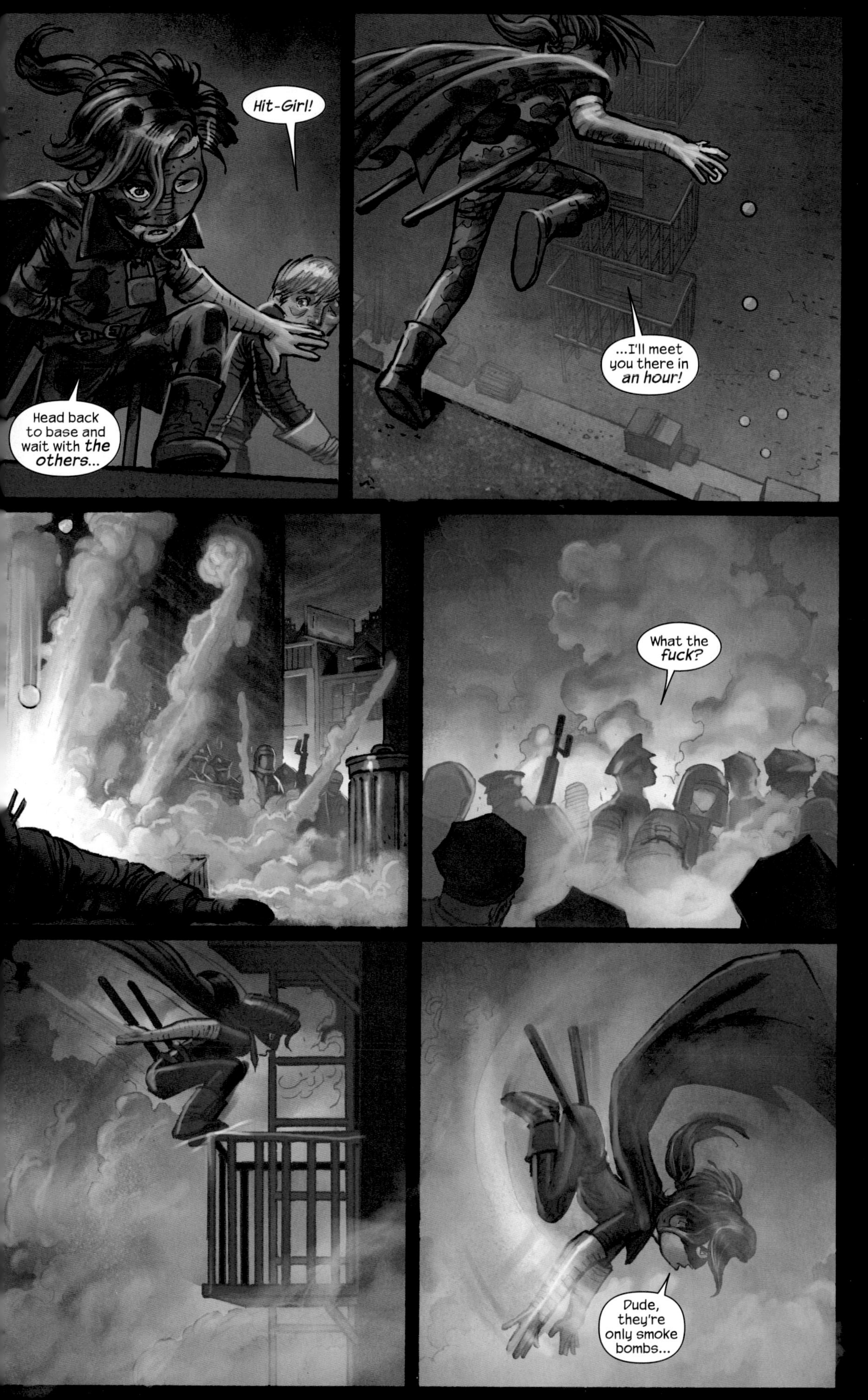
Hit-Girl!
Head back to base and wait with the others...
...I'll meet you there in an hour!
What the fuck?
Dude, they're only smoke bombs...

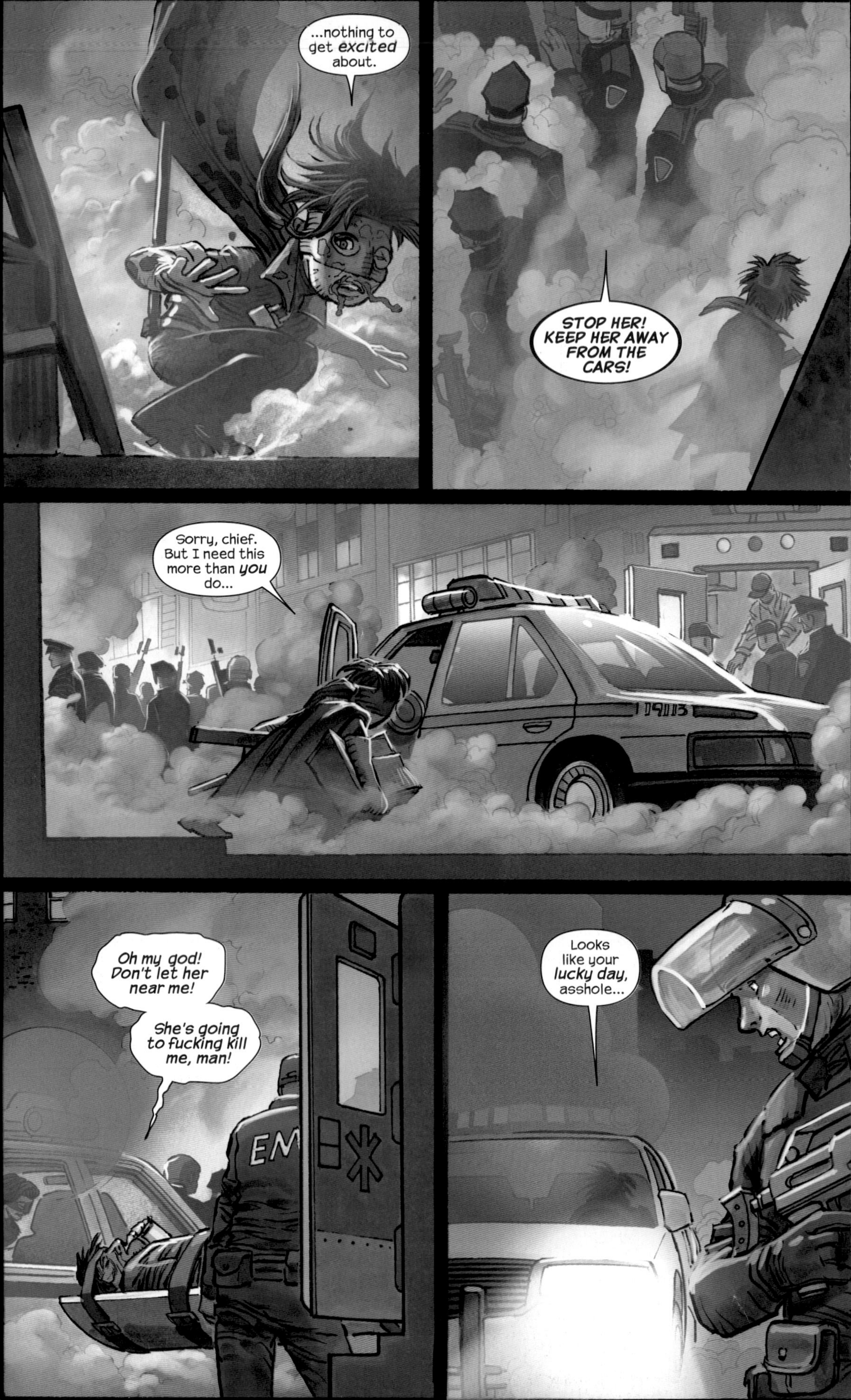
...nothing to get excited about.
STOP HER! KEEP HER AWAY FROM THE CARS!
Sorry, chief. But I need this more than you do...
Oh my god! Don't let her near me!
She's going to fucking kill me, man!
EM
Looks like your lucky day, asshole...

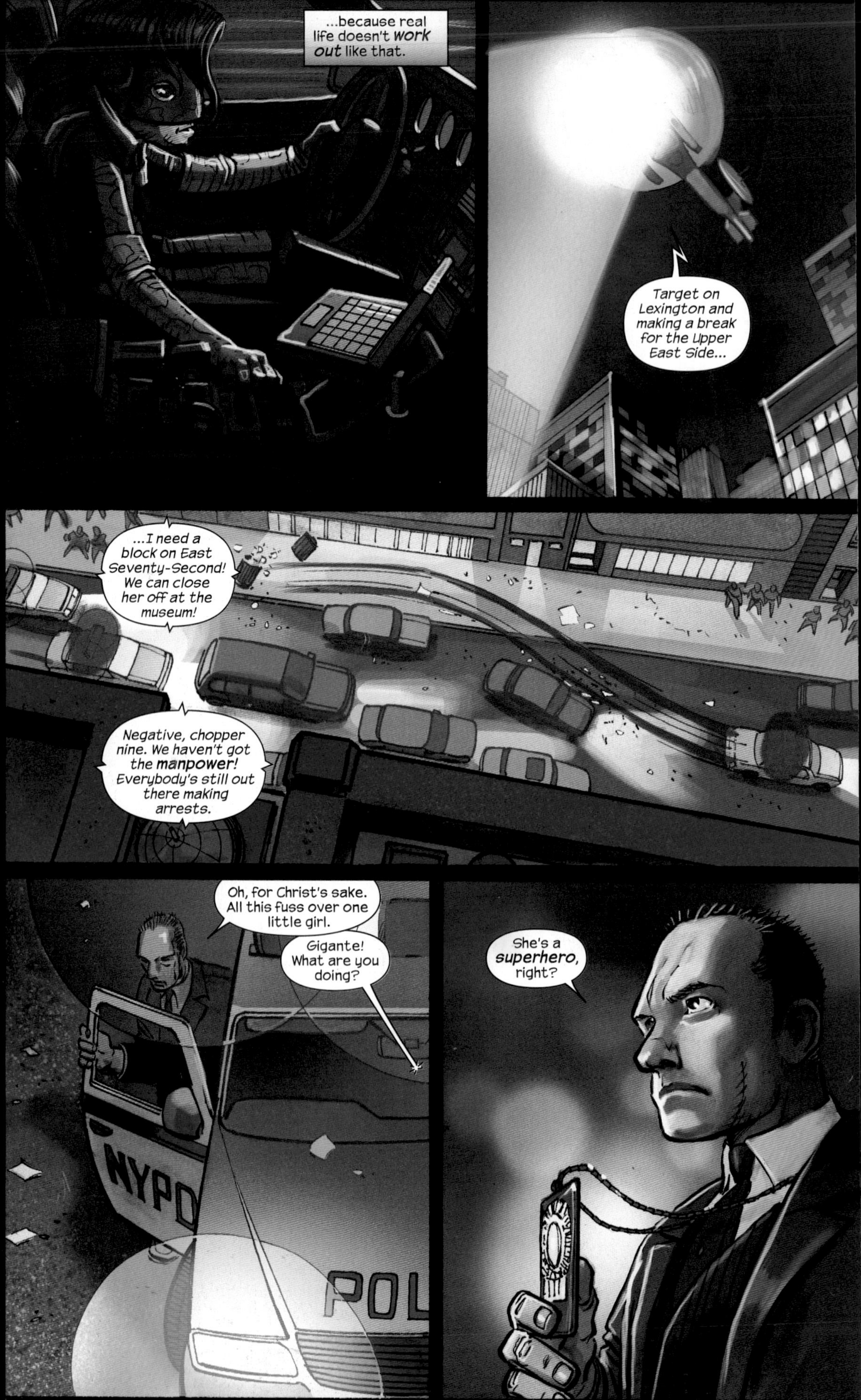
...because real life doesn't **work out** like that.
Target on Lexington and making a break for the Upper East Side...
...I need a block on East Seventy-Second! We can close her off at the museum!
Negative, chopper nine. We haven't got the **manpower**! Everybody's still out there making arrests.
Oh, for Christ's sake. All this fuss over one little girl.
Gigante! What are you doing?
NYPD
POL
She's a **superhero**, right?

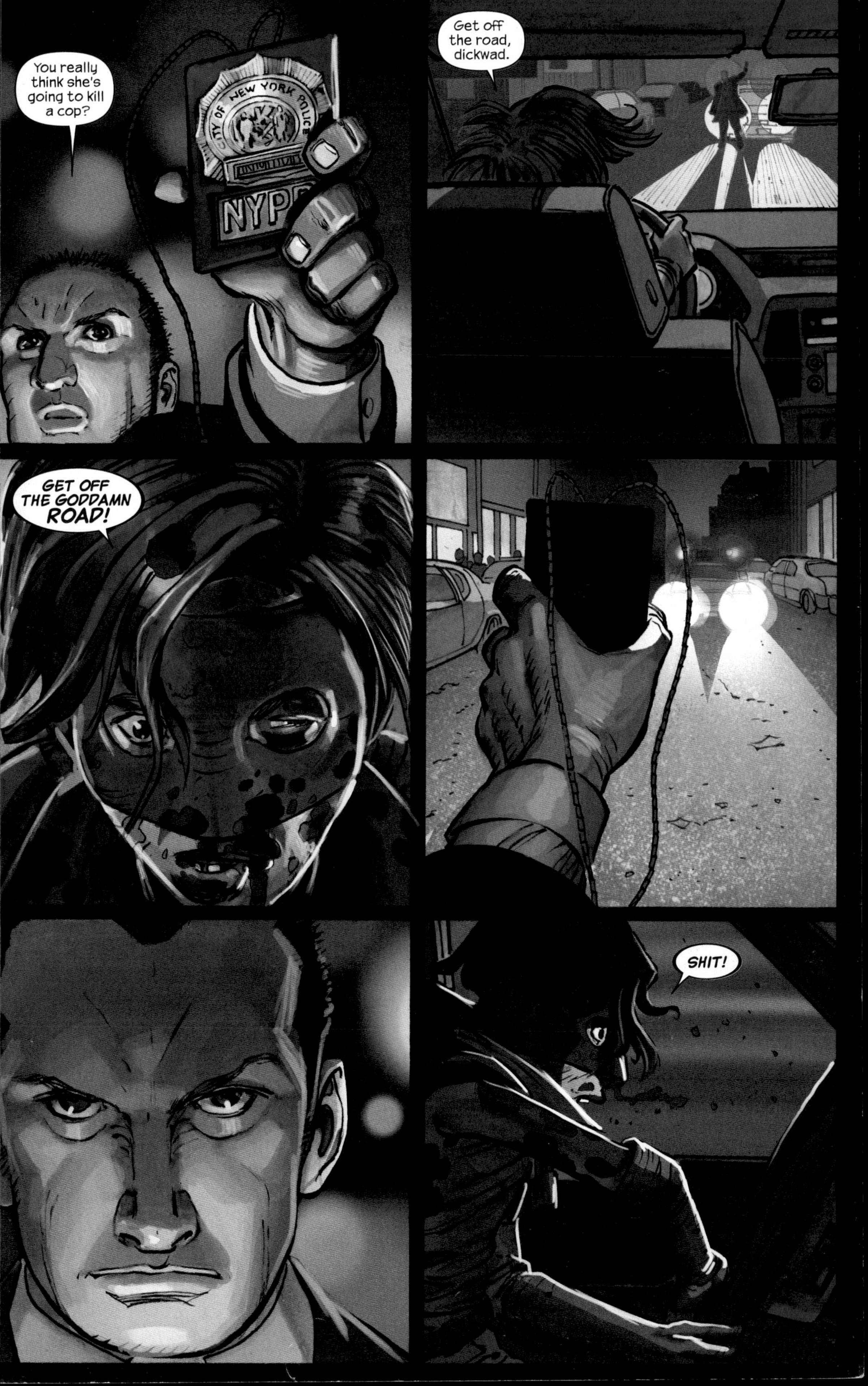
You really think she's going to kill a cop?
NEW YORK POLICE
NYP
Get off the road, dickwad.
GET OFF THE GODDAMN ROAD!
SHIT!

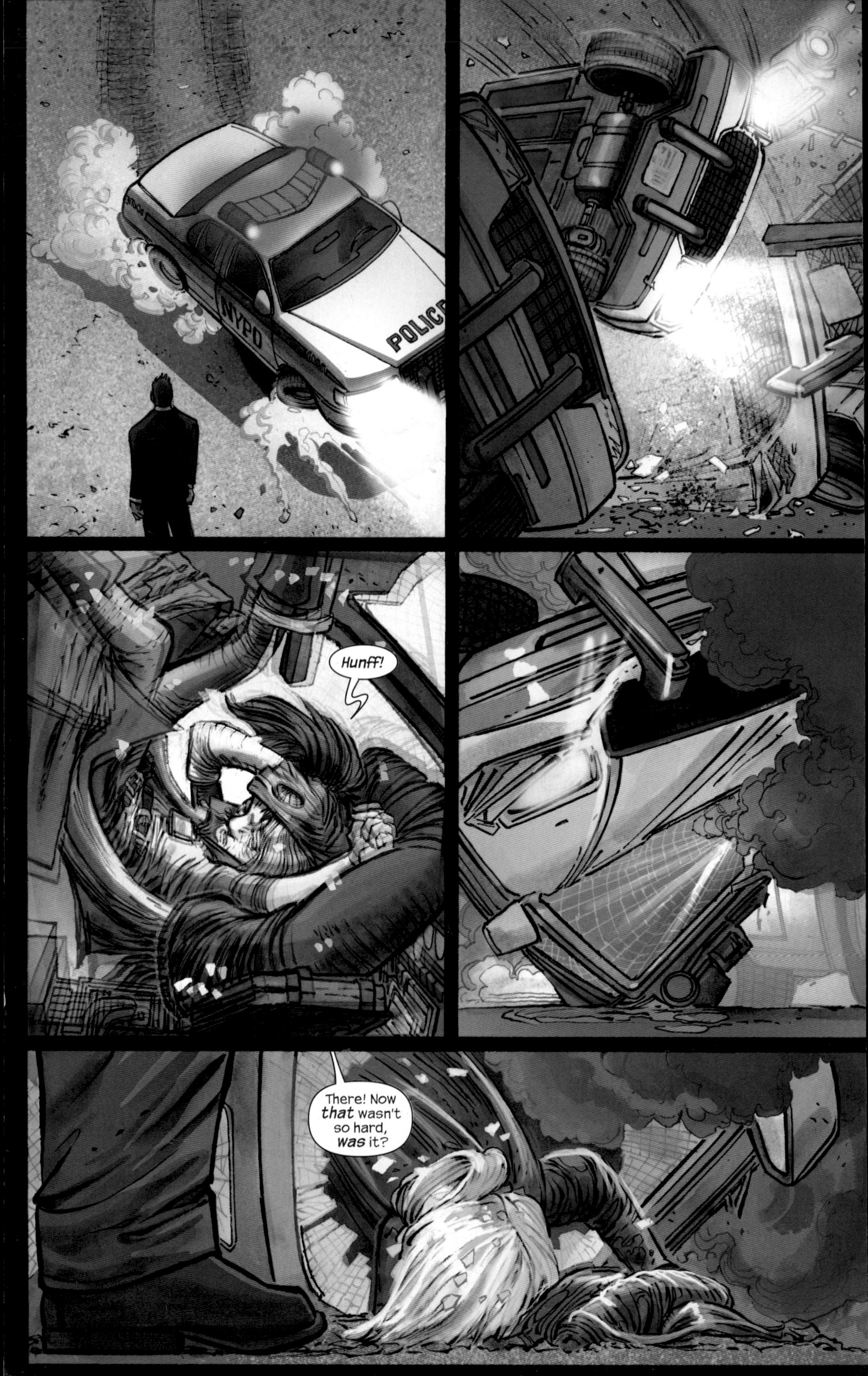
NYPD
POLICE
Hunff!
There! Now *that* wasn't so hard, *was* it?

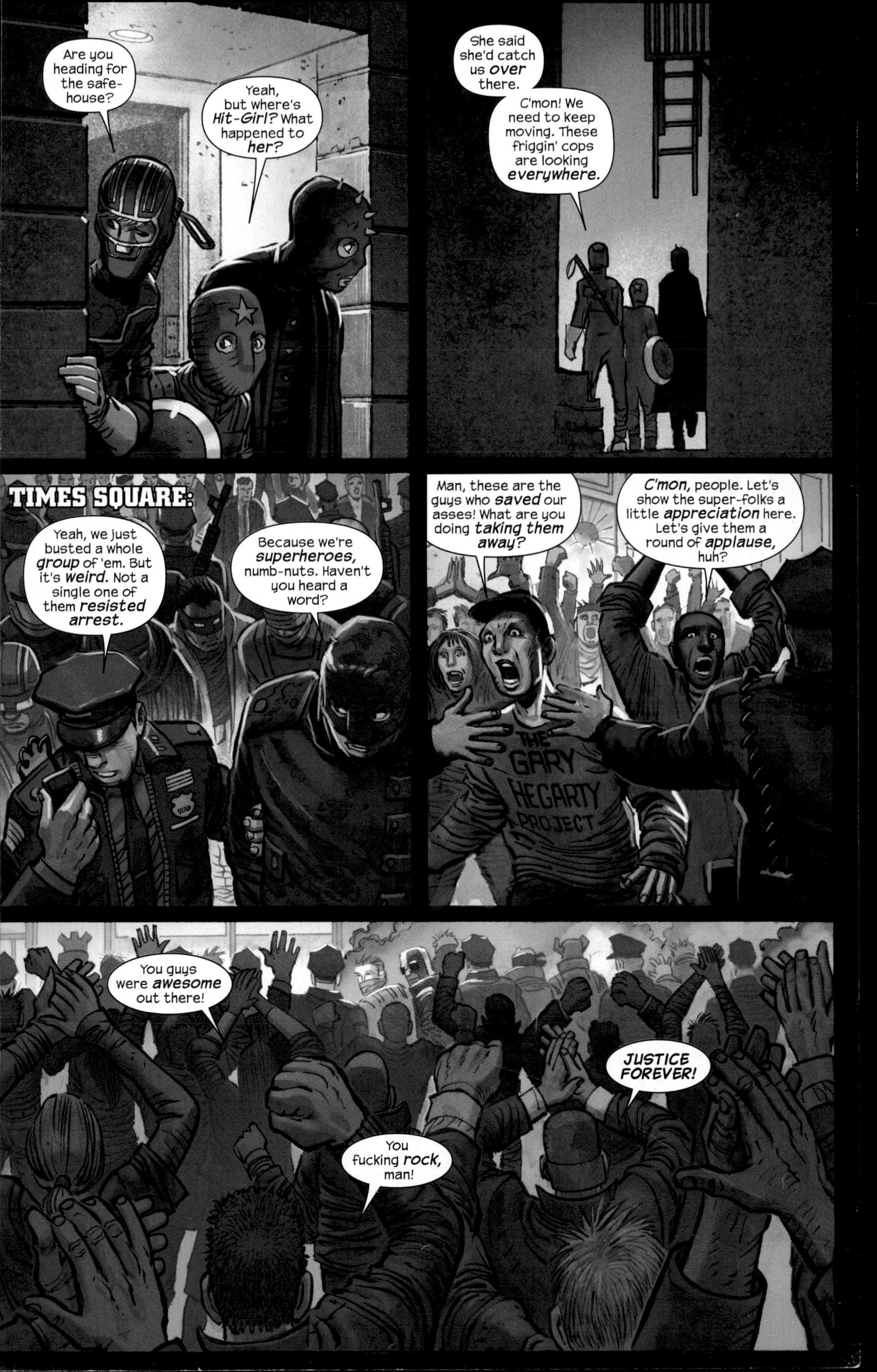

Are you heading for the safe-house?
Yeah, but where's Hit-Girl? What happened to her?
She said she'd catch us over there.
C'mon! We need to keep moving. These friggin' cops are looking everywhere.
TIMES SQUARE:
Yeah, we just busted a whole group of 'em. But it's weird. Not a single one of them resisted arrest.
Because we're superheroes, numb-nuts. Haven't you heard a word?
Man, these are the guys who saved our asses! What are you doing taking them away?
C'mon, people. Let's show the super-folks a little appreciation here. Let's give them a round of applause, huh?
THE GARY HEGARTY PROJECT
You guys were awesome out there!
JUSTICE FOREVER!
You fucking rock, man!

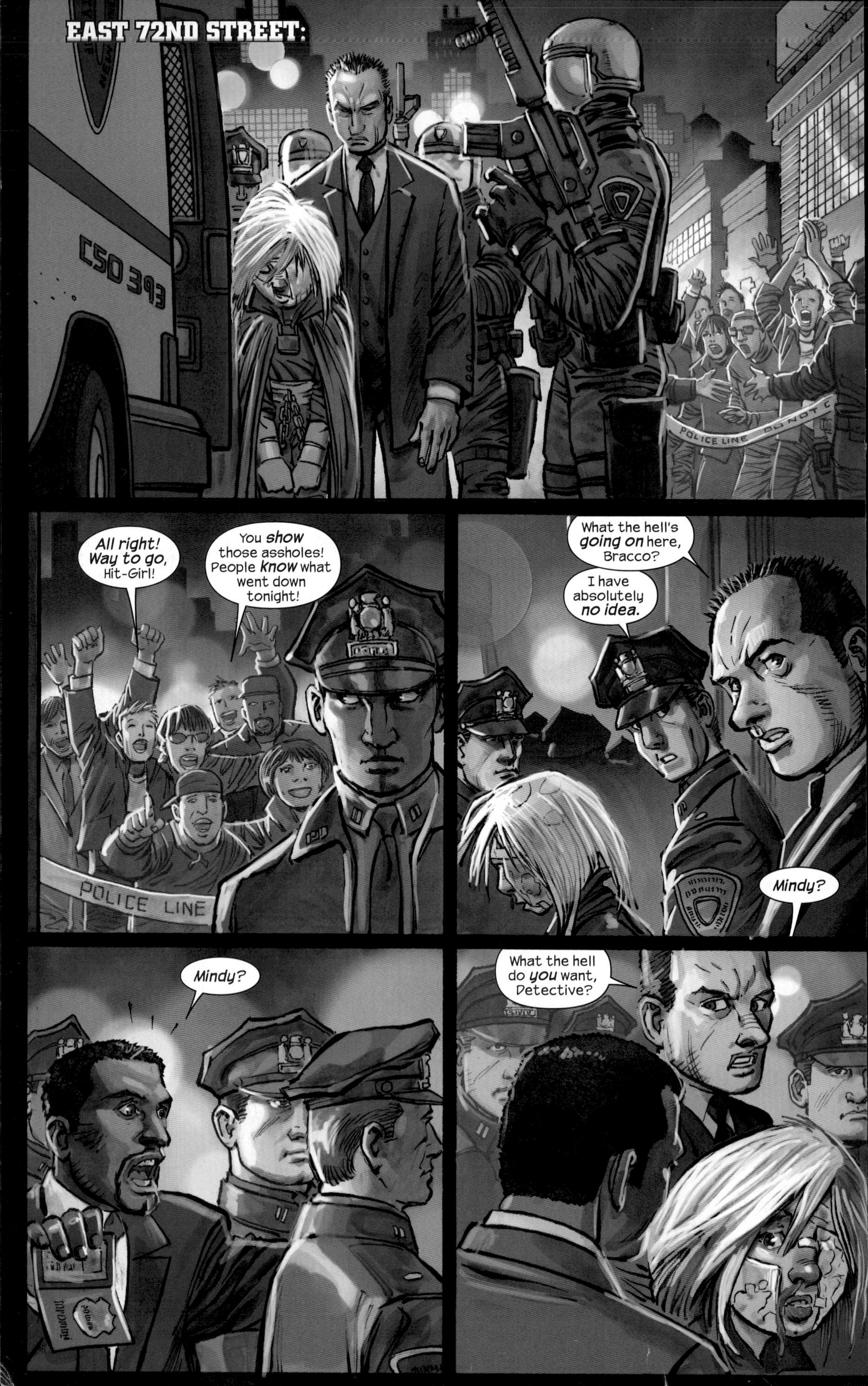
EAST 72ND STREET:
CSO 393
POLICE LINE
All right! Way to go, Hit-Girl!
You show those assholes! People know what went down tonight!
POLICE LINE
What the hell's going on here, Bracco?
I have absolutely no idea.
Mindy?
Mindy?
What the hell do you want, Detective?

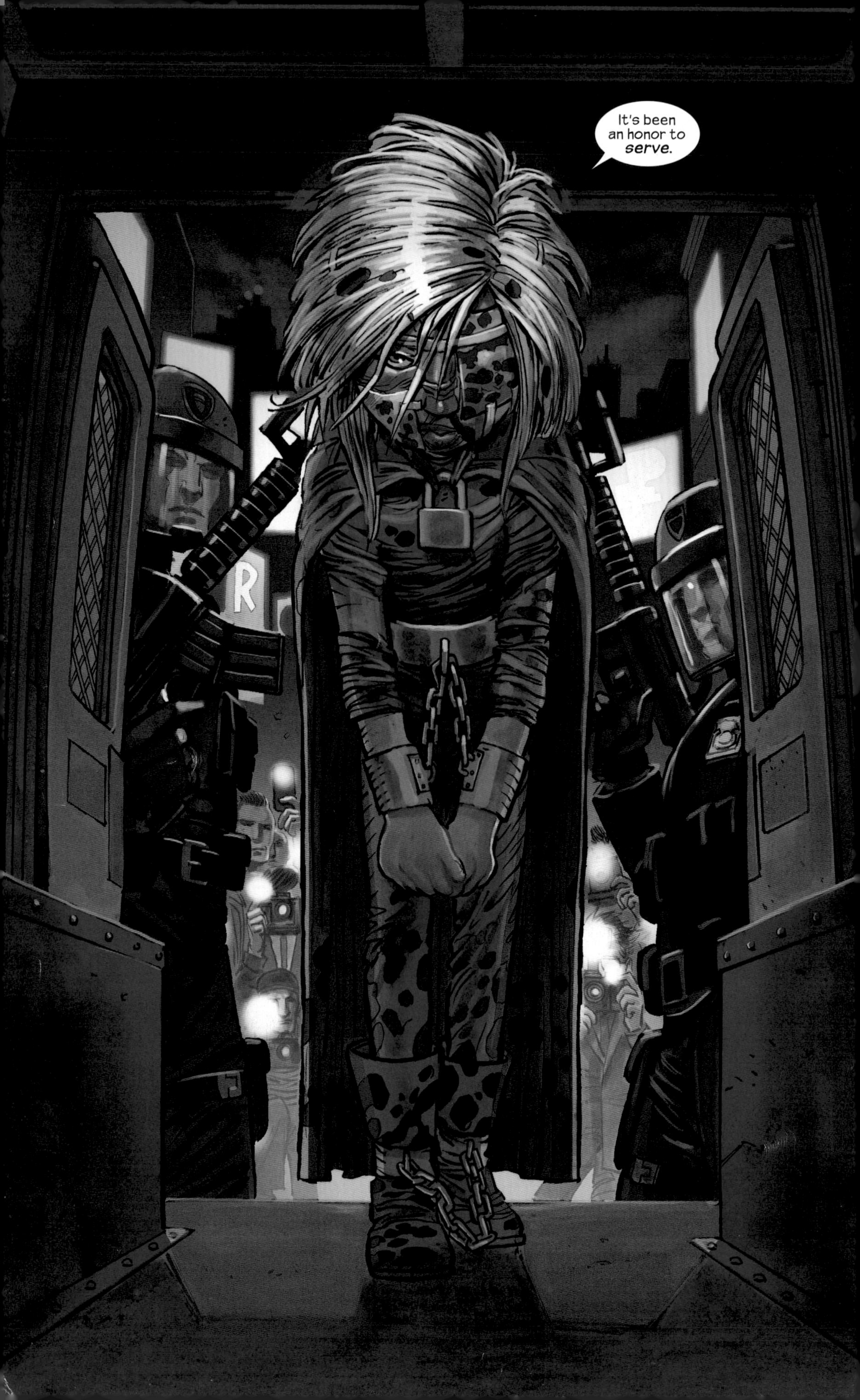
It's been an honor to *serve*.

END OF BOOK THREE

KICK

-ASS

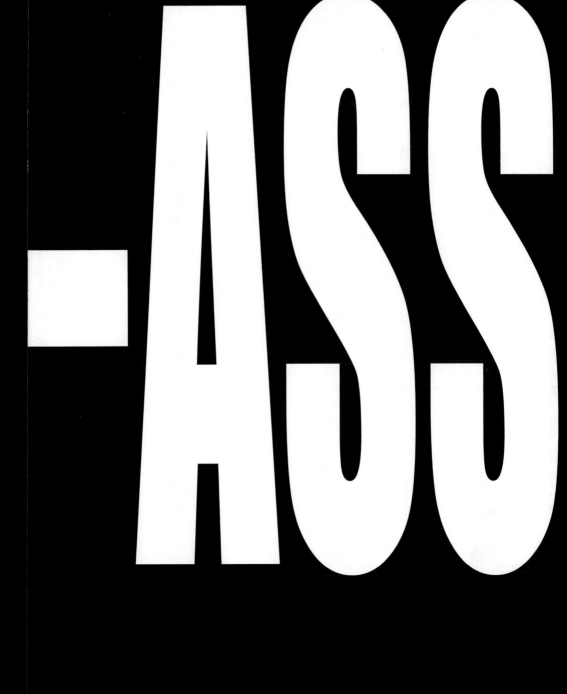

MARK MILLAR has written some of Marvel's greatest modern hits including *The Ultimates*, *Ultimate X-Men*, *Spider-Man*, *Wolverine: Old Man Logan*, and *Civil War*, the industry's biggest-selling series of the last decade. His Millarworld line boasts a roster of creator-owned smashes such as *Wanted*, turned into a blockbuster movie starring Angelina Jolie; *Kick-Ass*, which starred Nicolas Cage; and *Kick-Ass 2*, starring Jim Carrey. Millar is currently working on *Kick-Ass 3*, *Jupiter's Legacy*, and *Nemesis Returns*. In his native UK, he's the editor of *CLiNT* magazine, an advisor on film to the Scottish government, and CEO of film and TV company Millarworld Productions. He also serves as Creative Consultant on Fox's Marvel movies in Los Angeles.

JOHN ROMITA JR is a modern-day comic-art master, following in his legendary father's footsteps. Timeless runs on *Iron Man*, *Uncanny X-Men*, *Amazing Spider-Man,* and *Daredevil* helped establish him as his own man artistically, and his work on *Wolverine* and *World War Hulk* is arguably the most explosive comic art of the last decade. In addition to *Eternals* with writer Neil Gaiman, JRJR teamed with Mark Millar on the creator-owned *Kick-Ass*, later developed into a blockbuster feature film starring Nicolas Cage. Avid Spider-Man fans rejoiced at the artist's return to *Amazing Spider-Man* with the Brand New Day storylines "New Ways To Die" and "Character Assassination." He later joined writer Brian Michael Bendis on the relaunched *Avengers*. Recent titles include the blockbuster crossover *Avengers vs X-Men* and the relaunch of *Captain America*.

TOM PALMER has worked as an illustrator in the advertising and editorial fields, but he has spent the majority of his career in comic books. His first assignment, fresh out of art school, was on *Doctor Strange*, and he has gone on to lend his inking talents to many of Marvel's top titles, including *X-Men*, *The Avengers*, *Tomb of Dracula*, and more recently *Punisher, Hulk,* and *Ghost Rider.* He lives and works in New Jersey.

DEAN WHITE is one of the comic industry's best and most sought-after color artists. Well-known for his work on titles such as *The Amazing Spider-Man, Punisher, Dark Avengers, Captain America, Black Panther, Wolverine* and countless more, Dean's envelope-pushing rendering and color palette bring a sense of urgency and power to every page he touches.

CHRIS ELIOPOULOS is a multiple award-winner for his lettering, having worked on dozens of books during the twenty years he's been in the industry—including Erik Larsen's *Savage Dragon*, for which he hand-lettered the first 100 issues. Along with his success as a letterer, he also publishes his own strip *Misery Loves Sherman*, wrote and illustrated the popular *Franklin Richards: Son of a Genius* one-shots, and writes Marvel's *Lockjaw and the Pet Avengers* series.

AUBREY SITTERSON began his comics career as an intern at Marvel Comics, and went on to edit fan-favorite runs on *The Irredeemable Ant-Man, Ghost Rider* and more, before taking the plunge to write and edit comics freelance. Since then, he has edited *Kick-Ass, The Walking Dead* and other hit books, while writing comics for Marvel, DC, Image, Oni Press and Viz Media. Find him on the internet at aubreysitterson.com.

ONE (VARIANT BY TOMMY LEE EDWARDS)

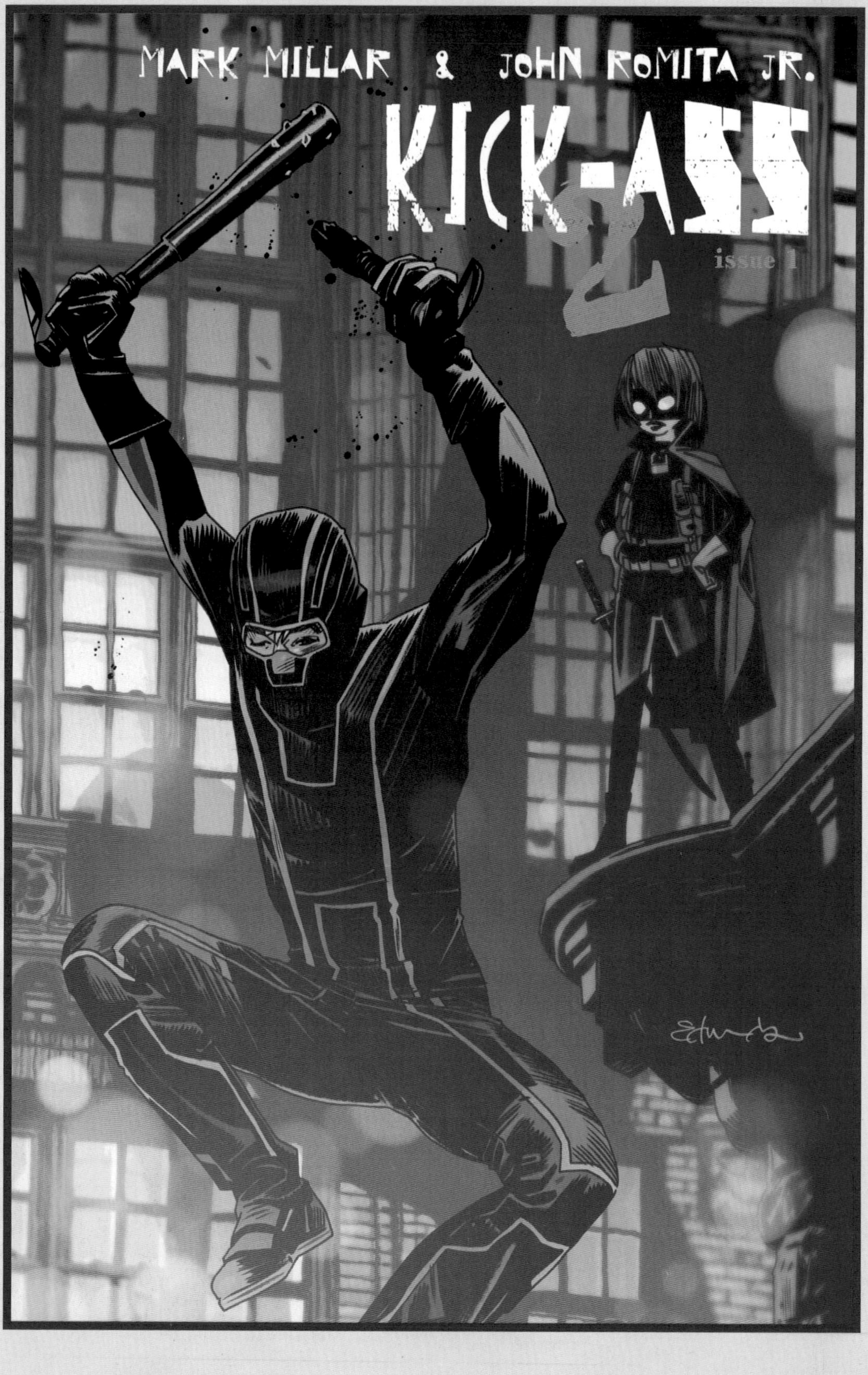
MARK MILLAR & JOHN ROMITA JR.
KICK-ASS 2
issue 1

TWO (VARIANT BY LEINIL YU)

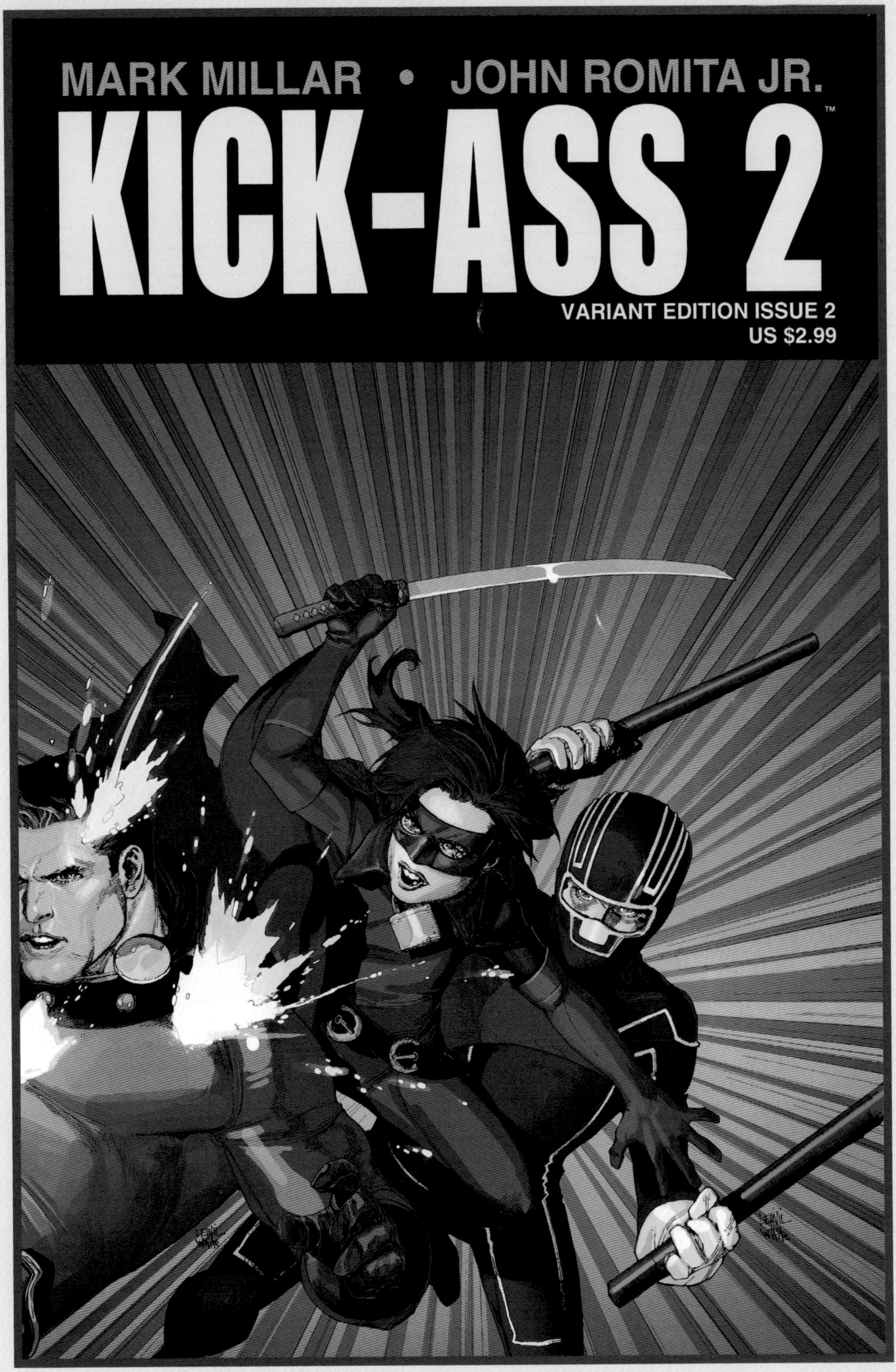
MARK MILLAR • JOHN ROMITA JR.
KICK-ASS 2™
VARIANT EDITION ISSUE 2
US $2.99

FIVE (VARIANT BY BRYAN HITCH)

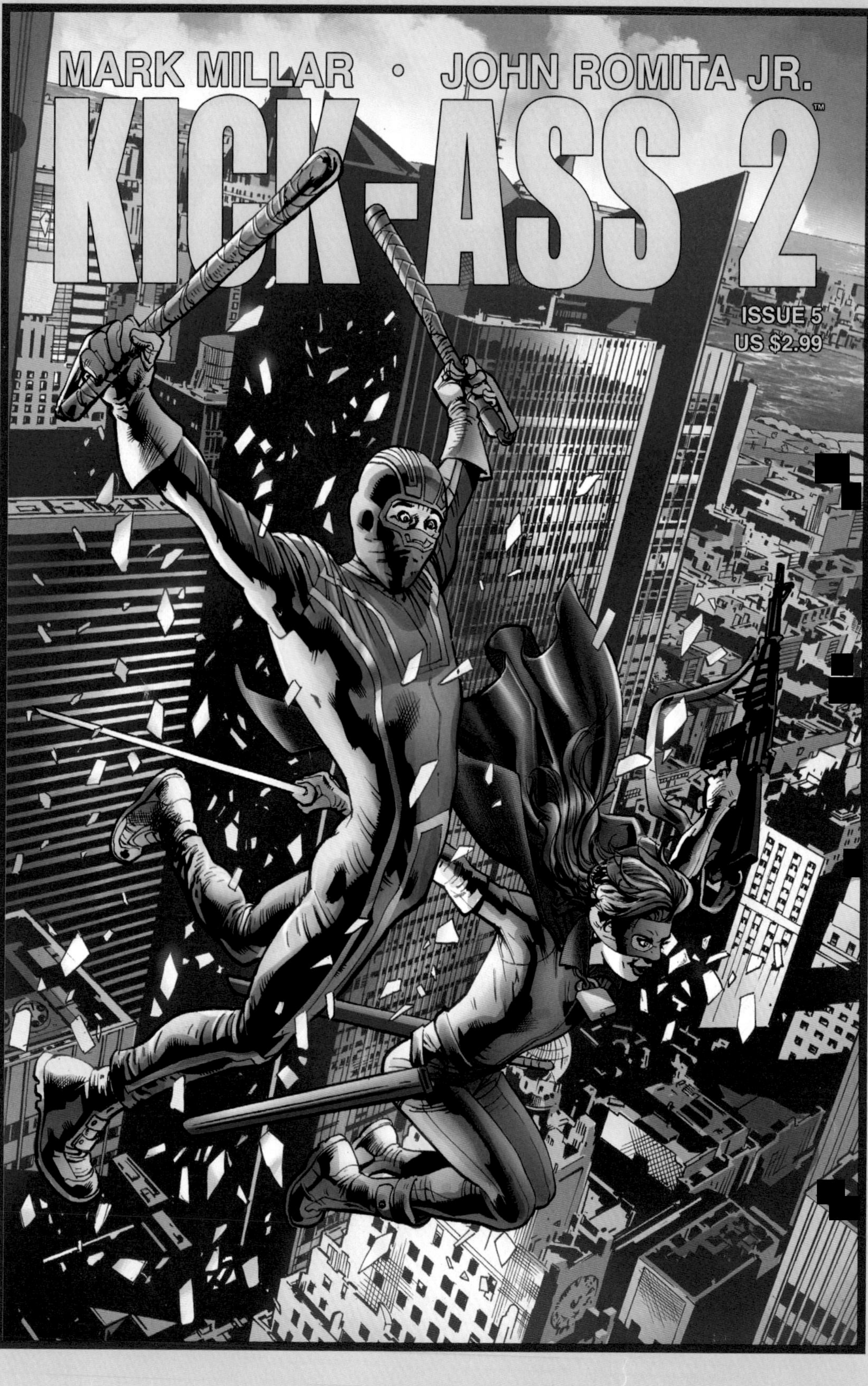
MARK MILLAR · JOHN ROMITA JR.
KICK-ASS 2™
ISSUE 5
US $2.99

FIVE (PHOTO VARIANT)

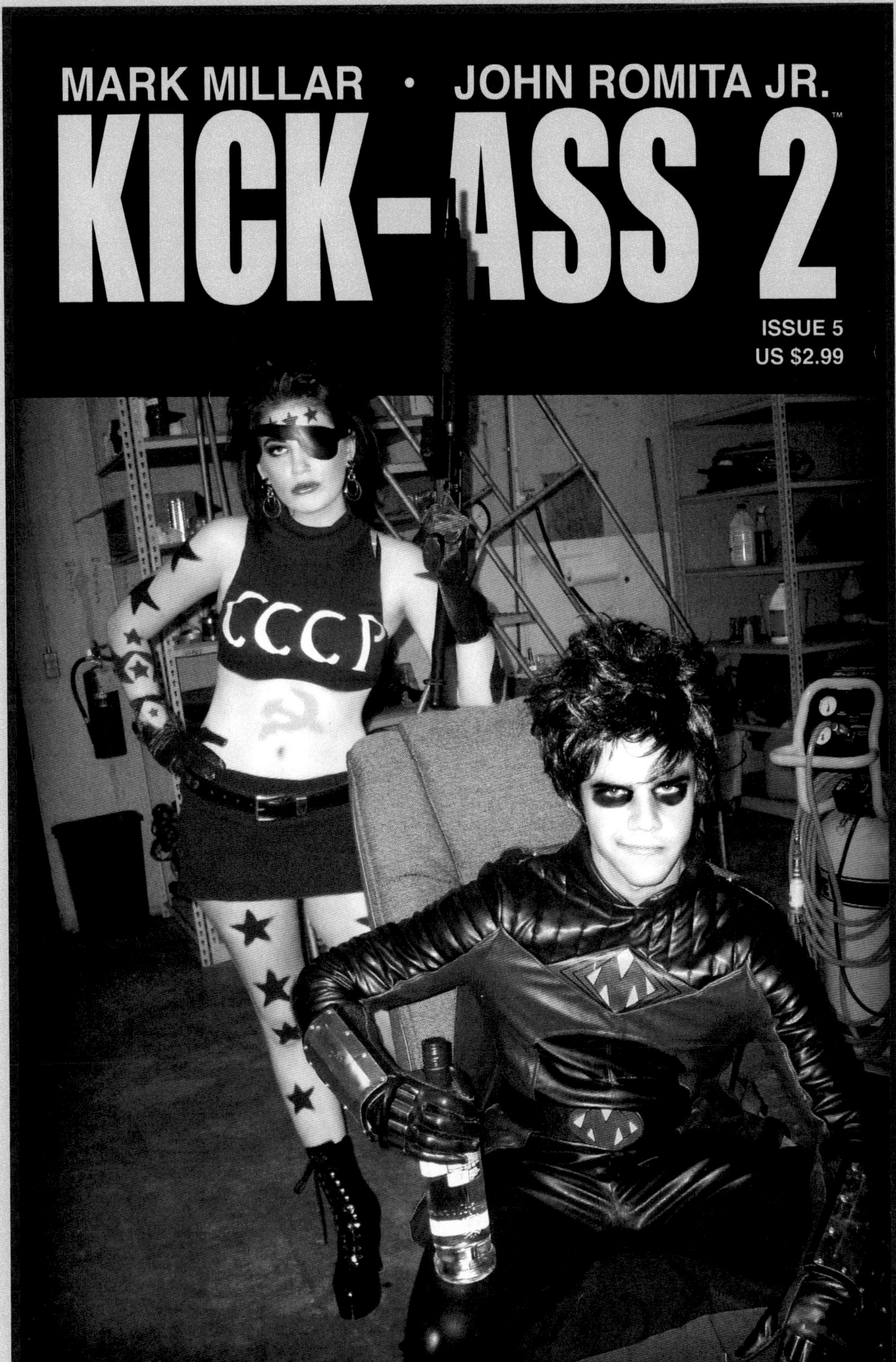
MARK MILLAR • JOHN ROMITA JR.
KICK-ASS 2™
ISSUE 5
US $2.99
CCCP

SIX (PHOTO VARIANT)

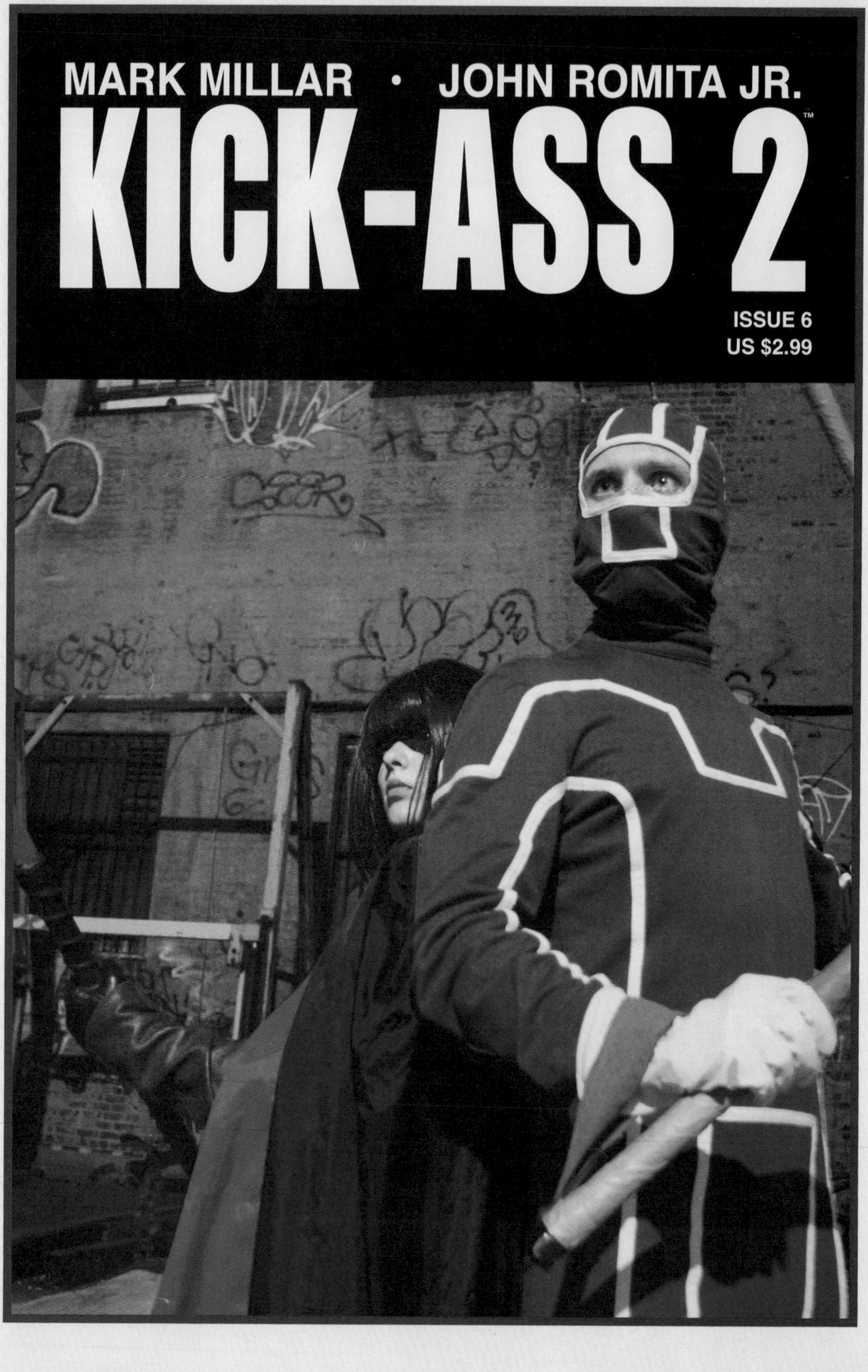
MARK MILLAR • JOHN ROMITA JR.
KICK-ASS 2™
ISSUE 6
US $2.99

SEVEN (PHOTO VARIANT)

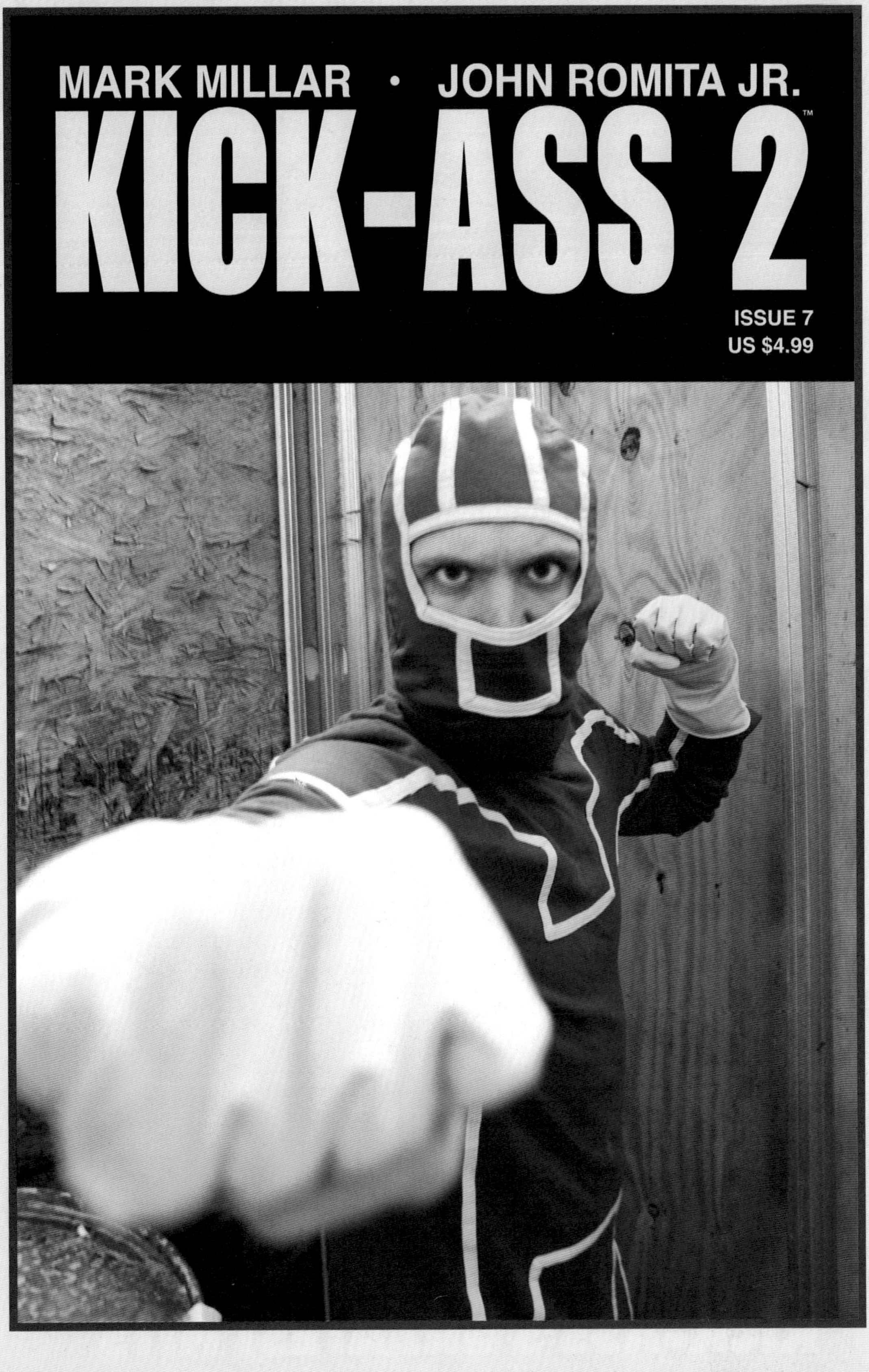
MARK MILLAR · JOHN ROMITA JR.
KICK-ASS 2™
ISSUE 7
US $4.99

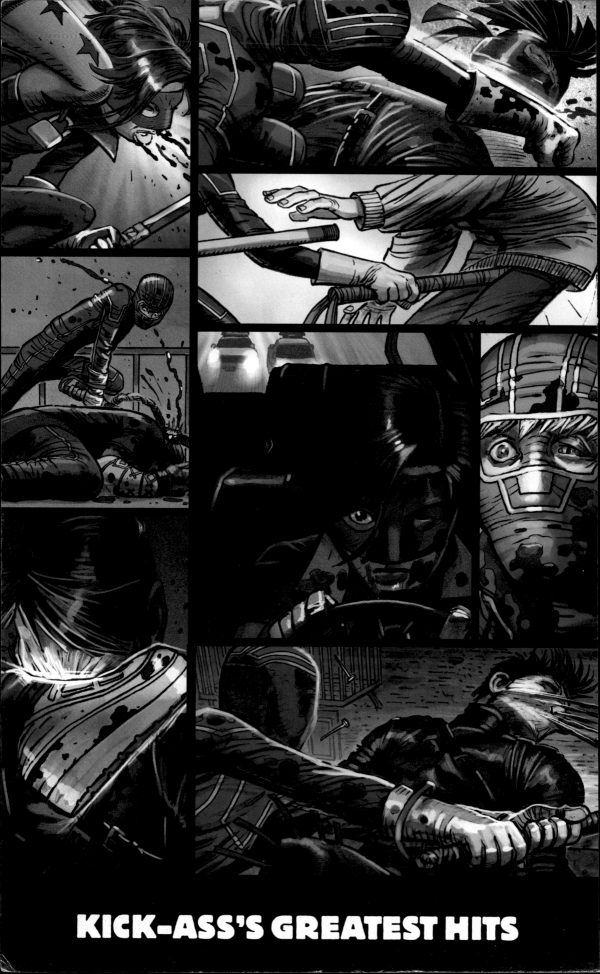

KICK-ASS'S GREATEST HITS

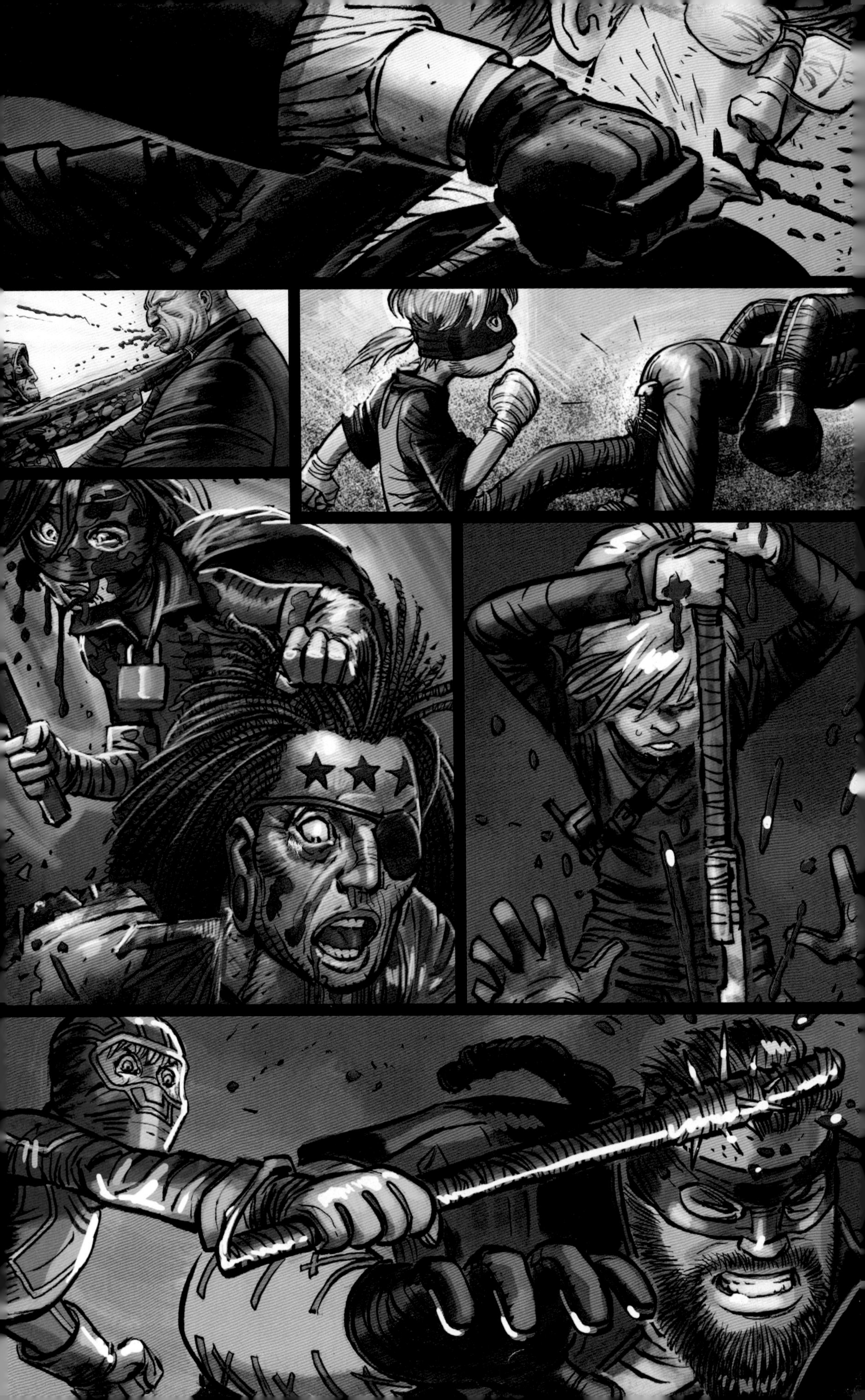

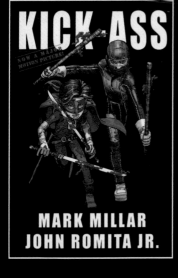

KICK-ASS

NOW A MAJOR MOTION PICTURE!

MARK MILLAR
JOHN ROMITA JR.

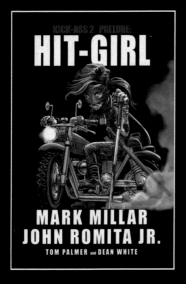

KICK-ASS 2 PRELUDE:

HIT-GIRL

MARK MILLAR
JOHN ROMITA JR.

TOM PALMER and DEAN WHITE

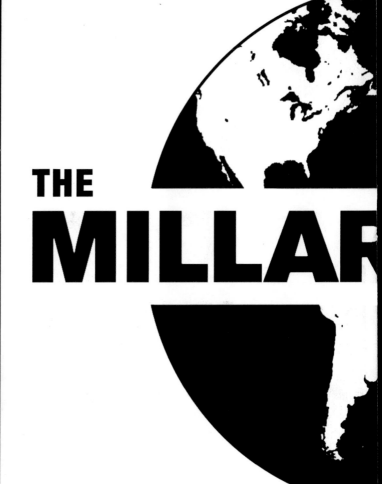

THE MILLAR

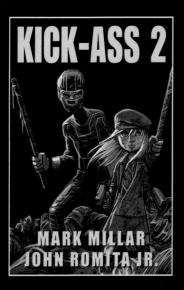

KICK-ASS 2

MARK MILLAR
JOHN ROMITA JR.

WANTED

MARK MILLAR • JG JONES • PAUL MOUNTS
NOW A MAJOR MOTION PICTURE FROM
UNIVERSAL PICTURES
WWW.MILLARWORLD.TV

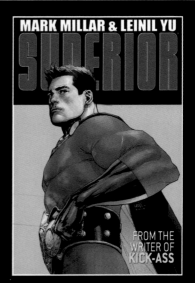

MARK MILLAR & LEINIL YU

SUPERIOR

FROM THE
WRITER OF
KICK-ASS

WORLD™ COLLECTION

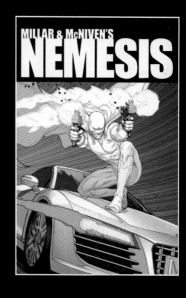

MILLAR & McNIVEN'S
NEMESIS

MARK MILLAR   DAVE GIBBONS
the
SECRET SERVICE

$2.99

MARK MILLAR · FRANK QUITELY
JUPITER'S LEGACY

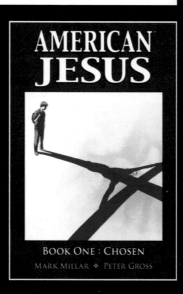

AMERICAN JESUS

BOOK ONE : CHOSEN
MARK MILLAR ✦ PETER GROSS

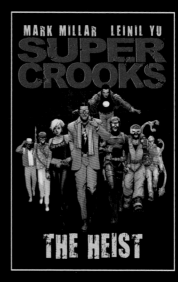

MARK MILLAR   LEINIL YU
SUPER CROOKS

THE HEIST

KICK-ASS CLOTHING!
T-Shirts With Attitude

TITAN MERCHANDISE

ALL T-SHIRTS AVAILABLE IN SIZES S, M, L, XL

AVAILABLE FROM ALL GOOD ENTERTAINMENT AND COMIC STORES. AVAILABLE IN THE UK & EUROPE FROM: FORBIDDEN PLANET.CO

MARK MILLAR'S
NEW, RETOOLED CLiNT!

#1 100 PAGES OF EYE-BLISTERING COMICS
INSIDE YOUR ALL NEW
CLiNT

SEX!

EXCLUSIVE!
DEATH SENTENCE
SIX MONTHS TO LIVE!

BOOZE!

NEW!
SECRET SERVICE
THREE WAYS TO KILL!

EYEBROWS!

EXCLUSIVE!
REX ROYD
ONE MIND TO F**K!

4 SHOCKING NEW COMICS EXPLODE!

NEED ONE LAST MEGA-HEIST? YOU BETTER CALL FOR THE...
SUPER CROOKS!

Plus! EXCLUSIVE INTERVIEWS: RAIDING THE DRAWERS OF THE BIGGEST NAMES IN COMICS!

Plus! / MASSIVE MILLARWORLD MELTDOWN / BADASS 101

100 BRAIN-SPATTERING PAGES!

FEATURING:
» **Mark Millar**
» **John Romita Jr**
» **Leinil Francis Yu**
» **Dave Gibbons**
» **Monty Nero**
...and many more!

On sale every 6 weeks!

SUBSCRIBE NOW!
GO ONLINE: WWW.CLINTMAG.COM
PHONE: 0844 815 5875

JOIN US: /CLINTMAG
FOLLOW US: @CLINTMAG

COMING SOON

JOHN ROMITA, JR.
HOWARD CHAYKIN

SHMUGGY &
BIMBO

WITH A TITLE LIKE THAT, IT HAS TO BE GREAT!

KICK-ASS
READING ORDER

PART ONE

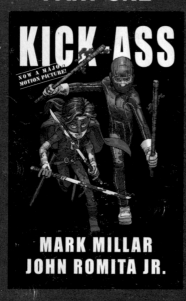

KICK-ASS

NOW A MAJOR MOTION PICTURE!

MARK MILLAR
JOHN ROMITA JR.

PART TWO

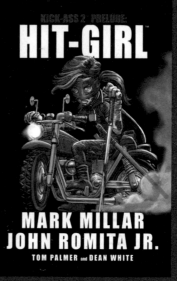

KICK-ASS 2 PRELUDE:
HIT-GIRL

MARK MILLAR
JOHN ROMITA JR.
TOM PALMER and DEAN WHITE

PART THREE

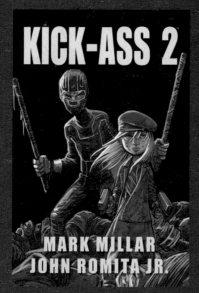

KICK-ASS 2

MARK MILLAR
JOHN ROMITA JR.

PART FOUR

KICK-ASS 3

THE GRAND FINALE

MAY 2013